# Emotional Equations

## Simple formulas to help your life work better

# Chip Conley

piatkus

PIATKUS

First published in the US in 2012 by Free Press, a division of Simon & Schuster, Inc.
First published in Great Britain in 2012 by Piatkus
This paperback edition published in 2013 by Piatkus

A CIP catalogue record for this book
is available from the British Library.

ISBN 978-0-7499-5625-7

Designed by Carla Jayne Jones
Printed and bound in Great Britain by
Clays Ltd, St Ives plc

Papers used by Piatkus are from well-managed forests
and other responsible sources.

MIX
Paper from
responsible sources
FSC® C104740

Piatkus
An imprint of
Little, Brown Book Group
100 Victoria Embankment
London EC4Y 0DY

An Hachette UK Company
www.hachette.co.uk

www.piatkus.co.uk

# Contents

## PART I

**EMOTIONAL EQUATIONS**      1

1. Emotions = Life      3
2. Emotions: *Your Owner's Manual*      14

## PART II

**DEALING WITH DIFFICULT TIMES**      27

3. Despair = Suffering − Meaning      29
4. Disappointment = Expectations − Reality      38
5. Regret = Disappointment + Responsibility      49
6. $\text{Jealousy} = \dfrac{\text{Mistrust}}{\text{Self-Esteem}} \quad \text{and} \quad \text{Envy} = \dfrac{(\text{Pride} + \text{Vanity})}{\text{Kindness}}$      60
7. Anxiety = Uncertainty × Powerlessness      73

## PART III

**GETTING THE MOST OUT OF YOUR WORK LIFE**      85

8. $\text{Calling} = \dfrac{\text{Pleasure}}{\text{Pain}}$      87
9. $\text{Workaholism} = \dfrac{\text{What Are You Running From?}}{\text{What Are You Living For?}}$      98

# Contents

10. Flow $= \dfrac{\text{Skill}}{\text{Challenge}}$     110

11. Curiosity = Wonder + Awe     123

## PART IV

## DEFINING WHO YOU ARE     135

12. Authenticity = Self-Awareness × Courage     137

13. Narcissism = (Self-Esteem)$^2$ × Entitlement     147

14. Integrity = Authenticity × Invisibility × Reliability     160

## PART V

## FINDING CONTENTMENT     171

15. Happiness $= \dfrac{\text{Wanting What You Have}}{\text{Having What You Want}}$     173

16. Joy = Love − Fear     185

17. Thriving $= \dfrac{\text{Frequency of Positive}}{\text{Frequency of Negative}}$     196

18. Faith $= \dfrac{\text{Belief}}{\text{Intellect}}$     208

19. Wisdom $= \sqrt{\text{Experience}}$     221

## PART VI

## DIY (DO IT YOURSELF)     235

20. Creating Your Own Emotional Equations     237

ACKNOWLEDGMENTS     249

NOTES     253

INDEX     275

# PART I

# EMOTIONAL EQUATIONS

# 1

$$\boxed{\text{Emotions} = \text{Life}}$$

On August 19, 2008, my heart stopped. Just minutes after my business presentation on stage, I passed out. Flatline. My memories of that day are opaque, but I can still see the image that was swirling around my brain as I came to in the emergency room: thick, sweet, fragrant oil slowly dripping down a set of dark wooden stairs. My version of "seeing the light," this was the ultimate wake-up call for me. The doctors could find no medical explanation for my heart failure.

Over the preceding few years, a series of wake-up waves culminating in my heart failure had hit me like an emotional tsunami and tested my sense of who I thought I was: a business I had built was sinking; a family member had been wrongly convicted of a crime and sentenced to San Quentin State Prison; a long-term relationship had ended painfully; and I had lost five friends and colleagues to suicide.

I know I'm not alone in experiencing these tragedies and setbacks. Many people have felt either out of control or stuck in an emotional logjam. At times, our emotions are crystal clear; we know what we're feeling and how to respond. At other times, we need guidance. And my heart failure, besides being a medical emergency, was also an emotional emergency. I felt as if I were treading water, gasping for air, my emotions acting like enemies instead of intuitive allies.

I had tried my best to put on a good "game face," because we CEOs like to portray a strong, steady image to everyone and a lot of people were relying on me. After all, my company is called Joie de Vivre (French for "joy of life"), so dour didn't really fit the profile. I'd started the company in 1987 and grown it to more than three thousand employees, the largest group of independent boutique hotels in the state of California, and had been adept at creating healthy "psycho-hygiene" at the company. I'd also written *Peak: How Great Companies Get Their Mojo from Maslow* about adapting for the workplace the theory of motivation created by the psychologist Abraham Maslow.

During the momentous days of the decade's first economic downturn, this mixing of psychology and business had let Joie de Vivre defy the general trend and nearly triple in size. It had also led me to lecture all over the world on how to become self-actualized—to become everything we're capable of becoming at work.

When the second economic downturn hit in 2008, however, I retreated to my home—once my sanctuary but now a place filled with beautiful things and ugly thoughts. I would take off my game face and wallow in an emotional darkroom where all my negatives were developing. I had a certain emotional awareness about what was going on inside me but little means to make sense of it, let alone find meaning in it. I felt almost paralyzed by a psychological fog.

As I was waiting for some revelation, one of my good friends, Chip Hankins, took his own life. He was my best "Chip" friend in the world and my insurance broker for more than a decade—a force of nature whom I deeply admired and, at times, emulated. We had more in common than just our names: we were both publicly extroverted but had an introverted, melancholy side as well; we both went for long periods of sobriety, even though we both owned bars. And we were both spiritual seekers who enjoyed throwing a frivolous party; we'd been planning to throw a "Chip" party someday to which we'd invite Chips from around the world to share stories of "The World According to Chip."

Instead, there I was at Chip's memorial service, where I listened to person after person get up and tell "Chip stories." It was surreal. The truth is, up to this moment, my mind had occasionally veered toward images of my own demise—by car crash or cancer—something dramatic that might help me escape from the mess of emotions my life had become. Clearly, I needed to push the reset button on my mind, and my life, and make some fundamental changes. The terror and despair I felt over this profound loss gradually gave way to a renewed sense that I could remake my experience here on Earth and a budding gratitude that I would have that opportunity even though others would not.

During that time, as four other friends also chose death over life, I learned more about the nature of emotional depression and suicide. Nearly a million people try to commit suicide annually in America; about 5 percent of them "succeed." Men are four times as likely to commit suicide as women, and suicide attempts by middle-aged people have spiked during the economic downturn (all five of my friends were men in their forties).

Shining the light on these sobering statistics gave me the incentive to look for a healthy way to make sense of my emotions.

## SEARCHING FOR AN EMOTIONAL ANSWER

I was compelled to revisit a book I'd read years before, the psychologist Viktor Frankl's landmark memoir *Man's Search for Meaning*.

Dr. Frankl's book was a spiritual salve for me. I figured that if this man could withstand the agony of a Nazi concentration camp, I could probably deal with the challenges in my own life. I was acutely aware that my company needed a new solution to its problems, but I was more focused on turning around my own life. Maybe if I could do that, a company turnaround would follow.

I would recount the story of *Man's Search for Meaning* to friends and colleagues, yet most couldn't understand why I was so fascinated with it. In spite of their blank stares, I kept reading Frankl's book and began to distill its wisdom down to one simple equation:

$$Despair = Suffering - Meaning$$

In other words, despair is what results when suffering has no meaning. In a recession (or, in Frankl's case, in prison), suffering is virtually a constant, so it's best to place your attention on growing your sense of meaning in order to decrease your feeling of despair.

This little mental rule of thumb or mantra became my lighthouse. Throughout the day, especially when I was feeling particularly tested, I would quietly recite this equation to myself as a reminder not to get caught up in the suffering and instead to place my attention on what I was supposed to learn. Because the worldwide hospitality industry was hit particularly hard by the Great Recession, the leaders of Joie de Vivre (JdV) were living lives of "quiet desperation"—in some cases, not so quiet. One day, as I facilitated a leadership series for senior managers, knowing that they were suffering, I decided to discuss my own vulnerability and worries and introduced my "Meaning" equation to the group. The managers really responded to it—they started texting and tweeting it to their staff, and, next thing I knew, they'd asked me to teach a whole class on Emotional Equations. To this day, I teach employees at JdV how to use Emotional Equations to create insight and perspective as well as happiness and success. Here are a few of the most popular:

$$Disappointment = Expectations - Reality$$

$$Workaholism = \frac{What\ Are\ You\ Running\ From?}{What\ Are\ You\ Living\ For?}$$

$$Authenticity = Self\text{-}Awareness \times Courage$$

$$Joy = Love - Fear$$

Though most people today aren't locked in a concentration camp or acting as CEOs of companies in distress, many people are prisoners of their own minds. So in this book I ask you, "What's your prison?" and I offer you some keys to unlock the door. Frankl's "Meaning" equation gave me a sense of freedom that liberated me from my habitual, fearful ways of thinking. Fear is a straitjacket. It incapacitates and isolates you. Yet the ancient root of "fear" is the word "fare." Passengers pay a fare to take a ship from one point to another, so perhaps in these rough economic seas our fare of fear will take us to a new place in our lives.

As Winston Churchill advised during World War II, "If you're going through hell, keep going." Today, too, we all need to come to understand that we can use our seasons of darkness as a means to find new reservoirs of strength—strength we didn't know we had.

You are no doubt faced today with situations that are testing you to be bigger than you've ever been in your life. Those challenges require you to become conscious of your emotions. As the poet Kahlil Gibran put it, "Your pain is the breaking of the shell that encloses your understanding." As I navigated my way through my treacherous time, the question that kept emerging from my work with the "Meaning" equation was "What is breaking open in my life that is meant to evolve into something new for me and those around me?"

## THE PARALLELS BETWEEN MATH AND LIFE

In most of the Emotional Equations in this book, we'll stick with basic math formulas—addition, subtraction, multiplication, and division—to get a handle on how emotions work together and how you can work with them. I want to note, however, that calculus is actually known as the mathematics of change. After inventing calculus, Sir Isaac Newton also crafted mathematical expressions of the laws of motion, capped off by the famous equation Force = Mass × Gravity (to be more precise, gravity is a form of acceleration).

Gravity is a universal force that affects the physical world, but you may not have considered how it also affects the human condition—and not just by keeping us on Earth. Gravity shapes our physical bodies; we often get shorter and closer to the ground as we age. Gravity can also shape our emotional selves. Emotional baggage, for instance, is a form of gravity; we acquire more of it as we get older, and it weighs us down. The more emotional gravity we're fighting, the more force we require to move forward. And force moving against gravity creates a lot of friction.

On the other hand, having a frictionless life is like being a rower gliding over the surface of the water—in rowing circles, this is called "swinging." Abraham Maslow called it "self-actualization," and Mihaly Csikszentmihalyi calls it "flow." It's a way of defying gravity.

When I went through the most difficult period in my life, I did not feel "in the flow." On some level, I felt as if mysterious natural forces—such as gravity—were conspiring against me. As one friend told me at the time, "Your internal math is haywire." That's what it can feel like when you are out of sync with the world—you feel trapped, heavy, full of friction and chaos.

Chaos is a math theory, but it also describes how many of us feel in troubled times. As one who has spent my life doing the left-brain/right-brain tango, I have often grasped for what I now understand to be an Emotional Equation to give me insight into what I was going through at home or at work, to distill some basic truths in life. Emotional Equations provide a new, visual lexicon for mastering our age of uncertainty.

When I was a teen, I suffered through algebra with its constants and variables, and somehow I seemed to always get the answer wrong. Today, many of us feel as though we're getting the answer wrong in life, and so we use prayers, mantras, and affirmations as a sort of adult form of algebra. The Serenity Prayer ("God, grant me the serenity to accept the things I cannot change, the courage to change the things I can, and the wisdom to know the difference") is an example of a kind of equation for serenity that defines constants and variables in life.

When I was at my lowest, the "Meaning" equation gave me the knowledge and conviction that if I placed my attention more on the meaning of this disparate collection of painful events, as opposed to the suffering, I would likely have less despair in my life. During my most troubled weeks, the equation felt as if it was my instruction manual for deactivating my emotional explosives. I didn't need to be a math whiz to figure out the emotional truth of the "Meaning" equation, I just needed to use it as my daily mantra and map to help me climb out of the deep well into which I'd fallen. In spite of my allergy to algebra, my solution to my personal inner chaos was to become an emotional mathematician.

Of course, there's no perfect formula or spreadsheet for solving the mysteries of life. Even so, the world and our emotions are filled with relationships, and that's what this book is about: the relationships between your emotions and how they can help you better understand yourself, your purpose, and your relationships with others.

## ADVERSITY REVEALS GREATNESS

Here's one major relationship that most of us can use some help sorting out: your mind and your wallet. They are inextricably linked. It's no coincidence that the word we use to describe the worst of economic times also describes a serious psychological disorder: depression. Economic gloom lightens your wallet while weighing down your spirit. Five of the ten most stressful life events are related to whether you are employed and whether the quality of your work experience is good. Your work does more than affect your self-esteem; it organizes your day, connects you with others, and can give you a sense of purpose.

Not since the Great Depression have we seen such a perverse connection between work and our psyche as we do today. We are more familiar with the kind of recession that comes and goes like a brief winter storm, and our capacity to handle it has a lot to do with knowing it won't last all that long. But what if this economic toilet bowl we're in lasts longer than any other recession in history? How do we find the internal resources to cope with that bad news?

It's encouraging to remember that some of the greatest American literature, such as *The Grapes of Wrath* and *Of Mice and Men,* came out of the Depression era. During the same decade, Napoleon Hill wrote the runaway bestseller *Think and Grow Rich* (1937), which urged readers to adopt a positive mental attitude and channel the power of their minds to improve their lot in life. And the theologian Reinhold Niebuhr created the Serenity Prayer, which was adopted by the USO during World War II and subsequently by Alcoholics Anonymous and other twelve-step programs. It seems as if the more the external world becomes chaotic, the more we need to create our own internal logic.

Why do misfortunes embitter one person while motivating another to become resourceful? What valuable coping skills can you acquire during difficult times that you would never have developed during a more tranquil phase of your life? Are there ways you can train your mind so that you don't waste so much time and energy on emotions and tensions that aren't serving you well?

Those questions are very personal for me. They're part of the reason I created my initial Emotional Equation about meaning, then more equations for the people I worked with, and now this book for you and others. In researching these equations, I reached out to psychologists and mathematicians, who generally welcomed me (and even gave me an honorary doctorate in psychology). Heck, one well-known academic told me that I'd clearly had a fascination with emotions going back to when I named my company after the French expression for "joy." And I was reassured to find that the psychology community was already using equations that defined happiness, positivity, and even the likelihood of a stable marriage.

In the next chapters, I ground my storytelling in the math and science that supports Emotional Equations, to provide you with a shorthand means of correcting yourself emotionally—to get clearer perspectives and more control—during both good times and bad. One way to think of Emotional Equations is as a grown-up version of finger painting. If you mix two primary colors, say, red and blue, you get a secondary color, in this case purple. In fact, psychologists believe that our primary emotions work together to create secondary and even tertiary emotions that have subtle distinctions. An Emotional Equation is like having a flash card that you can raise in front of you to remind yourself that emotions are related to one another and that you can cultivate your perfect emotion potion.

Certain Emotional Equations will likely be more meaningful to you than others, and one section of the book may be more relevant to where you are in your life today. It's a bit like an encyclopedia of emotions, so there's no need to read the chapters in order. In fact, I recommend that you read a chapter at a time and think about it for a while, letting it seep into your subconscious. Or consider selecting one equation to focus on for the week and incorporate the "Working Through the Equation" section into your daily life.

The last chapter of the book provides a practical framework for deconstructing your own emotions and creating Emotional Equations that will be personally meaningful to you. I invite you to participate in the growing, emotionally fluent community on the Emotional Equations website, www.emotionalequations.com, where people are sharing the equations that work for them.

## YOUR EMOTIONAL CONCIERGE

We all want a fully functioning heart and mind. Why shouldn't we want the same for our emotional state? I'm not a therapist, but I can still help coach you through your emotions. During the most challenging of times, these Emotional Equations bolstered my leadership skills and our company's performance. In fact, in 2010, Joie de Vivre was awarded the top American award for customer service in the Upper Upscale category of hotels by Market Metrix, beating Marriott, Hilton, Hyatt, Westin, Kimpton, and Peninsula. I believe the best CEOs are truly "Chief Emotions Officers," since great companies have great cultures and at the heart of a great culture are healthy emotions. You may not think of yourself as a leader, but you are already leading yourself—and maybe others—on a daily basis.

This is a very different attitude from when I graduated from business school. Then I believed that in order to become a successful CEO, I needed to be *superhuman*. But after nearly two dozen years of being a CEO, I've learned that the best leaders in life aren't superhuman; instead, they're simply *super humans*.

So just think of me as your emotional concierge. Or as your "street shrink." Even though we use the word "shrink" to describe an emotional counselor, I believe life isn't meant for shrinking. It's meant for stretching, and I'm hoping that Emotional Equations will stretch you and create a better life for you and those around you. After using Emotional Equations, you will find that your emotions will no longer get the best of you. Instead, your emotions can *represent* the best in you.

This is my operating manual for being a super human. I hope it serves you well.

# 2

$$\left[\begin{array}{c} \textbf{Emotions:} \\ \textit{Your Owner's Manual} \end{array}\right]$$

Over the nearly two dozen years that I was CEO of my company, I got smarter about how to read a balance sheet, how to efficiently develop and market a compelling hotel, and how to create a buzz when we launched. But the most profound thing I learned over all those years was probably the "smile index."

Upon entering one of our nearly forty hotels or while touring a competitor's property, I could quickly get a true sense of a place by observing the quantity—and quality—of the employees' smiles. My emotional antennae could pick up whether they were genuine or just a mask. Similarly, when interviewing job candidates, I could intuit a person's emotional state within ten minutes, so that I knew whether the position would be a healthy habitat for him or her—or not.

The most successful business leaders are often experts on emotions. The psychologist Daniel Goleman has shown that emotional intelligence (EQ) makes up two-thirds of the likely success of business executives, compared with intellectual capacity (IQ), which, along with the amount of working experience, makes up only one-third. Other academics have shown that we temporarily lose ten to fifteen points of IQ when we make decisions in an emotionally reactive state of mind. On the other hand, when we label an emotion *consciously* (as when working with an Emotional Equation), this thought reduces the intensity of the emotion and allows the more reasoning part of our brain—the prefrontal cortex—to take over from the reactive part of the brain.

Considerable research shows that emotions are contagious, especially in the context of the Petri dish of a family or an organization. Approximately 50 to 70 percent of the temperament of a work group is influenced by the emotional state of its leader, so a business leader can almost think of herself as the "emotional thermostat" of her work group. This is just as true in your family or any other closely knit group of people who regularly congregate.

Humanity's common currency, emotions, is how we connect, even when we have little else in common. Whether you speak Farsi or Icelandic, are male or female, are eight or eighty, emotions are universal to your experience of life. When talking to someone about how you feel, you probably refer to parts of your body to describe your emotional state; for instance, you say, "I have a broken heart," "I have a lump in my throat," or "I have a bad gut feeling about this." As my grandmother once told me, "No matter where you are in the world, you can always connect with someone by just being honest about your emotions, whether you're feeling sad, glad, mad, or bad."

Emotional fluency is the ability to sense, translate, and effectively apply the power of emotions in a healthy and productive manner. Yet most of us have more training in how to use our car or computer than we do in how to use our emotions in work and life. Welcome to driver's ed for your emotions. Fasten your seat belts, please.

# WHERE EMOTIONS COME FROM

Not long ago, my friend Tony Hsieh, Zappos' CEO, wrote a terrific book, *Delivering Happiness: A Path to Profits, Passion, and Purpose.* There are days I wish I could visit a website to order up some happiness and joy as well as shoes—or at least to get a little more internal sunshine. Emotional Equations offer a way to work with your emotions so that you can identify, change, and influence them much faster than even mail order can fulfill your order.

Our emotions even preceded our ability to put them into words. The emotional center of the human brain, the medulla oblongata, formed before the thinking part of the brain, the neocortex. Scientists from Charles Darwin and Paul Ekman to Frans de Waal and Jane Goodall have found common emotions in all animals, including human beings. And the pioneering work of scientists such as Antonio Damasio, Candace Pert, Joseph LeDoux, and others has shown that our thinking and feelings are part of a complex mind-body ecosystem. Whether it's the visceral "fight-or-flight" response that is built into our survival instincts or the love we have for a mate, emotions provide a means of protecting and propelling life.

In the nineteenth century, William James may have been the first psychologist ever to create an Emotional Equation when he suggested that self-esteem equals success divided by pretensions

$$Self\text{-}Esteem = \frac{Success}{Pretensions}$$

Of course, the solution would depend quite a bit on how we define success and pretensions. The way James saw it, if our perception of our actualities—what we have accomplished (success)—exceeds our potentialities—what we thought we should accomplish (pretensions)—we'll likely feel pretty good about ourselves.

Back in 1884, James wrote a landmark paper entitled simply "What Is an Emotion?" which stirred up a debate that still simmers. Ever since, psychologists have been arguing the "chicken-or-egg" question of whether emotions precede physical effects or vice versa. Does a stimulus cause you to get angry, your nostrils to flare, and your body to clench, or does the inner physiological reaction lead to the emotional reaction, which is what James argued? Experts acknowledge that because emotional responses are rather unconscious for most of us, we are at risk of having our emotions control us. One of the simple truths about life is that the more we ignore our emotions, the more likely they are to wield a powerful influence over us.

What does all this mean for you? The Latin root of the word "emotion" means "to move." Or Emotion = Energy + Motion. Emotions are vehicles for transforming or moving your life. They're not steady or stagnant states. The weather is an apt metaphor for this: sunshine or rainstorm, neither is stationary. They come and they go. Every weather condition is a function of a variety of ingredients such as barometric pressure, humidity, temperature, and elevation that help cook up the specific weather you're experiencing at any moment. That's also true of emotions. Disappointment might be a combination of surprise *and* sadness. Joy can be bittersweet.

When an emotion is stagnating and not moving through us, we find ourselves in a state such as depression, which is often defined as a condition of unexpressed anger. Bottling up an emotion can lead to an explosion. So learning how to let your emotional weather pass through you is the healthiest thing you can do for yourself—and others.

Think about it: Do you use the external weather as a means of distracting yourself from your internal weather? Becoming a savvy internal weatherman helped me understand what was brewing inside me during my roller-coaster years. It was also comforting to know that the frightening thunderstorm of emotions I might feel in one moment could be followed by sunshine in the next.

## HOW MANY EMOTIONS ARE THERE?

This question could launch a great parlor game. Philosophers and psychologists from Aristotle to Alfred Adler have been positing answers for thousands of years. Most academics agree that there are some basic human emotions, although the number varies in range from four to ten. The most widely agreed on emotions are fear, anger, sadness, disgust, surprise, and joy. Nonetheless, I'm among the many who believe that love is the most universal emotion.

I've seen tallies of the total number of emotions stretching from 558 to more than 800. What's fascinating is that in almost every study, nearly two-thirds of the words have a negative connotation. So for every gleeful, there is a gloomy *and* a greedy.

Because there are so many identifiable emotions, it can be challenging to read your own. You really can have "mixed emotions" when you feel some internal conflict. But over the past few decades, psychologists have identified the main combinations of basic emotions and how they can lead to other advanced or secondary emotions.

The psychologist Robert Plutchik created a compelling theory of how our emotions work. Patterning an emotional wheel after the primary color wheel, he created a circle of emotions. The eight primary emotions include joy, anticipation, anger, disgust, sadness, surprise, fear, and acceptance. Around those eight basic emotions are many other variations.

# PLUTCHIK'S WHEEL OF EMOTIONS

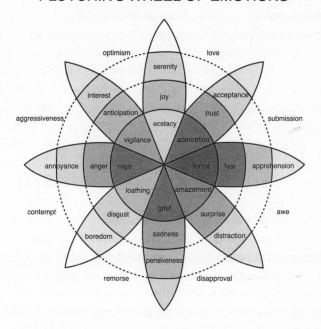

Fear and sadness are primary emotions, just as green and blue are primary colors. And joy and sadness are opposite emotions, just as yellow and purple are opposite colors. Next to and between all the primary emotions are other shades.

When adults are asked to look at photographs of faces showing different emotions, they are pretty universal in their ability to identify correctly what expression goes with which primary emotion. This is also true when most people are asked to distinguish between primary colors. But God help the color blind of the world (including me, although I call myself "color dumb") when we're asked to distinguish among various hues or a spectrum of colors. In fact, it isn't just the color blind who have a difficult time distinguishing among hues; many people who have not worked with colors cannot see much difference between periwinkle and lavender. The same difficulty can occur when we're face-to-face with someone who's showing mixed emotions (unless it's a child, since children are more inclined to exhibit clear emotions, whether sadness, surprise, anger, or joy). When you have trouble deciphering what message you're supposed to be picking up from someone, it can make you feel a little "emotion blind" or "emotion dumb," but Emotional Equations can give you a sort of corrective lens with which you can begin to "see" emotions in "Technicolor."

## EVENT + REACTION = OUTCOME

Many people do not distinguish between something that happens to them and their reaction to it. Yet it isn't the event or situation that holds the emotional charge; it's our beliefs that create our response. And when you create a response several times—you snap at your child, you get anxious when dealing with a boss or client, you get angry when someone cuts you off on the highway—you create an automatic reaction, a habitual response. In other words, you have an "ERO," or Event + Reaction = Outcome.

This description of a knee-jerk reaction is actually an important reminder that you do have some level of control over your emotions. As Viktor Frankl wrote, "Between stimulus and response there is a space. In that space is our power to choose our response. In our response lies our growth and our freedom." You have the power to choose how you respond. You are a product of your decisions, not your conditions.

In order to break your habitual response, you want to identify what an emotion is telling you. Think of your emotions as messages that give you the freedom, rather than the obligation, to respond. Fear protects. Regret teaches. Sadness releases. Joy uplifts. Empathy unites.

Emotions don't just happen to you, as if you are a willing victim.

Emotions are like clay, and you can mold them into the work of art that is your life. You have the capacity to transcend your set of petty grievances and emotional annoyances. The fact is that the biological life span of a particular emotion is about ninety seconds. It's the afterlife of that emotion that we mortals constantly revive and bathe in.


## RE-CREATING YOUR RELATIONS WITH EMOTIONS

Letting an emotion move through you is healthy. Letting an emotion define you is not. Moving it along requires a certain amount of "witnessing," or monitoring, of your emotions. For me, in business, that can mean "here comes that fear again" when our company—which has predictable, seasonal ups and downs—goes into the slower wintertime with tighter cash flow. In order to prevent that tight cash flow from translating into a tight chest and a taut demeanor, I need to be conscious of the first signs of an emotion, where it emerges in my body, and what shades from the "color wheel" of that emotion are accompanying it.

This is where Emotional Equations have become my ally. Over the past few years, when I was particularly overwhelmed by a pileup of emotions and feelings, I would go to a quiet place, take a few deep breaths, and then start writing down all of the physical feelings and emotional words that were flowing through me at that very moment. Then I would look at the lists and start making sense of how the various emotions and feelings fit together. Ultimately, I found that it was like solving a math equation. A little bit of this emotion plus some of that one led me to better understand the sum of emotions that filled me. Breaking them down, articulating them, and putting them into their places kept *me* from breaking down.

Emotional Equations became my psychological GPS, allowing me to navigate difficult or unknown terrain. They help to detect and translate, harness and channel emotions productively so they become rational and purposeful, rather than scattered and chaotic. Anger can become courage, and envy can fuel resilience.

So let's do a brief refresher course on mathematics that can help you better analyze the key Emotional Equations in this book.

## MATH: IT'S ALL ABOUT RELATIONSHIPS

An equation is just another way of expressing the relationship between two or more things—or two or more forces. Emotional Equations help illuminate relationships—the relationships between one emotion and another and how the mix of two emotions may lead to a third.

With the exception of two chapters (13 and 19), all of the Emotional Equations in this book keep things simple with pure addition, subtraction, multiplication, and division. Let's start with the simplest math functions, addition and subtraction, then go on to multiplication and division.

### ADDITION AND SUBTRACTION

When you add one thing to another, it gets bigger (and possibly more complex), and when you do the opposite, a positive number is reduced so that it's closer to zero. Now let's apply this to emotions. We talked about Robert Plutchik and his wheel of emotions earlier in the chapter. He suggests that if you add the primary emotions of anticipation and joy, you will get a secondary emotion of optimism. What happens if you take optimism and subtract the joy? According to basic math, that would give you anticipation.

$$Optimism - Joy = Anticipation$$

That sounds roughly right to me.

Try this one as an exercise. Let's assume that

$$Regret = Disappointment + Responsibility$$

What happens when you take regret and subtract responsibility? You are left with just disappointment, which is a basic, primary emotion. So Regret – Responsibility = Disappointment. (*Warning: not all of our equations can be mixed and matched like this.* For example, my favorite one, Despair = Suffering – Meaning, does not translate into Despair + Meaning = Suffering. So it's best to take the equations as they're presented.)

## MULTIPLICATION

Choosing multiplication as a means of relating numbers, compared with addition, means that you're going to end up with a more combustible effect. It suggests that there's a more potent relationship between the two elements.

The Emotional Equation featured in chapter 7 is Anxiety = Uncertainty × Powerlessness. Why do I multiply these two emotional states (or traits), as opposed to adding them together? I believe that the product of what you don't know (uncertainty) and what you can't control (powerlessness) creates the emotional condition of anxiety, which is greater than the sum of its parts. Research has shown—and your own personal experience may bear this out—that the scariest things in life aren't just the mysteries you face. It's even scarier when those uncertainties are matched by an ample amount of fear that you aren't well prepared for or powerful enough to address. In this case, trying to bring either your sense of uncertainty or your powerlessness closer to zero will have a big impact on the amount of anxiety you feel.

## DIVISION

My mathematician friends tell me that this type of equation is the most prevalent relationship in science, physics, and algebra. This is because changing the elements in a division equation creates more dynamic consequences than does addition or subtraction.

To work with division equations, we need to introduce two additional math words: numerator and denominator. The equation 12 equals 24 divided by 2, or $12 = 24 \div 2$, places 24 in the numerator (on top) and 2 in the denominator (on the bottom). Grow the denominator just a little—for example, go from 2 to 4—and you see a big change in the total. In this case, adding 2 to the bottom cuts the total in half, from 12 to 6: $6 = 24 \div 4$. So the denominator can have a profound impact on the equation.

As an example, one of my favorite equations is the one that I presented at the TED Conference in 2010:

$$Happiness = \frac{Wanting\ What\ You\ Have}{Having\ What\ You\ Want}$$

That may seem like a brain tease, but think of it this way: "Wanting What You Have" is like practicing gratitude. It means appreciating the good fortune in your life. "Having What You Want," to me, means that you are pursuing something that will give you gratification, potentially to the neglect of what you already have. In other words,

$$Happiness = \frac{Practicing\ Gratitude}{Pursuing\ Gratification}$$

The contest between gratitude and gratification is truly being played out in the modern world. Although we have many ways to build gratitude into our lives, as long as our need for gratification drives our wants, our happiness will be fleeting; we'll always be just one more object or experience away from obtaining it.

Understanding this equation helped me to see that most of us are on a treadmill in our "pursuit of happiness." This equation has helped many people I know identify the difference between practicing happiness and pursuing it. When my happiness feels elusive, I tend to ask myself, "What am I not being grateful for, and what am I pursuing that's distracting me from that gratitude?" In the chapters on division, you will see that I suggest that we "solve for" either the numerator (the top) or the denominator (the bottom). What I mean by "solve for" is to give extra attention to that part of the equation, because it can have a profound impact on your emotional state.

Now, as you get ready to dive into the equations, have no fear. Emotional Equations simply use math as a new lens to explore the mystery of the emotions inside you. So enjoy the adventure, and try not to let the math distract you from the bigger message in each chapter. In this case, math can be your friend!

# PART II

# DEALING WITH DIFFICULT TIMES

*We should not feel embarrassed by our difficulties, only by our failure to grow anything beautiful from them.*
—Alain de Botton

# 3

$$\boxed{\text{Despair} = \text{Suffering} - \text{Meaning}}$$

In the early 1940s, Viktor Frankl was a young psychologist in Vienna with a bright future. A newlywed, he was close to his extended family, and his new method of therapy was gaining respect in the European psychological community. Frankl believed that the primary human motivational force is our will to experience meaning. In this way, he differed from Sigmund Freud and Alfred Adler, whose theories were based on the will to pleasure and the will to power. Frankl often quoted Friedrich Nietzsche, who wrote, "He who has a *why* can bear with almost any *how*." Little did Frankl know that the imminent war would deeply test his character and his will to experience meaning. His profound postwar memoir, *Man's Search for Meaning,* chronicled his experience of living in the knowledge of this Emotional Equation.

On September 24, 1942, Frankl, his wife, and his parents were separated and shipped off to a series of concentration camps. Over the next three years, he experienced the living hell of being stripped of everything he loved and imprisoned by the Nazis. Tragically, everyone in his extended family perished.

What sustained Frankl, as well as many prisoners around him who were able to hear his day-to-day thoughts, was the idea that no matter how horrible the circumstances, with the right emotional tools he could find a sense of meaning. He saw that often, those who died weren't necessarily the ones who were the sickest or the weakest when they arrived in camp—they were the ones who focused on the suffering. The men who sought meaning, wisdom, or learning, even in such a horrific environment, were more able to, literally, stay alive.

In his book, Frankl noted that "The prisoner who had lost faith in the future was doomed." He tells the story of a friend who dreamed that the camp would be liberated on March 30, 1944, as his way of coping with the suffering. But as that day approached and there were no signs of a liberating army nearby, the man grew more and more despondent. On March 30, he gave up hope, and he died the next day, his will to live broken. Camp conditions were certainly a factor in shaping the prisoners' reactions, but their personal state of mental and physical health, and how they responded internally to what they were facing externally, determined whether they would perish or survive.

Frankl considered a person as a "being whose main concern consists in fulfilling a meaning, rather than in the mere gratification and satisfaction of drives and instincts." So for prisoners, finding meaning might translate into how they used this wretched experience as a life-changing catalyst when they emerged from the camps or imagined that there was some divine purpose in why they had been incarcerated. After his release from the camps, Frankl spent the rest of his life helping people understand that the search for meaning dispels despair, even when suffering is ever present.

As a practicing psychologist, Frankl often saw patients who were trapped in some form of mental prison, whether a bad marriage, a physical affliction, or an unfortunate career path. He coined the term "unemployment neurosis" to define someone who was jobless and who equated this idleness with uselessness. Since people who feel useless are also likely to feel they are living a meaningless life, Frankl counseled such patients to volunteer their time to a cause or organization that was personally meaningful to them. Not only did this exercise create some valuable discipline for the patients, it tapped into their will to experience meaning and led to finding gainful employment much faster.

Although most of us will never experience life inside a real prison, we can surely relate to a sense of suffering, whether that be facing painful outside circumstances or dealing with the inner struggles that go on between our ears. Have you constructed your own prison? If so, I invite you to think of this chapter as your "Get out of jail free" card.

## SUFFERING = PAIN × RESISTANCE

The equation above harkens back to the sixteenth-century Spanish Catholic saint and mystic Teresa of Ávila and even further back to the Buddha. Pain and suffering can be synonymous, but it's really the resistance to them that amplifies this relationship (or, as the Buddha said, it's our attachment to what was or what we think should be that creates suffering). Resistance is a voluntary action that can either accelerate or eliminate suffering. It's your choice. Based on the math, suffering might be considered voluntary, too, because if you take the resistance down to zero, it takes the suffering in that same direction.

The author Dan Millman suggests that pain is relatively objective and physical, but "suffering is our psychological resistance to what happens. Events may create physical pain, but they do not in themselves create suffering. Resistance creates suffering. Stress happens when your mind resists what is."

This may seem blasphemous to anyone who is dealing with a

tragedy right now. But as we learned in chapter 2, our circumstances aren't the primary causes of unhappiness; our reactions to situations are. Do we resist, or do we accept? This is one of the most fundamental questions in life, and it's not easily answered. How do you react to difficulties or circumstances out of your control? As someone who has spent most of my life trying to beat the odds with my accomplishments, I have found acceptance—or even that more docile word "surrender"—to be really tricky.

There are times when resisting—even amid the pain—is the right answer. This was my experience during more than five painful years when I was working diligently to help a family member defend himself against a wrongful criminal charge and conviction. He ended up being sentenced to time in San Quentin State Prison—which tested both of us in our abilities to find meaning in the situation—but ultimately our resistance led to justice being done when a federal judge released him.

The key is not to focus on your suffering. The Buddha taught that there are four Noble Truths; the first one is that suffering exists everywhere. Not just in concentration camps. Not just in prisons. Not just in historic recessions. Suffering is the constant in our life. It can also have a noble purpose once you stop focusing on it as a constant and instead start giving attention not just to relieving the pain but also to looking for the meaning that can come out of the experience. Once you modify your expectations and realize that suffering is ever present, just like oxygen and electricity, you can count on it; but if you don't fixate on it, you can shift your focus to what else life has to offer.

## HUMANS ARE MEANING MAKERS

Positive psychologists believe that making meaning is a basic need: we strive to make sense of our place in the world, especially as it becomes more complex. The more complicated our lives become, the more important it is to give attention to what it all means. A world without meaning is a world in which despair equals suffering, and we end up anesthetizing ourselves with distractions—TV, the Internet, alcohol—to kill the pain.

Jonathan Haidt, the author of *The Happiness Hypothesis: Finding Modern Truth in Ancient Wisdom,* suggests that the key to growth in life "is not optimism per se; it is sense making" and cites findings about the relationship between trauma and later health problems. The nature of the trauma—whether it was sexual abuse or losing a spouse to suicide (rather than illness or an accident)—turned out to be almost irrelevant. What mattered was what people did afterward: those who talked with their friends or with a support group were largely spared the health-damaging effects of trauma. Writing was an equally powerful antidote. But whether talking or writing, only people who extracted a sense of meaning from something awful had significant positive results.

Traumas are wounds. If a wound is cleaned and dressed well, it will heal well and the scarring may not be too visible. We all have scars, and despair is a natural human emotion. But our health has less to do with our actual wounds and more to do with our approach to healing them. An ancient Ethiopian proverb says, "He who conceals his disease cannot expect to be cured." Unattended wounds can turn into chronic "dis-ease." But heal your wounds, and you can move on with your life.

## MY LIFE MAKING MEANING

It has been said that the purpose of life is finding a life of purpose. The same could be said for meaning: the meaning of life is to find a life of meaning. Between my forty-fifth and fiftieth birthdays, I felt as if everything that could go wrong did. In retrospect, I see that I was experiencing an emotional and identity transformation analogous to a caterpillar turning into a butterfly. The only problem was, my metamorphosis took place inside a very public glass chrysalis.

Along the way, the writer in me felt the need to make sense of my overplotted world by writing in my journal. Although I don't enjoy journaling, during that time I imposed a certain amount of self-discipline. I kept coming back to the "Meaning" equation, Despair = Suffering − Meaning, and asking "What is the meaning in all of these disparate, difficult experiences?"

A life theme started to emerge from the rubble. Perhaps prophetically, the first hotel I had created when I was twenty-six years old was called "The Phoenix" in honor of the mythical bird that rose from its own ashes—an appropriate new name for what had been a "no-tell motel" popular with local prostitutes before we turned it into a successful (and infamous) rock 'n' roll hotel populated by everyone from David Bowie to Linda Ronstadt. And my midlife was my own rising from ashes. Once that became clear, I could see that all the crap was not happening just to me.

To shed some gravity-induced weight, I sold a majority interest in my company to an impeccably soulful guy (who happens to be a billionaire), and now the company is expanding rapidly again, in tandem with Thompson Hotels. I've dived deeper into my second calling of being a writer and speaker, which had been at odds with the demands of being a CEO. I've made peace with being single after nearly twenty years of sharing my life with two different partners. I've deepened my friendships, my relationship with my family, and my self-understanding. As a fiftieth-birthday gift to myself, I wrote a "mini" memoir called *Flatline on the Faultline,* which I shared with only my closest friends and family members—a testament to the sense of meaning I'd discovered. This process of rebirth healed my wounds and helped me move on, making my scars feel somehow like trophies.

## WORKING THROUGH THE EQUATION

$$Despair = Suffering - Meaning$$

Here are some suggestions for exploring meaning in your own life.

*Rethink your assumptions and link them with your "why."* Suffering often occurs at the intersection of old and new thinking. We suffer when we hold on to perspectives that no longer serve us and fail to see a new way to reframe our lives. Look for possible assumptions at the root of your suffering, and question whether these assumptions are still valid. Can you imagine a new way of thinking? Consider Bethany Hamilton, the teenage champion surfer who lost an arm in a shark attack. Bethany suffered great physical trauma, and most people assumed she'd never want to enter the ocean again. But less than one month after the incident, she got back up on her board and retrained herself to surf with just one arm, and today she continues to win competitions. Get in touch with your own purpose, and look for ways your difficult experiences can support you in living out your purpose.

*Find a way of expressing yourself.* For some people (right brainers), expressing themselves is cathartic because it means letting go of emotions. For others (left brainers), the process of communicating about a difficult experience may create some logic or rationale for why all this is happening. Whichever you are, you can transcend your suffering and get in touch with its meaning by developing a narrative, story, or theme that helps you see how, in the long run, this experience was a serendipitous match for you on your life's path. You can express yourself in a journal, in some kind of support group, in a religious or spiritual practice, or in collecting and displaying images and objects that represent what you're feeling. Take care, though, not to use those expressions to wallow in the suffering. Be willing to discover whatever meaning may come.

*Don't get so abstract that you lose sight of the concrete.* Frankl wrote that he felt compelled to teach other men in the concentration camp that "It did not really matter what we expected from life, but rather what life expected from us. We needed to stop asking the meaning of life, and instead to think of ourselves as those who were being questioned by life—daily and hourly. Our answer must consist, not in talk and meditation, but in right action and right conduct."

Lots of people are so distracted by searching for the light at the end of the tunnel that they cannot see clearly what's right next to them. Creating an abstract idea of meaning can just become another distraction. What is life asking of you right now? Can you light a figurative candle in your hand to illuminate this moment so that you and those around you can make a difference today?

When I was faced with two "once-in-a-lifetime" economic downturns in the same decade, I looked for ways to improve the mental health of those around me on a daily basis. It felt as if life were asking me, "What's our company culture going to look like when this is over, and what can I do in this moment to breathe life into that culture?" You could apply this same thinking to your family: "How can I show up as a role model when I get home tonight?" What can you do to take attention away from the bad news (suffering) and focus it instead on that which you can control (meaning)?

*Describe the "new you."* Consider how much you have grown as a result of the challenges you've faced. Make a list of five adjectives—for example, creative, patient, compassionate, wise, or resilient—that describe you as a result of what you've gone through. Then imagine how this "new you" will make a real difference in the world and help you to become a role model for others. Don't worry, I'm not asking you to be the next Mahatma Gandhi. Just define the new habits or behaviors that have sprouted from this difficult time that will support and strengthen your character as you move forward.

I also recommend reading one of Frankl's favorite books, Leo Tolstoy's novel *The Death of Ivan Ilyich,* the tale of a man who suddenly learns he is about to die and is confronted with the fact that he's wasted his life. This insight floods him with a new sense of inspiration that carries him into becoming a "new person" even though he had only a few days of life remaining.

When we can't find meaning, we often seek stimulation or distraction instead. That's not the end of the world, but don't wait until you have only a few days left to experience your meaningful life. This equation is relevant to you whether you prefer Dolly Parton to the Dalai Lama or your idea of a good time is the Las Vegas strip, not a Buddhist temple. Meaning can find you anywhere—in a park with your kids or in a lunch conversation with a coworker—just be open (and willing) to be found. To paraphrase Nietzsche, the measure of ourselves is how we transform pain or suffering into something worthwhile or meaningful in our lives.

# 4

$$\boxed{\text{Disappointment} = \text{Expectations} - \text{Reality}}$$

When Abraham Lincoln was seven, he and his family were forced out of their home and he had to start working to help support his parents. When he was nine, his mother died. As a child, he was kicked in the head by a horse, and once he nearly drowned. Throughout his life, he suffered from malaria (twice), syphilis, and smallpox. At age twenty-one, he failed in business. At age twenty-three, he ran for the state legislature, lost his job, and was turned down for law school. That same year, he started another business on borrowed money, but a year later he was bankrupt. At age twenty-six, he was engaged to be married, but his fiancée died; soon afterward, his only sister died during childbirth. Lincoln hit an emotional low and took to his bed for six months.

At age twenty-eight, he was defeated as speaker of the state legislature. At age thirty-three, he ran for the U.S. House of Representatives and lost. He tried again at age thirty-nine and lost again. He ran for the U.S. Senate at age forty-five and lost. He tried for his party's vice presidential nomination at age forty-seven and lost. And lost again for the U.S. Senate at age forty-nine. Despite all this, at age fifty-one, Abraham Lincoln was elected the sixteenth president of the United States.

During the course of his life, Lincoln would write long, sad poems, one of which contemplated suicide. His contemporaries, as well as most historians, describe him as melancholic; some believe that he suffered from depression. His writings display pain, doubt, and a dash of inferiority. Those attributes and his melancholy served as building blocks of his success later in life.

Lincoln wrote, "I have been too familiar with disappointments to be very much chagrined." In other words, he had a realistic view of life. There would be large and small tragedies and disappointments, but he would move on. He had little sense of entitlement. Lincoln's humble roots and unvarnished view of himself didn't stop him from achieving, but they did temper his expectations. One expert suggests that what gave him the ability to continue moving ahead was "a search for meaning that Abe Lincoln pursued throughout his life."

Lincoln seemed to use disappointment as a lesson in diligence and discipline. His story has been called one of integration rather than transformation. He didn't do all his great works as a result of solving the problem of his melancholy; the problem actually motivated him to do great work. His adaptation and resilience show just how much disappointment can empower a midlife sense of fortitude.

In the mid-1990s, psychologists conducted an exhaustive American/German survey of the frequency and intensity of people's emotions. Of thirteen unpleasant emotions, including guilt, loneliness, embarrassment, and sadness, disappointment was, by far, the emotion that scored the highest intensity among those surveyed. Disappointment came in a close third place behind anxiety and anger in frequency. Other studies have shown that disappointment can be highest right around midlife, when what we'd hoped to accomplish doesn't measure up with the reality of what we've achieved.

Yet Lincoln might have negotiated any midlife crisis of his own in a highly constructive and more positive manner than other people because he had come to terms with the upheaval and darkness of dashed expectations. Such repeated defeats can expand our consciousness and view of possibility, moving us beyond the limitations of our views of ourselves, of what our egos decree as being who we are and what is ours. As the British satirist and poet Alexander Pope put it, "Blessed is he who expects nothing, for he shall never be disappointed."

It's easy to misunderstand Pope's quote as an excuse to crawl under the covers when things go wrong. Yet Lincoln is a perfect example of someone who might have learned to curb his expectations while continuing to pursue his ambition and hopes and his purpose in his life. Let's explore what we mean by disappointment, expectations, and reality.

## THE BLESSINGS AND CURSES OF EXPECTATIONS

Disappointment resides in the same apartment building as regret, just on a lower floor. Regret (which we'll get to in the next chapter) has a higher charge because it relates to choices you have made that have led to unsatisfying outcomes—your responsibility for or role in causing a problem, loss, or tragedy. Feeling disappointed means you didn't get what you wanted. You feel frustration, on the other hand, when you still have a sense that you could affect an outcome.

Is something in your life right now not going the way you want it to? If you had to define it as disappointing or frustrating, which would it be? Disappointment recognizes that something is over. That's why it often comes with a sense of deflation or defeat.

From the moment we wake up in the morning, we're walking expectation machines, whether we are expecting something as mundane as good weather or something more essential such as a promotion at work. It can be the buyer's remorse you feel a week after you bought your highly anticipated new car or the tinge of melancholy at the end of a honeymoon. Yet the psychologist Barry Schwartz, in *The Paradox of Choice: Why More Is Less,* suggests, "We probably can do more to affect the quality of our lives by controlling our expectations than by doing virtually anything else." The math in this equation is very clear: the higher your expectations, the more the potential for disappointment.

Based on this equation, you have two options to reduce your potential for disappointment. Either you reduce your expectations, or you influence reality—or at least your sense of reality.

If you believe your high expectations fuel your success, it can be hard to stomach the first option. In fact, there's quite a bit of evidence showing that Asian-American teens tend to score higher on standardized tests partly due to the high expectations that have been instilled in them by their parents.

Some researchers believe that a "disappointment effect" causes people with high expectations not to prepare themselves or "emotionally cushion" themselves for disappointment, so that they are less able to deal with it when they experience it. Those who expect the worst in life know that disappointment lurks when they get their hopes up, and they tend to give themselves a low ceiling. Others believe it's not really healthy to abstain from so much life nourishment just to play disappointment dodgeball.

Clearly, this equation leads to a slippery slope when you try to determine where to place your expectations set point. Do your expectations fuel you, or do they deflate you?

This brings us to the definition of reality, a key actor on this equation's stage but one that is rarely given any lines. Reality is what you make of it, and it can be a critical variable in this equation. Olympic athletes who win a silver medal are generally unhappier than those who win a bronze. Why? Because more of the silver-medal winners expected to win a gold medal (or make the upward comparison to what they almost won), whereas more of the bronze-medal winners weren't sure they were going to win a medal at all (or downwardly compare themselves with those who ended up empty-handed). Again, expectations influence happiness here.

What if these athletes were to reframe their emotional response to these results? Let's look more closely at what we consider reality in order to understand this equation.

## SHIFT HAPPENS

The social scientist Alex Michalos has studied people's perceived quality of experience—in other words, their sense of reality about what has happened. He's argued that people establish a perceived level of satisfaction based upon comparing three gaps: what you have versus what you want ("I want a beautiful green lawn"), what you have versus what you think other people have ("The neighbor's grass is greener"), and what you have and the best experience of what you've had in the past ("I don't like AstroTurf. I miss my old grass"). I would add a fourth: the gap between what you have and what you feel you deserve ("I've been working my tail off for this grass").

One problem with respect to these gaps is that modern society tends to live on a "hedonic treadmill." We adapt to pleasure and our situation—we get used to it—and come to expect more and more from life. I call this the "gravity effect." What initially "floats our boat"—whether it's our favorite resort or the bay view from our office—starts to wear off over time. Quite often, it's this shifting upward of expectations and downward of our appreciation of what we have that leads to larger gaps in Michalos's model.

We also downshift our definitions of reality relative to others. H. L. Mencken once said, "Wealth is any income that is at least one hundred dollars more than the income of one's wife's sister's husband." I get it. I always brace myself before going to my Stanford Business School reunions because I tend to feel like an underachiever—relative to the wealthy, retired classmates of mine who became investment bankers and venture capitalists. I know that the reunions trigger some sense of lack in me, so now before I go, I prepare myself with a "reality check" and explore my current definition of "wealth" a little more deeply. How do you define wealth? Is it how much money you make annually or how many zeroes you have on your personal balance sheet? Or is it the wealth of time? Or family love? Or freedom?

Have you experienced "reality inflation" the past few years? What if you stopped looking over the fence? I love the saying "Never compare your insides to someone else's outsides" because we never really know what's going on with "the Joneses" next door or with anyone else. We can only make assumptions that often lead to our feeling "less" than someone else.

I believe the secret to cracking this equation is to realize that it's not our expectations that we necessarily need to curb; it's our sense of entitlement that leads us to be so bitterly disappointed when things don't go our way. A shift will happen when we're willing to make this adjustment to accept reality—when we stop focusing on some delusional idea of the way life "should" be. Have you shifted your own expectations about income, retirement, future education or career prospects, or where you'll live as a result of the economic downturn? Can you assume that this shift is something that may become permanent? Does this expectation feel comfortable to you?

The physicist Stephen Hawking was diagnosed at the age of twenty-one with amyotrophic lateral sclerosis, a crippling neuromuscular disease that has progressed over the years and left him almost completely paralyzed. But that hasn't stopped him from making astonishing discoveries in theoretical physics and becoming the most widely read scientist in the world. As one of the longest survivors of Lou Gehrig's disease, as ALS is also called, he has said, "Concentrate on things your disability doesn't prevent you doing well. Don't regret the things it interferes with."

One means of dealing with disappointment is to initially be optimistic when you're in the process of trying to influence an outcome but to brace yourself against a potential negative outcome by ratcheting down your expectations over time once it's out of your control. A Dutch experiment proved that, as a coping mechanism, people will lower their expectations only if a particular outcome is important to them. And the closer they get to the outcome, the more they lower their expectations. We've all done this to manage our anxiety while waiting to hear about a second job interview or for the phone to ring for a second date. It's healthy behavior as long as we don't lower our expectations so far that we begin to feel disdain toward a prospective employer or date. Anyone who feels that just obsessing on an outcome will actually change it may need to seriously consider a reality check.

Another coping mechanism is to dilute the importance of reality. In some cases, you may have to ask yourself how important the result is. Disappointment may be just a mosquito bite that you can forget twenty minutes later. On the other hand, it may feel like more than a bee sting to find out that you came in second place in the Olympic 100-meter breaststroke—by one one-hundredth of a second. Your expectation was first place. Your reality was second place. And there was no time to reduce your expectations.

Is a silver medal all that bad? The harder you've worked toward a goal, the more entitled you may feel, but you may derive great value from reframing the results. This is where friends and family can help you interpret your situation and the events around you.

## IS YOUR REALITY CHECK BOUNCING?

In 1999, my company opened a luxury campground called Costanoa on California's scenic Highway 1. There was something sort of experimental about this 240-acre development surrounded by thousands of acres of pristine coastside wilderness (even the oxymoronic phrase "luxury campground" defined this place as an original). It took nearly four years for us to open after navigating an obstacle course of local politics through the approval process, challenging design planning with the California Coastal Commission, an extended construction schedule through an El Niño winter of record-breaking rains and winds, and a difficult financing environment for such an oddball project.

I felt a deep resonance with Costanoa and set up residence there during the construction process, renting a shack for a half year at the nearby historic lighthouse. Though I'd spent my share of time as an Eagle Scout sleeping on the ground, I quickly became a convert to Costanoa's concept of cushy camping. Who could argue with the idea of staying in a small, safari-like tent with a heated mattress, down comforter, lavender sprigs on the pillows, and fluffy bathrobes for the walk to the nearby bathrooms that had heated, polished concrete floors and roaring fireplaces? Within a couple of months after the opening, *USA Today* did a front-page spread on Costanoa as the future of camping for a new generation. The media flocked to Costanoa, as did customers—initially.

Unfortunately, a combination of factors—some operational, some related to rigid development rules that limited what we could offer guests, and some due to having the wrong mix of partners—led to a financially rocky start after the high expectations that accompanied our opening. And then the Bay Area dot-com bust dried up all of our weekday corporate retreat business. The next thing we knew, our majority partner was pushing to sell Costanoa for a fraction of what we had paid to build it. Given that my company wasn't in a position to buy the property, another real estate investor bought Costanoa and we were quickly out on our ears.

Saying good-bye to the staff was heart-wrenching. It was months before I got my leadership legs underneath me again. I was full of disappointment, partly because after investing so much blood, sweat, and tears in the project I felt entitled to its success. My friends and family knew that there wasn't much they could do to change the expectations part of the equation for me, so they tried to help me reframe my sense of reality instead. One of my development guys on Costanoa sent me three clear glasses of varying sizes, along with a note to remind me that most people view their glass as either half empty or half full but my ambitious optimism tends toward "Why can't I have a bigger glass?"

Another note came from a friend after a family trip to Costanoa. He said, "I know losing Costanoa is like losing a family member, Chip. But just know there are many families in the Bay Area who are lucky that you had the vision to create this miraculous place. Don't ever forget that." This supportive reality check took me from viewing Costanoa as a financial and professional failure to seeing it as an innovative experiment that had turned into a rich family tradition for many people. With time, my disappointment started to evolve into a sense of pride and legacy for having conceived and pursued such a wild-eyed idea.

So when you're bathing in disappointment and can no longer influence your expectations, ask yourself whether your definition of reality is truly serving you or if you need help to modify that definition to shift this equation.

## WORKING THROUGH THE EQUATION

$$Disappointment = Expectations - Reality$$

*Ask yourself, "Am I frustrated or disappointed?"* I know that, when I'm not getting what I want, I spend an awful lot of time on the island of frustration before I cross over to the mainland of disappointment. You can tell the difference between these emotions based upon whether you still feel like you can influence the outcome or not. If you're frustrated, use that energy and shift it into the determination you need. Frustration can serve as a temporary bridge to a better outcome. That may mean studying harder for a final exam after having not done so well on a term paper. Don't fall into a state of disappointment prematurely. But if the outcome is fixed and you're frustrated, it's time to evolve that hot emotion into disappointment, as that emotion is more likely to dissolve quickly. If you're disappointed, lick your wounds and move on. Just remember that the worth of an emotion has a lot to do with the outcome it is intended to serve. Frustration moves forward. Disappointment retreats.

*Ratchet down your expectations in anticipation of an outcome.* If there's one clear message in all the studies of disappointment, it's that there's an inverse relationship between expectations and disappointment: the more of the former, the greater potential for increase of the latter. The key is to know when to ratchet down your expectations. Don't do this prematurely, as you risk creating a self-fulfilling prophecy—psyching yourself out by negatively affecting your performance, which will create exactly the disappointing result you were expecting. So much of this has to do with letting go of what you can't control and knowing when you have lost your ability to influence the outcome.

*Learn a lesson from the stock market.* Over the years, I've recited this mantra to just about everyone I've ever worked with: "Disappointment is the natural result of badly managed expectations." If you have to deliver disappointing news, do it as early as possible. Companies on the stock exchanges have learned this lesson the hard way, because when stock analysts aren't given any indication of a likely quarterly earnings disappointment disclosure, they tend to punish earnings surprises with excessive reductions in the stock price of the company. Does your "stock price" with your boss or spouse take a beating when you don't give adequate warning about an upcoming disappointment? Be proactive about managing expectations.

*Ask yourself, "In terms of my lifetime, how important is this disappointing result, and what can I learn from it?"* At the moment, a disappointment can feel as though a big, oppressive, heavy blanket has been thrown over you. Just remember what we learned in chapter 2: Emotions are momentary. You determine whether to stew in your own sad juices. Abraham Lincoln had all kinds of disappointing results through his lifetime, many of which could have been considered life- or career-altering, but he learned from those experiences and they made him into a better statesman and more empathetic person.

And we can all gain perspective from Stephen Hawking's comment on expectations, which he made in reference to his diagnosis of ALS: "My expectations were reduced to zero when I was twenty-one. Everything since then has been a bonus." How can you make that kind of mental shift in your life so that your glass isn't half empty or half full? How about simply being glad that you have a glass?

# 5

$$\boxed{\text{Regret} = \text{Disappointment} + \text{Responsibility}}$$

"M rs. Dalloway said she would buy the flowers herself." This is the famous opening line of Virginia Woolf's acclaimed novel *Mrs. Dalloway,* the story of a post–World War I London socialite who is strained by the complexities of her life. This first line suggests that Clarissa Dalloway will take it upon herself—so that her house staff isn't troubled—to choose and fetch the flowers for an evening party, but one can sense an undertone of tension in her proclamation.

Regret is the wistful, yearning older sister of disappointment. It's a more mature emotion, suggesting that dissatisfaction with a result may be due to unfortunate personal choices. Taken to the extreme, regret is responsibility with a magnifying glass—a painful indulgence that we choose because we're so used to blaming ourselves.

Virginia Woolf herself had a rich interior dialogue, yet she also suffered from mental illness (she ended her life by filling the pockets of an oversized trench coat with rocks and walking into a river). But her ability to capture the nuances of emotions makes her one of the twentieth century's greatest novelists.

Michael Cunningham won a Pulitzer Prize for adapting *Mrs. Dalloway* into his novel *The Hours,* which was made into a film. One particular sentence from this exquisite book captures the constancy of regret: "There's just this consolation: an hour here or there when our lives seem, against all odds and expectations, to burst open and give us everything we've ever imagined . . . Still, we cherish the city, the morning; we hope, more than anything, for more."

How often do you hope for more? Virginia Woolf, as exemplified in her character Mrs. Dalloway, was blessed with many choices but hoped for more. Mrs. Dalloway is surprised by a visit from Peter Walsh, an enigmatic man she had chosen not to marry years earlier; she also has deep feelings for her intimate friend Sally Seton. She chose a reliable, safe husband in Richard Dalloway, but—in the hours a well-to-do woman has to herself—she seems to regret the choices she's made and the passion and adventure she gave up.

Meryl Streep, who starred in *The Hours,* also starred in *Sophie's Choice,* which could have been called "Sophie's Regret," given the consequences of the agonizing decision the character has to make. Robert Frost's poem "The Road Not Taken" captures the idea that life is full of choices and ends with the following stanza:

> *I shall be telling this with a sigh*
> *Somewhere ages and ages hence:*
> *Two roads diverged in a wood, and I—*
> *I took the one less traveled by,*
> *And that has made all the difference*

Anyone with a sense of responsibility can feel regret, which can be sharp, bittersweet, or deeply haunting, a cloud that hovers over you for years. When you regret your actions more than your choices, regret can become remorse.

Regret = Disappointment + Responsibility

$$\left[\ \textit{Remorse = Regret + Guilt.}\ \right]$$

Remorse may sting more than regret, but regret has it over disappointment because if you "woulda, shoulda, coulda" taken a different path, you wouldn't be feeling this sorry emotion now.

## "IF ONLY . . ."

These have been called the two saddest words in the English language, and they succinctly summarize the mental anguish that comes with regret. There's a lot going on with this emotion, but regret isn't wholly negative. It can be a call to action to correct our mistakes and to learn from them, which assists us in the future. Regret doesn't just result from the actions we take; it also comes from those actions we wish we had taken. Regret is different from many other emotions because it lacks immediacy and tends to come from reflection or after insight that comes with time.

I call regret a "First World emotion," not because it doesn't exist as much in the developing world (although there are surveys that show this) but because it's a function of the modern world's plenitude of choices. The more choices we have, the more possibility we have for regret. In the West, we tend to glorify plentiful choices without recognizing the pain they exact. Alexander Solzhenitsyn, the Soviet dissident who understood how few choices the USSR provided for its citizens, reportedly said, "America is full of choices; unfortunately, all of them are mundane." Choices need to be meaningful.

Sheena Iyengar, the author of *The Art of Choosing,* developed an experiment in which she set up two jam-tasting kiosks in an upscale supermarket. One offered samples of twenty-four different flavors, and another offered just six. The kiosks with twenty-four flavors tempted nearly 60 percent of shoppers passing by, while the kiosk with fewer choices attracted only 40 percent. But only 3 percent of the people who had the choice to sample twenty-four varieties actually purchased the jam, while 30 percent of those who sampled one of the six varieties bought some. Having lots of choice can be a pleasant distraction, but too much choice leads to a certain level of paralysis and, in some cases, stress. Do you find yourself stressing out with so many choices in your life? Can you reduce the number of "jams" you have to taste in order to simplify your choices?

Choosing jam is mundane, but the fact is that any choice contains the potential for regret since it's hard to shift the blame for a decision you've made. For example, one of the pleasures of our modern life is choosing where to live and work, a privilege that is less available in the developing world. Conventional wisdom suggests that life is better when we don't have to live our adult life next door to our parents, doing the work that has been prescribed for us since we were born. Choice can be liberating. But the process of making choices can be challenging, and psychic costs that we haven't factored in can later lead to regret.

A classic American middle-class decision is choosing to take a job in a downtown metropolitan area because the salary is attractive but to live in the suburbs for the bigger homes and the better schools. The psychologist Daniel Kahneman found that commuting is by far the most unpleasant part of the average person's day, and spending even an extra twenty minutes in transit is 20 percent as harmful to your well-being as losing your job. So regret can be hiding behind the veil of choice.

Choice can be both a blessing and a curse. It can increase the burden of gathering information, increase the likelihood that you'll make no decision due to "analysis paralysis," increase the expectation of how good the chosen option should be, and, most relevant to this chapter, increase the likelihood that you'll feel regret and a sense of blame when you make the "wrong" choice.

## THE MANY FLAVORS OF REGRET

Regret comes in all shapes and sizes. Understanding a few of them can help you deal with your own—and perhaps make you more conscious of ways to prevent yourself from creating more. One way it can arise is by our protecting ourselves against loss. When making choices among alternatives that involve a certain amount of risk, we may prefer a small, sure gain to a larger, uncertain one. Mrs. Dalloway may have been calculating this way when she chose the matrimonial path with her husband. Losses can have twice the psychological impact on us as equivalent gains. We tend to prefer satisfactory middle-ground solutions to extreme highs or lows.

In *The Paradox of Choice,* Barry Schwartz outlined two kinds of regret: "anticipated regret" and "postdecision regret." We're more familiar with the latter when we're sorry for a choice we made. But anticipated regret can be worse, as it lasts longer and you start ruminating on it earlier. Schwartz suggested, "Both types of regret—anticipated and postdecision—will raise the emotional stakes of decisions. Anticipated regret will make decisions harder to make, and postdecision regret makes them harder to enjoy."

Most of us have a two-to-one predilection toward loss aversion. This gets more interesting when you anticipate regret and try to protect yourself from it. If given the choice between a guaranteed $100 now or the potential of $200, based upon choosing the correct outcome of a coin flip, most people will take the $100, as there's less risk of regret. But if you choose the $100 and are forced to flip the coin to see the results, a different emotional phenomenon occurs. We've introduced the potential for much more postdecision regret, and studies have shown that if a situation is set up this way, we are more likely to take the risk.

Once we've made a decision, we tend to put our heads in the sand to limit our "regret aversion." (Imagine if Mrs. Dalloway had known that her former beau might live only a block away for the rest of her life, which would have affected her decision to marry Mr. Dalloway.) This may explain why that old flame of yours doesn't want to stay in touch with you after you choose to marry someone else.

Mark Twain didn't dabble in psychological focus groups, but he certainly knew something about human nature when he wrote, "Twenty years from now you will be more disappointed by the things that you didn't do than by the ones you did do. So throw off the bowlines. Sail away from the safe harbor. Catch the trade winds in your sails. Explore. Dream. Discover."

A series of surveys explored the premise that time is an important variable in this equation. Researchers asked a random sampling of people, "When you look back on your experiences in life and think of those things that you regret, what would you say you regret more, those things that you did, but wish you hadn't, or those things that you didn't do, but wish you had?"

The results found that regrettable "failures to act" outnumbered "regrettable actions" by a two-to-one margin and that this was true for both sexes. Most surprisingly, older people had only slightly more regret than younger folks about what they hadn't done. The clearest regret is, as Twain suggested, that we wish we had lived less timidly. As you think of your own life, what are two or three "failures to act" that you wish you could do over? Is it too late to do anything about them, or can you take the steps to act now so that this regret doesn't linger any longer?

The researchers went on to surmise that the story of regrettable actions tends to close: you do something; you feel regret for some period; then you move on. The story of a failure to act, however, is open. It carries a big cloud of "if only"; it's unfixable and probably leads to more mental hypotheses about how the outcome would have been different if you'd just done something. So, as Mark Twain suggested, seizing the moment is the antidote to the fact that we are so heavily influenced by the immediate sting of regrettable action that we favor inaction over action without calculating the long-term toll of this choice.

## MODERN-DAY REGRET

Regret is an emotional bouillabaisse. Its stock is your sense of choice and responsibility. The more advanced a culture is in giving its citizens a sense of freedom to choose and access to information, the more regret they may feel due to bad results. That's why the financial meltdown of 2008 led to such a heavy sense of regret. So many people wished they'd been a little smarter and made better choices. But perfect choices rarely exist.

If you bought or refinanced your home during the past few years, you may have assumed—as many others did—that the double-digit appreciation in home values would continue forever. Instead, quite the opposite happened, and all that joy turned to grief. Some decisions we make in life are pretty dispassionate, but others are deeply rooted in our emotional core: who we choose as a life partner, whether we have kids, where we choose to live, and what kind of home we choose to own or rent long term. These kinds of decisions carry with them many more upsides and downsides because they're integral parts of our lives.

Millions of people have lost their homes during the financial wreckage of the past few years. My best friend, Vanda, had an instructive lost *and* found experience around her sense of home when she lost her apartment in London. Fortunately, she'd moved to California and the apartment was not her primary residence anymore, although it was her only financial asset, so it wasn't the crisis it has been for many individuals and families who have become homeless. Even so, she felt a deep level of regret along with a great deal of shame. Today she wishes she'd created some kind of conscious ritual to benchmark the experience and learn from it, rather than allow it to negatively affect the way she felt about herself for years.

The "found" part of her story was realizing that home was her true sense of ballast. A couple of years after she lost her apartment, although she couldn't afford to buy a home like her fashionable flat, she was able to invest in a tiny houseboat on San Francisco Bay that gave her some of the same psychological and emotional currency her London pied-à-terre had provided. She described her feelings about the eventual outcome, saying, "While I may occasionally feel a twinge of regret, I don't feel the sense of loss that I once did. Loss has loosened to nostalgia and prepared me in some small way for the time when I will have to give up this home, too, as inevitably I shall. I believe each loss brings its own medicine, its curing of the soul, so that ultimately when death calls us to give up everything, we can."

I was once asked in a leadership workshop to make a list of the five biggest regrets I'd had during my business career. My list included everything from not securing more growth capital in the early days of Joie de Vivre to not purchasing an apartment building on Los Angeles's Sunset Strip that later became a very successful boutique hotel. The workshop leader asked us to look at what was common to all these regrets. I could see that four of mine had been failures to act, as opposed to mistakes I'd made. In each case, my gut had told me to act, but my rational mind (and the conventional wisdom of others) had taken me in a different direction. Finally, the leader had us write down our five regrets on a separate piece of paper, along with one sentence for each that described the key learning we could carry for the rest of our lives. We went outside and lit each of the five regrets on fire, then poured all of our regrets together into a roaring fireplace.

How can your regrets light a fire to propel you in making better decisions from here forward?

## WORKING THROUGH THE EQUATION

$$Regret = Disappointment + Responsibility$$

*Examine your sense of responsibility.* The equation is very clear: what distinguishes disappointment from regret is your sense of responsibility in the matter. But I've found that feelings of regret are not necessarily logical; I've felt sharp stabs of regret even when a milder disappointment would have been more appropriate to the situation. Maybe I exaggerated my sense of control or responsibility in those instances or I tended to think of myself as a perfectionist who wasn't allowed to err. In any case, if a specific regret keeps eating at you and it feels a little misplaced, talk it over with a friend or colleague who has some understanding of the situation and your responsibility in it, in order to get an objective reading on whether you're overidentifying with the responsibility part of the equation.

*Deem short-term pain to be less significant than long-term angst.* That's easier said than done. But I have two simple questions you should ask yourself when determining whether to do something or not: Is it repeatable? Can it be repaired? If it's not repeatable, beware of saying no. If it can't be repaired (if something goes wrong), beware of saying yes. In my junior year at college, I had the opportunity to study at Stanford's British campus, which at the time was set in an enormous mansion on nearly four hundred pristine acres on the Thames River just outside London. My concern was that if I took my junior spring quarter there, which would then merge into summer, I wouldn't have a summer job on my résumé when going into my senior year looking for a full-time job after graduation. Fortunately, I had a wise counselor at school who gave me the following advice: "Over the course of your lifetime, you will have many, many jobs, but you will never have the opportunity to experience studying and

57

traveling overseas during college. You'll regret it later if you don't do this now." Those five months of studying in a castle and traveling as a carefree student with friends are some of my best college memories. Stick Mark Twain's quote on your bathroom mirror.

*Turn regret into a lesson.* The deeper the regret, the more you'll learn from it. You can ritualize regret in such a way that you'll see it as a bolstering experience in your life. First, use the experience as a wisdom builder for how you make decisions in the future. Second, if you're open to it, share your story. Teaching others about your regret and your lessons can be a truly healing experience (part of the reason I write books). Third, if amends are to be made, don't hesitate just because you're in a raw place. If your regret relates to others who may have been disappointed by your choice, be open to expressing how you feel; in some situations, this can be cathartic for them, as it shows how important it was to you. Regret can be a temporary emotion that means you just haven't found the meaning of the experience yet.

*Be a "satisficer" as opposed to a "maximizer."* Some people agonize over their decision-making process in order to maximize their options and make the best choice. Others are more comfortable satisficing—figuring that the time, money, and anguish aren't worth it and assuming that setting a lower bar of expectation will likely lead to less regret. *The Paradox of Choice* has a test on pages 80–81 that will help you determine which of these two breeds better defines you. Why is it relevant? Modern society, with all its choices, is exactly what a maximizer doesn't need. It just adds to the investment that goes into each choice and leads to a greater potential for regret as a result. Become more comfortable with "good enough."

What about a person who says he has lived a life with no regrets? There are three likely explanations: Either he is living an unexamined life and just says he has no regrets because it makes him feel and look confident. Or he has a low baseline of expectations or an ability to reframe reality such that he never has disappointments. Or, as the equation suggests, he doesn't take responsibility for anything.

Life is full of choices, and it's also full of ways to deal with regret. Oscar Wilde opined, "To regret one's own experiences is to arrest one's own development." But this is also the man who lived by the rule that yielding to temptations is often the fastest way to get rid of them.

Benjamin Franklin, arguably the father of the modern self-help movement, offered a more serious and logical approach for how to deal with choices in our lives as a means of reducing our regret later. He recommended what many of us have done at some point: create two columns on a piece of paper, writing "Pro" on one side and "Con" on the other. He explained, "Then, during three or four days' consideration, I put down under the different heads short hints of different motives, that at different times occur to me, for or against the measure. When I have thus got them all together in one view, I endeavor to estimate their respective weights; and where I find two, one on each side, that seem equal, I strike them both out. If I find a reason pro equal to some two reasons con, I strike out the three. If I judge some two reasons con, equal to three reasons pro, I strike out the five; and thus proceeding I find at length where the balance lies. . . . I think I can judge better, and am less likely to make a rash step; and in fact I have found great advantage from this kind of equation, in what may be called moral or prudential algebra."

Wise people have been using equations to solve life's problems for centuries.

# 6

$$\left[ \text{Jealousy} = \frac{\text{Mistrust}}{\text{Self-Esteem}} \right]$$

$$\left[ \text{Envy} = \frac{(\text{Pride} + \text{Vanity})}{\text{Kindness}} \right]$$

In kindergarten, Lisa was enchanted by Neil Armstrong's 1969 moonwalk. When she reached her teens, she so admired the first young women who entered the NASA space program that she decided to pursue that path herself. She graduated from the U.S. Naval Academy with a degree in aerospace engineering, went on to naval flight officers' school, married a classmate, received her master's degree, had three kids, and began advanced test pilot studies with a nine-month-old baby in tow. She was a superwoman.

Captain Lisa Marie Nowak logged more than 1,500 hours of flight time in thirty different aircraft as she rose up the naval ranks. This smart, ambitious woman spent ten years in NASA's astronaut corps preparing for her lifetime dream: a trip to the International Space Station. During her thirteen days in space, Lisa was responsible for operating the robotic arm of the space shuttle. She came back to Earth a hero, one of a small number of women in the world who had ever traveled into space. But although she had "the right stuff" to conquer space, Lisa's life unraveled when she couldn't control the beast of an emotion from which virtually no one is immune: jealousy.

At the time of her space shuttle excursion, Lisa was married. She was also having an affair with a recently divorced fellow astronaut. Six months after her space trip, Lisa separated from her husband, seemingly with the hope of building a new life with her lover. But unbeknownst to Lisa, the boyfriend had started dating Air Force Captain Colleen Shipman.

Overcome with jealousy when she found out about the other woman, Lisa's emotions sent her on a dangerous and life-threatening mission. Armed with a knife and a pistol and packing black latex gloves, a drilling hammer, rubber tubing, and plastic garbage bags, Lisa donned a pair of NASA-issued diapers so that she could drive from Houston to Orlando without having to stop to go to the bathroom. She then proceeded to drive nearly a thousand miles to find her romantic rival. Arriving in Orlando, disguised in a trench coat and black wig, she confronted Colleen Shipman in an airport parking lot, pepper-sprayed her, and then attempted to kidnap her. Colleen escaped. Within an hour, Lisa Marie Nowak was in custody and her story of modern-day jealousy soon became fodder for the media.

Twenty-five hundred years ago, the Greeks were telling the tale of Medea, the jealous wife who killed her own children to exact revenge on her husband, Jason, after he left her for a younger woman. The expression "green with envy" dates back to Greek times, as the Greeks believed that jealousy and envy resulted in the overproduction of bile, which they believed turned skin a light shade of green. Jealousy and envy are often mistaken for each other, but there's a fundamental difference between the two.

Jealousy is the fear of losing something that one has to someone else, often in a romantic kind of way. Envy is the frustration of witnessing someone else have what you want. Romantic jealousy involves three people: you, your love interest, and your rival. Envy typically involves just you and the person who got what you wanted.

Whether it's the fear of loss (jealousy) or the wish for gain (envy), in small doses these emotions are tame and manageable. But with both emotions, when jealousy or envy escalates—as it did in Lisa Nowak's case—it can lead to very ugly consequences. Is jealousy or envy more familiar to you? What can you do to temper the mania that can be associated with these hot-blooded emotional cousins? Let's start by focusing on jealousy.

## THE CAR WRECK WE CALL JEALOUSY

If I'm driving on the freeway and see a collision on the side of the road, I slow down, partially to be cautious but also to sneak a guilty peek at the wreckage and to see the impact on the people involved. Our fascination with jealousy has similarities. It's why celebrity tabloid magazines scream headlines about jealousy—"bad" behavior sells. A complex emotion, jealousy is familiar to most of us. And when it strikes, a whole collection of other emotions—from anger to humiliation to betrayal to sorrow—follow in its wake. Jealousy is the leading cause of marital homicide, yet, compared to most other well-known emotions, there is far less research on its origins and manifestations.

Part of jealousy's intrigue is that it can masquerade as love. The fine line between devoted love and compulsive jealousy has kept many a poet up late at night. The British psychologist Havelock Ellis underlined the paradox of this emotion when he wrote, "Jealousy, that dragon which slays love under the pretense of keeping it alive."

Research proves a strange paradox: most of us want our partner to demonstrate a little jealousy. As the French writer André Gide wrote, "To be loved is nothing. What I want is to be preferred." I was once in a relationship with someone who didn't seem to have a jealous bone in his body. That got under my skin and made me feel a little more self-conscious about my own level of jealousy. Jealousy might give us a hint of what's stewing in our partner's heart—if there's something stewing at all—and it can feel (however unreasonable) like an indication of his or her level of commitment. Some might see its expression as a way of testing whether it's safe to invest more emotion in a partner—although this is not the healthiest gauge of real security in a relationship.

What's fascinating is that men and women's brains respond quite differently when in the midst of a jealous fit. Jealousy activates regions in men's brains that are rich in testosterone receptors, which are involved in sexual and aggressive behavior. In women, by contrast, the activation is greater in a region associated with trying to understand others' intentions and trustworthiness. Maybe this is part of the reason that 40 percent of women admitted to having deliberately provoked a bit of jealousy in their partners in order to get a reading of the strength of their bond. Though we may be wired differently, both men and women experience a dark enchantment with the possessiveness known as jealousy.

## THE LEADING INGREDIENTS OF JEALOUSY

You'll notice that this is the first chapter in *Emotional Equations* to employ division in its equation. When you're feeling jealous, what's going on inside you? The denominator (the bottom) in a division equation is very weighty. It has a significant influence on the final product. If you can solve for the denominator in most Emotional Equations, you'll make great strides in solving the emotional puzzle. I believe that two key variables affect jealousy: your level of mistrust and your sense of self-esteem. I'll start by addressing the denominator, self-esteem, because it has a more profound impact on the overall equation.

A *Psychology Today* survey found that people whose responses indicated a high degree of jealousy tended to exhibit any of three personality characteristics: (1) they had a low opinion of themselves; (2) they saw a large discrepancy between how they really are and what they would ideally like to be; or (3) they valued such visible achievements as being wealthy, famous, well liked, and especially physically attractive. Those who were less jealous had higher self-esteem, felt good about who they were (rather than bad about what they hadn't yet become), and were less interested in the external trappings of success.

So at the root of self-esteem is a sense of worthiness. Do you feel worthy just as you are? Not based on what you do or what you're going to do. Or on what you're wearing, where you live, who you know, or how much money is in your bank account. You are susceptible to the jealousy virus when your sense of worth is running on empty.

Since jealousy is an anticipatory emotion, someone who isn't feeling very good about him- or herself may try to prevent loss by imagining the worst. People tend to imagine the worst to soften a blow—in case something bad is going to happen. For someone whose self-esteem is low, imagining a partner being attracted to others may be a coping mechanism for the expectation of disappointment. Yet it's this unhealthy circular reasoning that can lead to the self-fulfilling prophecy of you and your suitcase out on the street.

What if jealousy were just a signal, an indicator that something is askew in you, not in your partner? I know how easy it is to start blaming your partner or, even better, blaming the person who is preying on your partner. But before you "pull a Lisa Nowak," ask yourself, "What's the state of my own self-regard?" When I've been jealous of someone else, it's often because the other person emanates an aura of magical attributes that feel unrealized in myself. Jealousy is often thought of as an emotion that is associated with protecting yourself, but imagine instead if it were an invitation to open up, to consider a more enriching life and enhanced self-esteem.

Another key variable is your level of relational confidence with respect to your partner. Are you a good match, or do you feel like you're dating the equivalent of a Julia Roberts or a George Clooney, someone with endless other romantic partners to choose from? Your choice of partner and whether you are dating someone whom you perceive as either "above" or "below" you can influence your feelings of relationship stability. Being well matched with someone who feels like an equal tends to give a greater sense of confidence that a relationship will last. Be careful when assessing, however, because, based on your emotional condition, your ability to recognize an equal—or feel like one—may be skewed.

Now let's turn to the numerator. The reason I use the word "mistrust" rather than "trust" is that the less you trust your partner (or the world in general), the more jealous you're likely to be. Where does this mistrust stem from? Some people are naturally skeptical of the world. When this transfers over to their romantic life, I call it "skinical"—the protective mechanism of being extra cynical when you have romantic "skin in the game." A study found that people who had a tendency toward being neurotic or were anxious about the world being a dangerous place were less likely to be trusting. On the other hand, those who were agreeable and by nature trusting, cooperating, and compassionate were less likely to feel jealous. That makes sense. Which pair of glasses are you wearing? If your glasses are slightly skewed toward seeing risk, just know that it will take you much longer to build the kind of trust in a relationship that allows love to flourish, so make sure you have a patient partner.

Now let's move beyond your worldview and whether you are naturally trusting or not. In the context of your current relationship (or when reflecting on the last relationship you were in), do you feel that your partner is trustworthy? There may be many elements that influence your answer to this question. Does he or she tell the truth? Does he or she admit to cheating on you? In past relationships, did your partner tend to leave when the going got rough? You can ask these same questions of yourself, because our partners can be mirrors. In therapeutic terms, blaming others or labeling them with your own issues is referred to as "projecting," and it can do real harm to a relationship if you don't take responsibility for your own insecurities. Jealousy is an opportunity to look within at what is prompting intense emotions. And those who have cheated are much more likely to imagine being cheated on.

In sum, jealousy may be more painful than envy since it is more personal and involves losing something that you already have. For some people, this means the stakes are higher. But rather than falling into the bottomless well of jealousy, first make sure you do a checklist of (1) your sense of self-esteem, both independent of and within the relationship, and (2) your level of trust, your natural tendency *as well as* whether you feel your partner is trustworthy. Feeling good about yourself, feeling well matched in your relationship, having a generally trusting perspective on the world, and feeling confident in the trustworthiness of your partner will help dissipate any of the natural jealousy that can arise when you're "crazy" about someone. Being conscious of the ingredients of jealousy will help you moderate its influence.

## ENVY: THE POWERFUL EMOTION YOU DON'T WANT TO ADMIT

We often say, "I envy you." But using the textbook meaning of this word, we usually mean we "admire" the other person or want to have similar circumstances in our own lives. Envy isn't a small distraction; otherwise it would never have made it to the list of Seven Deadly Sins. Envy has the risk of becoming covetous and leading to conniving, shameful behaviors. In Shakespeare's famous tragedy, Othello is jealous—not envious—of the affections of his beautiful wife, Desdemona. The character in the tragedy that resoundingly exemplifies envy is the arch villain, Othello's pretended friend Iago.

Jealousy erupts. Envy simmers. Envy is often an emotion we try to disassociate from, as if we're not feeling it.

But haven't you felt envy in the following type of situations? You have a workmate who works fewer hours and isn't quite as smart as you, yet gets a promotion and now makes more money. Your neighbor's kid just got accepted to an Ivy League school, even though he has lower grades than your daughter. Your little brother just got a new wife, a new sports car, or tickets to the Super Bowl. Perhaps you feel genuinely empathetic and happy for these other people and have a low envy quotient. But maybe you see the world as a zero-sum game in which your fortune has to mean my misfortune.

At the heart of this zero-sum game is social comparison, our natural tendency to measure ourselves relative to the benchmarks around us: what is often called "neighbor envy." Though we may compare ourselves to Martha Stewart or Donald Trump, envy is usually more localized to people we know. We envy people who live much as we do because it seems possible that their gains could have been ours.

Though jealousy tends to be a little more socially acceptable and redeemable, envy lurks in the shadows. That's part of the reason the envious mind can create an imaginary world of justification. When we envy someone else's gain, one of the ways we can rationalize the emotion is to imagine he didn't deserve what he received. In fact, indignation can be a side effect of envy. The next time you feel a little indignant or resentful toward someone else, ask yourself if there's a thread of envy—the desire to have what he has—behind your emotion.

Brain researchers have shown that resentment follows envy and schadenfreude, the pleasure derived from the misfortune of others, follows resentment. This German word, the petty foil of envy, is familiar in cultures that enjoy seeing people on pedestals fall from grace. It isn't just the Europeans who relish in this "sorrow for another's good" (as St. Thomas Aquinas called it); the Japanese also have a saying, "The misfortunes of others are the taste of honey." And of course, in American culture, reality TV is our source of schadenfreude. We seem to take great joy in the very public sorrows of others. As with jealousy, low self-esteem is a contributor to schadenfreude, which gives people who celebrate others' downfall a sense of false redemption.

Take a step back for a moment and imagine the emotional toll envy has on a culture or society. Imagining the worst for those around you and those who've gained more gifts does nothing to better your own situation. Some people use envy to motivate themselves to achieve more, but for most, envy is a spectator sport that creates flabby character traits. Bertrand Russell wrote, "If you desire glory, you may envy Napoleon. But Napoleon envied Caesar, Caesar envied Alexander, and Alexander, I daresay, envied Hercules, who never existed." Envy may make the world go round, but it also flattens your spirit.

$$ENVY = \frac{(PRIDE + VANITY)}{KINDNESS}$$

Benign envy might lead to admiration and a motivation to make change in one's life, but I don't think Dante had this in mind when he suggested that the envious have their eyes sewn shut in Purgatory because they have gained sinful pleasure from seeing others' misfortune. As with jealousy, envy is a division equation. The emotions on the top (the numerator) of a negative Emotional Equation will have qualities similar to the emotion of envy, while the solution of an equation, focused on a negative emotion, will come in the denominator on the bottom.

Envy has an awful lot to do with self-image. Envy and narcissism (which we'll address in a later chapter) went to the same school. Someone with an inflated self-image has taken pride (another of those Seven Deadly Sins) and vanity too far. Jane Austen wrote, "Vanity and pride are different things, though the words are often used synonymously. A person may be proud without being vain. Pride relates more to our opinion of ourselves; vanity, to what we would have others think of us." As is true with jealousy or envy, a moderate amount of pride or vanity isn't corrosive, but when greediness is mixed in, those two emotions in the numerator are the kindling of the envious fire that can emerge.

The virtue that directly counteracts envy is kindness or a spirit of generosity. When you have a generous spirit, you feel encouraged and enthused about your neighbor's good fortune, as opposed to diminished by it. It is damn near impossible to be both envious and kind at the same time.

Try this: Imagine someone who feels like a rival. Though the person may not know it (as is often the case), you see her as a competitor in the game of life, and somehow her positive fortune makes you feel as though you're losing the competition. Sound familiar? Now think of this person receiving some honor, award, financial benefit, or other gift that could easily have been bestowed on you. Feeling a little bit envious? Now imagine you are that person for a moment. What kind of elation would you be feeling? How does it feel to consider the good feeling she may be feeling? Most people who do this exercise are surprised that they are able to empathize with their rival. In activating that empathy, you move out of pride and vanity's confining closet.

Most of what happens in life isn't a zero-sum game, and there may be collateral benefits from your sister getting a promotion at work (she'll be easier to be around) or your friend building a backyard swimming pool (your kids won't have to go to the public pool). On a personal level, I have found that adding a drop of kindness to my heart and mind when I'm most envious of someone else helps dilute the resentment and turn it into either motivation (to work a little harder to achieve similar gains) or empathy (to get out of my own selfish way and live a more expansive life basking in others' good feelings).

I've spent much of my work life relating to the small, rebellious side of the David-and-Goliath relationship. Joie de Vivre's archrival, Kimpton (it's the largest boutique hotelier in the United States, while we're the second biggest), has always been a company we've compared ourselves with and occasionally competed with for talented executives and hotel management contracts. Given that its headquarters is only two blocks from ours, there's a certain amount of neighbor envy in this relationship. Both companies compete in listings of the Best Companies to Work For, both in the Bay Area and nationally. Joie de Vivre has always aspired to be featured on *Fortune* magazine's annual list of the 100 Best Companies to Work For.

Three years ago, Kimpton made the list, and I have to admit that I (as well as many of our top execs) was quite envious and even a bit resentful about the fact it had made it and we hadn't. Internally, I could see that this corporate form of envy could turn corrosive if we didn't turn it into a positive. First off, I congratulated Kimpton's CEO and asked him how the company had made the list and what his biggest learning had been from the experience of getting there. Similarly, I suggested that our CPO (chief people officer) reach out to Kimpton's top HR folks to tap into their wisdom as well. As a result, rather than just accepting our "loss" and nurturing a collective envy, we used it as an experience to raise our game a notch.

## WORKING THROUGH THE EQUATIONS

$$Jealousy = \frac{Mistrust}{Self\text{-}Esteem}$$

$$Envy = \frac{(Pride + Vanity)}{Kindness}$$

*Identify what you can learn from your jealousy.* Jealousy can be a wise teacher and a great test of your sense of reality. Beware of negative obsessive thinking about yourself or your partner, as it typically means you are in a loop that isn't willing to let new information into your analysis of the situation. Look for an objective friend who knows and respects your partner as a means of talking through whether your thinking is rotten or realistic. And start pondering whether it's low trust or low self-esteem that has allowed jealousy to raise its head. If the answer is that your partner doesn't deserve your trust, maybe it's time to move on. If instead it's time to build your sense of esteem or trust, take a look at the next suggestion.

*When in doubt, build your self-esteem.* A big denominator is the quickest means of melting your jealousy, so ask yourself what activities give you a sense of feeling good about yourself. For many, the best way to build self-esteem is either to be of service to someone else or to focus on a talent or activity that puts you in a timeless sense of enjoyable flow. For me, running on the beach with my faithful dog clears my mind faster than just about anything else. Also, writing a few grateful emails to friends or colleagues creates a feedback loop that typically makes me feel good and leads to esteem-producing responses from the recipients. The key thing to consider is whether your sense of confidence is poor in all parts of your life right now or specific to your relationship.

*Ask, "What can my envy teach me?"* Pinpoint what makes you envious of the other person, as it's a great indicator of what you truly value. Now that you've identified it, is it really that important? If it is, what can you learn from the success of the other that you can apply to yourself? Are you spending too much of your time being prideful and vain about how deserving you are without spending the necessary time in the trenches to create the results you're wishing for? Find a way to measure your growth and success, not compared to your rival, but compared to your past and your own standards for the future.

*Forget schadenfreude. Embrace "mudita."* The solution to the denominator of the envy equation is to find "sympathetic joy"—what Buddhists call *mudita*—in the good fortune of even your most competitive rivals. This isn't easy, especially if you feel the twin justifications of indignation and resentment. More often than not, the way to happiness and a more charitable spirit is to find empathy in appreciating just how the sweet taste of victory may feel to someone else. Isn't that sort of delight what you would want from them if you were the lucky one?

Jealousy is angry, agitated worry. Envy masquerades as indignation and resentment. These very normal emotions share many similarities, and in the end both equations are best solved by asking, "What do I hope to gain from my jealousy or envy?" Wouldn't it be ironic if jealousy were the doorway for you to find a more trusting, compassionate, and self-affirmed sense of who you are? Similarly, what if envy was the means of stepping up your desire to maximize your potential *and* your ability to empathize and celebrate the victories of others? Learn from your emotions. Jealousy can teach you about what you treasure in your life today. Envy can teach you about your future.

# 7

$$\text{Anxiety} = \text{Uncertainty} \times \text{Powerlessness}$$

A gregarious outdoorsman and intrepid traveler, Charles Darwin spent his early twenties voyaging around the world to study native plant and animal species. But by the end of the decade, he succumbed to a mysterious, debilitating condition that, at the time, was attributed variously to tropical diseases, arsenic poisoning, intellectual exhaustion, and bad nerves. Psychiatric experts now believe that Darwin more than likely suffered from severe anxiety attacks, possibly due to agoraphobia, the fear of crowds and people. It's odd to think that the man responsible for understanding how we human beings evolved may actually have been "allergic" to us.

Darwin describes the malady in his journal as a "sensation of fear . . . accompanied by troubled beating of the heart, sweat, trembling muscles." The uncomfortable palpitations and regular vomiting bouts started about the time he began writing in a secret notebook that, twenty-two years later, would become his theory of the origin of species. Over the next few decades, he stayed in bed for months at a time, consulted with more than twenty doctors, and even tried unusual therapies such as a belt that delivered electrical shocks to the abdomen.

Some scholars have speculated that Darwin's revolutionary work was assisted, ironically, by his becoming more reclusive during the last forty years of his life. In his autobiography, he wrote, "My chief enjoyment and sole employment throughout life has been scientific work; and the excitement from such work makes me for the time forget, or drives away, my daily discomfort. I have therefore nothing to record during the rest of my life, except the publications of my several books." That was written by a tortured soul who today might have sought relief in medication and therapy, along with the millions of others who suffer in the throes of anxiety.

Sir Isaac Newton, Emily Dickinson, Howard Hughes, John Madden, Katharine Graham, Charles Schulz, Michael Jackson—countless famous people have been afflicted with some form of anxiety. What about you? Or someone you know and love? Whether it's generalized anxiety, obsessive-compulsive disorder, panic attacks, or social phobia, anxiety is commonly a preoccupation with the likelihood of danger and the feeling that you are ill equipped to cope with what you're about to face. Sounds like just another day at the office for me!

When anxiety overtakes me, I feel like a skinny kid in college thrown into a wrestling ring with someone twice my size: I have difficulty breathing, I sweat profusely, my heart races a mile a minute. In those moments, it would make sense to reach out and ask for help. But when anxiety hits me, it often feels too scary to admit it to others. It makes me feel small, ugly, and impotent—not an easy thing to share.

About 20 percent of the population struggles with some kind of anxiety disorder—a club I never wanted to join. The good news is that, whether through the miracles of modern medicine or the healthy coping mechanisms I'll outline in this chapter, you no longer have to feel like the weakling in the wrestling ring when that bully named anxiety comes looking for a victim.

# ANXIETY IS HERE, MY MIND IS THERE

Think of something that makes you anxious. The economy? Parenting? Public speaking? Regardless of the cause, much of anxiety's potency comes from your anticipation of an event or experience that hasn't happened yet. Mark Twain put it this way: "I am an old man and have known a great many troubles, but most of them never happened." We tend to overestimate a perceived danger and underestimate our ability to handle what may come. Anxiety is anticipatory. It is fueled by the fear of the unknown and the belief that we have no control over some impending doom. We imagine that we will be unemployed and homeless, that our children will not be safe, or that an audience will break out into laughter or be completely bored by what we have to say. As a high school water polo player, I would get so anxious that I would throw up ten minutes before our big games. The coach got so used to it that he'd come looking for me in the bathroom to make sure I was okay. Anxiety is the hatcher of a thousand "butterflies in your stomach"—but there are ways to tame them.

Let's start by recognizing that we essentially welcome anxiety when we let our minds race into the future, imagining the worst. In the extreme, death—the ultimate future trip—is the most pervasive anxiety-producing experience we fret over. One of the best coping mechanisms I was taught long ago is staying in the present moment. When I feel my anxiety level rise, I sit down and focus on the sensation of my feet on the ground, with my hands resting on my legs, and breathe slowly and evenly through my nose, taking full breaths from my belly into my chest. It's amazing how five minutes of this kind of "being-present awareness" can steal the power from the anxiety bug.

There are two variables in this equation: what you don't know (uncertainty) and what you can't control (powerlessness). Typically, the combination is combustible: the more uncertain you feel, the more powerless you feel. Because feeling powerless is debilitating, this equation uses multiplication to produce an exponential result. Yet if you can influence one of the variables, so that you reduce it closer to zero, you can significantly reduce your anxiety quotient. Generally speaking, feeling less anxiety doesn't just make you feel better, it puts you in a better place to respond to life. Feeling certain about something yet powerless to affect it may not be comfortable. In fact, you may feel resigned, but you're less likely to feel anxious. Similarly, feeling uncertain yet powerful means that you're comfortable with your ability to respond to whatever is thrown at you, and that means your anxiety dissipates.

If anxiety is the lead actor in your life's movie of the week, there's a 60 percent chance that depression is either the lead actress or a supporting character. The way I see it, depression is almost like a stunt double for the risks we must take on a daily basis. Anxiety feeds on our fears of being unable to deal with what life throws at us, but there's a certain security in being depressed or disappointed and sad about life. When you're depressed, you don't expect much and you certainly aren't interested in taking risks. If anxiety is a fear of the uncertain and unfamiliar, depression is as certain as that old coat that smells and feels the same every time you take it out of the closet. And although it may not be right for the part you are playing today, it sure feels comfortable. When you're anxious about life, it is reassuring to slip into a place where your expectations are low.

You can try to slip into something comfortable by ingesting something, too. When feeling anxious, many people experience discomfort in the stomach (those "butterflies") or queasiness in our "second brain," as the gastrointestinal tract is sometimes called. In fact, most of our neurotransmitters (which regulate our mood) are produced in the digestive system. More than 95 percent of serotonin (the "happy" chemical) is produced and stored in the gut. So today there are myriad antianxiety/depression drugs that doctors prescribe in alarming numbers. Don't get me wrong; they can be absolutely lifesaving for some, but they can also cause adverse reactions, from addiction to worsening symptoms, for others. Then there's the "self-medication" route, from cocktails to cookies, to temporarily calm the anxiety beast. Caffeine, alcohol, and sugar can all exacerbate rather than quell your symptoms. So be careful about what you're digesting, as it can positively or negatively affect your "gut reactions."

## SHOCK ME NOW

Most people cannot tolerate the distress of waiting. Studies show that when faced with the choice between a mild electric shock at some unexpected time in the future or a more intense shock now, most people prefer to get it over with even though they're choosing more pain. The fear of suffering is worse than the suffering itself when anxiety has taken us hostage. This is part of the reason why a long, brutal economic downturn can have such a psychologically debilitating effect. We'd rather just experience the pain once and get it over with. Yet an economic decline can persist like a bad winter cold.

If anxiety is the by-product of uncertainty and powerlessness, what does the opposite of the equation look like? When someone is certain about everything and thinks of him- or herself as all-powerful, we generally think of the person as an arrogant know-it-all. Can you think of someone who fits this profile? Or have you ever overcompensated this way? Some anxious people use false bravado as a coping mechanism. The truth is that anxiety exposes our vulnerability, our humility, and our willingness to admit that we don't have a solution readily in hand. Though it's no fun having a friend or family member who is constantly anxious, being with someone with a little too much "puff" can be equally challenging.

Anxiety is an emotion, not a character defect. People with the greatest need to control their lives are often hit hardest by anxiety symptoms. Those who experience high anxiety levels tend to be high-functioning, high-achieving, strong individuals who exercise a lot of influence over their lives, yet can't understand when things go wrong. For me, anxiety is a big clue that something in my life is out of balance—whether my mind is too future-oriented, my desire for control too amplified, or my sense of my own power too unappreciated. Anxiety is not an equilibrium condition; it's not what we should strive for. But we can welcome it into our lives and then ask ourselves what we need to do to reduce our uncertainty or feeling of powerlessness.

## THE ILLUSION OF CONTROL

I'll admit it, I love control. Like many people who are driven to succeed, I am motivated by both my desire to perform well and what kind of reception I will get at the finish line. I learned long ago to creatively visualize myself winning a 100-yard breaststroke race or giving a powerful speech in my race for seventh-grade class president at school. My imagination was my ally. It helped me believe that I could control or influence my results.

But at some point, my imagination also became my heckler. Especially during times when the future was unclear and I lacked self-confidence, I could get swept away by imagining myself completely out of control and unable to "shoot the rapids" of life. Turns out I'm not alone. Fifteen years ago, anxiety overtook relationship concerns as the number one mental health problem being raised by college students in academic counseling centers across the United States.

Let me tell you a story about how I hit the reset button on a bout with anxiety. In the summer of 2009, when my life was in full disarray—my company on the rocks and my relationship about to end—I was invited to give a talk at the 2010 TED Conference. The TED Conference (www.ted.com) is a world-renowned gathering of thought leaders dedicated to spreading great ideas. Speakers run the gamut from both Nobel and Pulitzer Prize winners to academics, heads of state, designers, entertainers, and CEOs. Each speaker has eighteen minutes to tell his story to an audience filled with the likes of Bill Gates, Jane Goodall, Al Gore, and Isabel Allende, along with tens of thousands of people watching online around the world. It was both an honor and a thrill to be invited. But the anxiety bug soon permeated my excitement. In an instant, my mind was back at that water polo match—with me vomiting in the bathroom.

TED had requested that I talk about the intangibles of happiness and how both business and political leaders need to start learning to measure and value what's most meaningful in life. It seemed a cruel irony that I was tasked to take the stage as an expert on a subject that felt so elusive to me at that time. No matter that my book *Peak* had espoused a self-actualized way to do business; I had lost my mojo.

I got into the mind-set that I was unworthy and the only way I could overcome this challenge was to write the speech of my life and practice it hundreds of times. I expected that perfection would be my antidote for anxiety. You may have put yourself into this position, assuming that a goal would give you comfort. But the fact is, striving for perfection only amplifies anxiety.

For the next few months, I labored painfully over a speech on happiness, completely at odds with how I normally prepare for a presentation. My style is more extemporaneous and intimate, not robotic and over-rehearsed. The closer I got to TED, the more anxious I became.

My talk was scheduled on the last day of the conference (right before that of the film director James Cameron). So when I arrived, I had five excruciating days to become even more anxious as I watched all the other speakers do their thing. At some point during the week, I realized that my obsession had become laughable. One friend asked me, "Where is the love in all of this, Chip?"—just as a blimp appeared in the sky above us, revealing a big red heart on its side. A red heart is the visual icon for my company, so it was a fateful moment of synchronicity that reminded me that my performance-driven self-obsession was getting in the way of the bigger message—the one I needed to get *and* the one I needed to give.

In the twenty-four hours before my speech, I turned my anxiety into a mantra to help me get on stage. My fear of embarrassing myself in front of so many influential people dissipated when I got past my ego and need for approval and embraced the amazing opportunity to be of service. When my anxiety peaked, I channeled that intense energy into this statement: *I am powerful because my message is resonant.* Those words, plus a positive mental image of simply being a vehicle for the message, calmed me down. By telling myself, "The message is perfect, so I don't have to be," I released the fear and tension and tapped into the "flow," which we'll explore further in chapter 10.

I gave the speech of my life. When I got out of my own way and allowed my message, not my ego, to take precedence, I was able to move out of the indulgent obsession of my fear of failure. Fortunately, the message did resonate with the audience, leading to the twenty-first-century leaders in the audience asking how they could start measuring and valuing the intangible assets in their organizations. Perhaps if I'd taken a few more baths with my mantra—instead of pitifully practicing in front of a mirror—I might have enjoyed the experience even more.

## WORKING THROUGH THE EQUATION

$$Anxiety = Uncertainty \times Powerlessness$$

*When anxiety strikes, create a balance sheet of what you know and what is within your influence.* First, unravel the sense of mystery about what you don't know. Anxiety lurks in the dark, so shine a flashlight on what it is that's disturbing you. Is this situation as uncertain as you think it is? Are you overestimating the danger associated with this mystery or the importance of the event? Then explore whether you are truly ill equipped to address the experience. If you are, what resources can you tap into to help you feel a little more powerful? Make a list of your strengths, your coping skills, and the resources available to you. Sometimes the best solution is just to focus on what you can control; that may be as simple as your breathing. Fear is excitement, only deprived of breath. Get in touch with how the anxiety feels in your body. Gain some control over your breathing, then shift to how you can influence your thinking. As you build some momentum in seeing your ability to cope with a widening sphere of influence, you'll build your sense of confidence so that you can handle what life is throwing at you. I've worked with many anxious business leaders to create a balance sheet of uncertainty and powerlessness. Here's how: Create four columns on a piece of paper. Label the first column "What I know" and the column next to it "What I don't know." Label the third column "What I can influence" and the final one "What I can't control." Then fill in the columns. In the process of making these factors explicit, people are often surprised by how much certainty and influence they actually have.

*Create a "worry period," and indulge in worry as much as you want during that time.* Anxiety can be free-floating. Like a bird seeking prey, it can swoop down and carry you away in its clutches. Imagine if you opened yourself up to anxiety only during certain periods of the day. Let's say you give yourself thirty minutes of worry time in the morning and afternoon (à la Holly Hunter's five minutes of scheduled crying time in the film *Broadcast News*). During that time, focus all your attention on worrying. Make lists of all the potential things that can go wrong, all the collateral emotions that are stemming from this anxiety, and how your life feels awful as a result. Then, once you've finished your worry period, banish those anxiety thoughts from your brain, knowing that you'll have another space for them in a few hours—or tomorrow. For some of us, that's how we use therapy. It's our prescribed time to let all those anxiety vultures gather above us, but under the protective care of a therapist who can help us see that most of the vultures are imaginary.

*Think extreme.* Anxiety is like a game of dominos. "Catastrophic cascading" is when you take an idea and let it turn into something worse through a domino effect. Let's say you're scared that your date on Saturday night will reject you. So take yourself through the dominos. Let's say the date goes badly. What's next? Your date tells his friends. You become known as a loser in your community. People make fun of you. No one else asks you out. You spend the rest of your life alone. Once you've created that scenario, ask yourself, "Is this the worst-case scenario, and what's the probability of each domino falling?" When you become conscious about how extreme anxiety thinking can be, you realize how lacking in logic it is. Similarly, think extreme in the opposite direction. The author Marci Shimoff suggests that we ask ourselves, "If this were happening for a higher purpose, what would it be?" Maybe all this pain and suffering is preparing you for a life you haven't even imagined. Think big and creatively about what more profound message may be emerging as a result of the anxiety you are feeling. This is how I turned my self-obsessed TED speaking experience into something much bigger than myself.

*Use "paradoxical intention" as a means of dissipating your anxiety.* Viktor Frankl believed that one means of coping with anxiety is to detach from it. Instead of trying harder, just let it go. For example, if you have insomnia and get anxious about your lack of sleep, "paradoxical intention" would suggest that you get up when you wake up in the middle of the night rather than trying harder to fall back to sleep. If you and your partner are at odds with each other, make a rule that you aren't going to have sex for the next couple of months and see what happens (usually, just reducing the anxiety associated with the performance pressure opens up new potential for a connection to be made). By restaging the relationship you have with sleep or sex, you short-circuit the habitual anxiety response that typically makes the situation worse.

Even in good times, anxiety can be a habit and can turn anything—even going on an exciting date or winning the lottery—into just another burden. One other element that could be added to this equation would be to put parentheses around "Uncertainty" and "Powerlessness" and multiply the sum by "Severity of Consequences." There are some things in life that are worth worrying about, and there are others you just need to let go. My best advice is to focus on what you do know and can influence: your body and your mind. Reduce your caffeine, sugar, and alcohol intake, and eat foods that provide you with healthy fuel. Physical exercise is one of nature's remedies for stress, and getting plenty of bed rest allows your body to rejuvenate itself. Kevin Cashman, the CEO of LeaderSource, says that typically, before any great mental breakthrough, there needs to be a "pause-through" when you let your body and subconscious take over from your conscious mind. When the world is uncertain and overwhelming, breathe, and miraculously, you may find that your mind moves from a war zone to a refuge.

Congratulations on making it to the end of the "Dealing with Difficult Times" section of the book. You may choose to continue on to the next section in a linear fashion, but don't hesitate to venture out and explore other chapters that may catch your fancy first. Heck, after reading about all of these difficult emotions, you might want to skip ahead to "Happiness" or "Joy." Reading this book—like life—isn't meant to be done in a straight line.

# PART III

# GETTING THE MOST OUT OF YOUR WORK LIFE

*What really matters for success, character, happiness and lifelong achievements is a definite set of emotional skills—your EQ—not just purely cognitive abilities that are measured by conventional IQ tests.*
—Daniel Goleman

# 8

$$\left[ \text{Calling} = \frac{\text{Pleasure}}{\text{Pain}} \right]$$

Agnes Bojaxhiu heard the call twice, first as a teenager, leading her to leave her Albanian home, never to see her mother or sister again, and travel to Ireland and then India to become a nun, and the second time in her late thirties, which set the destiny for which she is known. While traveling by train from Darjeeling to Calcutta, Mother Teresa, as she was known by then, distinctly heard a "call within a call": "I was to leave the convent and help the poor while living among them. It was an order. To fail would have been to break the faith."

Mother Teresa found this second call to be particularly difficult, because it required her to leave her sisterhood of two decades for an uncertain life surrounded by pain. She wrote, "I was on the street, with no shelter, no company, no helper, no money, no employment, no promise, no guarantee, no security." At first she had to beg for food and supplies for her mission, but by doing so she experienced poverty and suffering firsthand. She has been quoted as saying "By faith, I am a Catholic nun. As to my calling, I belong to the world."

Mother Teresa's Missionaries of Charity has grown to more than 5,000 sisters and brothers operating 600 missions in 120 countries.

"Where did Mother Teresa find the strength and perseverance to place herself completely at the service of others?" Pope John Paul II asked at her beatification ceremony. This is the kind of question you yourself might ask when watching anyone follow a calling, which usually requires surmounting major impediments.

The concept of a calling can be daunting, as many people associate having a calling with being chosen for some kind of divine service. But you don't have to be a saint to find your calling. Julia Child was a government spy delivering intelligence documents to agents in the field during World War II. She didn't enter cooking school until age thirty-six, after her husband introduced her to the sophisticated cuisine of Paris, where they were living. Child describes the culinary revelation when her taste buds woke up as "an opening up of the soul and spirit for me." She went on to teach cooking to American women in Paris and then, well past the age of fifty, started delivering intelligence about the culinary arts worldwide.

You might be called to other more familiar but important jobs: a butcher, a baker, a website maker. The poet Khalil Gibran asked, "Who can separate his faith from his actions or his belief from his occupations?" The world is full of nonreligious people who feel a sense of purpose in what they do and a deep emotional connection to their work. I prefer to think of a calling as one of three ways in which we relate to our work—with or without a paycheck, either by choice or circumstance: (1) a job, (2) a career, or (3) a calling. There are no other options.

If you aren't currently living your calling, think of someone you know who is truly inspired by what he or she does. Do you admire the spring in his step and the sense of purpose in how he lives? Ask him how he found this calling, and you may hear a serendipitous story of a gravitational pull that drew him to his destiny—as if some kind of invisible guidance counselor had been standing by his side.

My hero the very secular Abraham Maslow wrote, "One must respond to one's fate or one's destiny or pay a heavy price. One must yield to it; one must surrender to it. One must permit one's self to be chosen." To pursue your calling can feel like breathing in life in a whole new way; it's tapping into what you were meant to do and be on this planet.

Although a calling need not be religious, it does imply that someone or something is calling . . . and you are responding. I feel most captured by a sense of calling when I see myself as a vehicle for something much bigger than I am, whether it's in my role as a father, CEO, or close friend. This feeling of acting in a larger role is an important element of a calling. When we've been successful by following our calling, it's easy to forget that we aren't the caller, we are just responding. When we show almost a childlike respect or humility for the master or caller—however we perceive that energy or entity—we settle into a conscious commitment to our calling.

For some, a calling feels like a constant tug on the shirtsleeve. And that can be a real irritant when we're not listening. How many of us spend our lives distracted from our destiny and deafened to its call? When you allow yourself to be called, something rather miraculous happens. A calling energizes you. A job with no meaning depletes you. Living your calling means tapping into an emotional energy that emanates from a deep inner reservoir.

## THE PLEASURE AND PAIN OF A CALLING

Pleasure has gotten a bad rap in modern society and is generally associated with short-term gratification or comfort, although Aristotle defined pleasure more expansively. Suggesting that some pleasures were more beautiful and others more corrupt, he even ranked our senses based upon which was associated with a higher quality of pleasure. He believed that pleasure was inextricably connected with living a good life—as long as one remained conscious about what was driving the will to pleasure. Pleasure for its own sake grows old quickly, but when it is a by-product of doing something that fulfills you, pleasure is divine indeed.

Pleasure is an anesthetic. That is both its best and worst quality, since we can use it as a distraction and it can divert attention from pain. Think of Lance Armstrong, who's had two obvious callings in his life: as a professional cyclist and as a well-known spokesman for organizations that fight cancer. He wrote, "If something hurts so much, how can it be enjoyable? At the point where physical stress begins to take you beyond what you imagine to be endurable, you enter new territory of understanding, an expanded psychological landscape. . . . The pleasure comes when you grasp just what has happened inside your head and spirit. It doesn't stop when the bike stops, when you reach the top of the col or peel off at the end of the ride, so tired you can hardly think or stand straight. That's where the pleasure begins." Lance has also written, "Pain is temporary. Quitting lasts forever."

You don't have to be a world-champion cyclist to understand the paradoxical relationship between pleasure and pain. Any woman who's experienced childbirth understands it. The philosopher Meister Eckhart wrote, "If you want the kernel, you must break the shell." Our shell is often the pain that contains us, the false boundaries that keep us from completely surrendering to the full pleasure of our capacity to live a calling. It's the pain that gives us the sense that we're breaking through something—and perhaps letting go and leaving something or someone behind that no longer serves our greater vision.

Mihaly Csikszentmihalyi writes that someone living his calling is likely in a state of "flow" (which we'll look at in chapter 10) such that "when attention is focused, minor aches and pains have no chance to register in consciousness." He's found that people tend to report more physical symptoms, such as headaches and backaches, on weekends or at times when they are not in the midst of the flow of their work. Work can be an anesthetic that takes our attention away from pain. The more you're living your calling, the more likely you're in the pleasure zone that distracts you from your minor aches. When you're living your calling, pleasure predominates pain.

## PASSION AND PEACE OF MIND

Eighty percent of Americans say they would continue to work even if they inherited enough money that they no longer needed to work. This doesn't suggest that people would stay in their current jobs if they suddenly became rich, just that they wouldn't retire and give up on the working world. Khalil Gibran also wrote, "Work is love made visible." On some deep emotional level, we long to do work that feels as though it's an extension of who we are. Indeed, one of life's universal pursuits is searching for that kind of work. What would you pursue if money weren't an issue?

You fit into a job. A calling fits into you. Passion and peace of mind—one a hot emotion, the other a calming one—are the two emotional states that best define someone living their calling. When Silicon Valley venture capitalists bet on a high-tech entrepreneur, they plumb the psyches of the people in whom they might invest. There's a fine line between a promising entrepreneur who's a driven workaholic (what we'll cover in the next chapter) and one who seems enraptured by his business plan. Both of them may have a certain level of grandiosity, an elevated mood and expansiveness. What separates the person living his calling from the one who isn't is the fact that his passion for the business is matched by a sense of tranquility that this is exactly where he's supposed to be right now.

Quiet confidence is a hallmark and enduring trait of a person who has transcended work beyond a job or career. Someone living her calling is intrinsically motivated. It's not money, fame, a fancy title, or some other external motivation that drives her. Whether

Oprah Winfrey or Richard Branson, the person living a calling has created a work experience, and sometimes a company, that is a direct extension of who he is as a person. This isn't reserved for entrepreneurs. Elizabeth Gilbert, the author of *Eat, Pray, Love,* has said that her experience of writing is almost otherworldly—as if a genie inhabits her soul and helps her create great work. Those of us who have been lucky enough to experience a calling in our work have a certain faith and peace of mind that it's exactly what we're supposed to be doing.

## JUGGLING TWO CALLINGS

Work is not the only place to find your calling. You may find it in being a triathlete, a political activist, a grandmother, or a garage band guitarist. I've found my calling two times, both in the context of work. The collision was not comfortable. In fact, I felt as if I was cheating on my spouse when I came to realize that one calling was starting to decline while the other was ascending.

If you've ever had a calling decline, the first thing you notice is that the anesthetic is wearing off—as if you were coming out of surgery and the drugs had stopped working prematurely. Ouch! I'd spent more than twenty years loving the fact that I had found my calling at age twenty-six as one of the first American hoteliers to create unique boutique hotels for people who were tired of generic chain hotels.

On my twenty-sixth birthday, a week before I started my company, I made a list of the key qualities that I was looking for in my work: something that would leverage my commercial real estate background, a design-oriented environment, the opportunity to serve others, the opportunity to revolutionize an industry, and an employee-centric workplace where creating a compelling company culture made a difference. After having worked in the rough-and-tumble worlds of investment banking and real estate development, I longed for work that allowed me to be creative—where my relationships were defined by collaboration, not by adversarial negotiation.

For more than twenty years, I felt a deep sense of calling in being the founder and CEO of what became California's largest boutique hotel company. Friends and outsiders would often ask, "How do you do it?" They would see that my dedication to the company meant very long hours, lengthy stretches of not getting paid, and sometimes dealing with issues 24/7 since the hotel business never closes. But for me, it wasn't an addiction most of the time (which we'll talk about in the next chapter, "Workaholism"). What drove me was a sense of purpose. The pleasure of creating a unique, culture-driven organization that was a role model for others outweighed the pain associated with some of the day-to-day tasks that outsiders shook their heads at.

When I was twelve years old, I told my dad that I wanted to be a writer when I grew up. He said that writers were either poor or psychotic, and most were both. So I shelved that aspiration and wouldn't even allow myself the pleasure of taking an English or writing class in college. Then, in the first decade of the new millennium, I started writing about my experiences as an entrepreneur and CEO. I wrote three books in less than eight years and loved writing them. It was such a high to take a step back, reflect on what I'd learned as a business leader, and then communicate it to others in such a way that it made a difference in their lives.

I loved the introversion of writing as well as the extroversion of giving speeches about the principles expressed in my books. After nearly two dozen years of being laser-focused on my own company, it was liberating to meet with other business leaders throughout the world to see how my experience could influence them and their companies. Plus, I was learning so much in the process. It was a bit of a schizophrenic life: hibernating while writing, then giving eighty speeches per year, made more complicated by the fact that I was still the CEO of the company.

In August 2008, the pleasure-divided-by-pain equation appeared like a life-sized flash card in front of me. I had recently broken my ankle playing baseball at a friend's bachelor party in the San Francisco Giants ballpark and was on strong antibiotics to kill a bacterial infection that had taken over my leg. I lay low for a few days before crutching my way onto a flight to St. Louis, where I was scheduled to give two speeches, followed by another in Toronto and capped off by a half-day seminar with 140 entrepreneurs in Houston the following day.

Toward the end of my first speech in St. Louis, I started feeling nauseated and ultimately slumped down unconscious in my chair while signing books on stage. A handful of folks laid me on the floor. I was unresponsive for about three minutes. Paramedics arrived and put me back into my chair. I passed out again. They put heart monitors on me and placed me on a gurney. My heart stopped completely. Flatline. Just as they were getting the paddles out, my heart slowly started again. But for the next hour, my heart rate was no more than thirty beats a minute—half its normal rate.

Through my time in the emergency room and in the midst of more than twenty tests over the next day and a half, they couldn't figure out what was wrong with me. Other than my heart rate plummeting to zero, my vital signs looked good. My father flew into town to be at my side. As I started to feel less fuzzy, I asked him to fly to Houston with me so that I could give that workshop (the rest of my speaking tour had been canceled). Everyone back home thought I was crazy, but it was almost as if I saw this workshop as an alternative means of breathing.

In Houston, the half-day entrepreneurs' workshop was a tremendous success. And in the midst of the four-hour experience, I felt a supreme sense of being in the right place. On our way back to the airport, my dad said, "I came to St. Louis thinking you might die, and now I'm leaving Houston seeing how you want to live." He saw my calling in action and told me that he was going to do everything in his power to support my transition from being a CEO to becoming a writer and speaker as my primary career.

If we are lucky in life, we get to experience a day equally significant to the one when we were born: the day when we discover *why* we were born. That day, both my dad and I discovered at least part of the reason.

Because of the crumbling economy, it took almost two years for me to make the transition of selling a majority share in my company and stepping down from my role as CEO. During that time, it became glaringly apparent that the anesthetic of my first career had worn off. What once had given me joy was now drudgery. I would come home from a vacation and look at how much I had to accomplish in my first week back and couldn't imagine how anyone could ever get all of it done. Yet when I had been in a different state of mind, I used to get all that done—and more—without feeling the pain.

During this transition from one calling to the next, I kept two photos on the wall of my office, both taken of me on that gurney in St. Louis. There I was with paramedics surrounding me, no heart rate, and oddly enough, with Maslow's Hierarchy of Needs pyramid as a PowerPoint backdrop. In Maslow's model, we need to meet the most basic level of needs before we can "move up" the pyramid to higher needs—becoming all that we can be. The image was my daily reminder that life is precious and that within forty-eight hours of being flatline, I had been back up onstage feeling the deep pleasure associated with living my calling.

## WORKING THROUGH THE EQUATION

$$\text{Calling} = \frac{\textit{Pleasure}}{\textit{Pain}}$$

*Reflect on a time or experience in your life in which your sense of deep pleasure overrode any pain a normal mortal might have felt.* Was it while running a marathon? Having a baby? Writing your dissertation? Spending late nights creating the ultimate Christmas gift? Volunteering at a homeless shelter? Did you feel something calling you? If you can think of multiple experiences like this yet you don't feel a calling in your work today, consider what is consistent in these out-of-work callings. Is it because of whom you're doing it for, such as your kids or family? Is it the pleasurable feeling that seems to come through you whenever you're doing that activity? Or is it an inexplicable kind of energy that is directing you in some way? At the end of the day, we all long to be able to experience our life, and possibly our work, as an extension of who we are at our best. Don't worry if your true calling is beyond your work. That's true for many of us. The key is to make sure you can invest sufficient time into your nonwork calling that it gets the attention it deserves. You never know where it will lead you.

*Evaluate the "want-to" versus "have-to" equation.* Professor Tal Ben-Shahar's "How to Be Happy" class was once the most popular course at Harvard. One of his revelations was that how happy we are depends to a large degree on the ratio between want-tos (pleasure) and have-tos (pain) in our life. The more have-tos you have in your day, the more exhausted you are when you imagine your day ahead. Take a look at your satisfaction with your current work. Was there a time when you felt your work was more of a calling than it is today? If so, is it possible that more have-tos have crept into your day-to-day work life? Take out a piece of paper, create two columns, "Want To" on the left and "Have To" on the right, and write down all the elements that make up both your day-to-day existence in your job and the overall theme and purpose of your work. Has your work become one big have-to? Which parts of your work that represent the want-to can you nurture and grow such that the pleasure can override the pain? An obligation is not a calling. Beware of being suffocated by your sense of responsibility to the have-tos in life.

*Does your work energize you, or does it deplete you?* When people ask me whether their current work is a calling or not, this is the simple question I ask them. A calling energizes. A job depletes. That's a generalization, as there will be days when a calling kicks your rear end and your job fills you with great joy. But over the course of a year—not just a day—what is this work doing for you? One question many of us ask is "What am I getting from my work?" Instead, consider the question "What am I becoming as a result of my work?" You have to fit into the parameters of a job, but a calling fits into you.

*Do you feel "invisible hands" guiding you?* The author Joseph Campbell suggested that when you are "following your bliss," you put yourself on a track that has been there all the while, patiently waiting for you. The emotional experience of finding one's calling can feel like surrender. For people who are highly willful, surrender sounds like defeat. Yet when you let go and trust that you are on a path with a purpose that is bigger than you'd ever imagined, you realize that surrendering is one of the most courageous and powerful acts anyone can ever pursue. If you find your calling, it's just as though you picked up the telephone. You're answering the call. You're worthy of the invitation that is being extended to you. Don't shrink from it. Otherwise, I'll force you to read that darn "Regret" chapter again. The key in life is to attune our ears and our sense of knowing so exquisitely that we can hear a calling like a dog hears a high-pitched whistle.

Don't fret if you haven't been smitten by your calling yet. One's calling isn't easy to discover, and, as I've learned, you aren't issued just one calling in your life. It requires much reflection, dialogue with others, trying things out, a certain amount of persistence, and, yes, faith (which we'll explore in chapter 18). And though this part of the book relates to your work, many find their calling outside work. Just know that living your calling is definitely different from being a workaholic, even though an outside observer may think they're the same. Now let's explore the combustible equation that defines workaholism.

# 9

$$\text{Workaholism} = \frac{\text{What Are You Running From?}}{\text{What Are You Living For?}}$$

Thirty-year-old Kenichi Uchino's future seemed predestined. Following in the footsteps of his father and grandfather, both lifelong Toyota employees, Kenichi ascended the company ladder to quality control inspector for the booming new Prius model in Toyota City, Japan. He was also the quality-circle leader, which placed him in a leadership role with his fellow employees, with whom he focused on weekly meetings to discuss how to improve this new hybrid car model that was quickly becoming the rage. At home, Kenichi had a three-year-old daughter, a one-year-old son, and a loving wife.

Like many of his colleagues, Kenichi had a tendency to work overtime. Japan's rise from the devastation of World War II to becoming a major economic power just three decades later had a lot to do with the intense work ethic of its people. A typical Japanese worker commuting to Tokyo might spend as much as three hours traveling in each direction. He might begin each day by being "packed" onto a train in a Tokyo suburb by a white-uniformed "packer," who pushed him and other commuters into their train car at the station. Upon finishing his day, the typical worker might have a drink with colleagues before going back to work for a couple of hours to tie up loose ends and then brave the long commute home. Kenichi logged an average of 80 hours of overtime per month (once working 150 overtime hours in just one month).

On February 9, 2002, Kenichi never made it home. At 4:20 a.m., thirteen hours into what would have been his regular fourteen-hour shift, he collapsed at the office from a heart attack. The Japanese have a word to describe this modern phenomenon: *karoshi,* literally, death from overwork. Kenichi's story isn't new. In the 1980s, Japanese public health officials estimated that *karoshi* was responsible for the deaths of 10 percent of the country's working men. What made Kenichi a posthumous cause célèbre was the fact that his wife sued and won against the government and Toyota under a new law that qualifies *karoshi* as a sudden-death occupational accident.

I've always been fascinated by the language we use to describe our relationship with work. We have "drop-dead dates" and "deadlines." We are "terminated" when we lose our job, and at the same time we're "drowning in debt." People say that they're "dying to get a job," and some who are either unfulfilled or "waiting for the ax" say that they're "killing time." An old boss of mine spelled the last day of the workweek "Fried-day," since that's what we were typically feeling. The pejorative psychological term we commonly use to describe our workload is "crazed" or "crazy-busy"—which on its own is a symptom that our relationship with work is in need of a healthy makeover. Even the word we use to describe work, "occupation," sounds oppressive.

Americans haven't created "*karoshi* courts," but we're neck and neck with the Japanese in overtime. In fact, Americans put in enough overtime hours to equal three more weeks of work annually. The Koreans aren't far behind us and have even coined the term *kwarosa* as their form of *karoshi.* Americans work almost two months more per year than average Germans, French, and Italians, who are incredulous at our average of a paltry two weeks of vacation time per year. And overtime doesn't even include commuting time, emailing at all times of the evening and weekends, and the obligatory work-related social events. The term "workaholism" first appeared in American lingo in 1971, yet today we work 200 hours per year more than we did then. That's an extra five weeks of work each year!

It's fitting that this chapter on workaholism follows on the heels of our discussion of calling, because quite often the two seem indistinguishable. Are you a workaholic or a "work-a-frolic"? Believe me, I've asked myself this question many times over the past couple of decades when I felt completely under the spell (or the gun) of my work. This particular equation was a godsend for me, and in fact it's one I started using more than a decade ago as a mental reminder about what's important in life. Yes, there were some great excuses for why I was burning the midnight oil—the deadlines, running with a "skeleton crew," expense cutbacks, or just my desire to do an over-the-top job. I came face-to-face with my own mortality when I pushed myself too hard one too many times. I was fortunate to have some pretty fearless people in my life who confronted my workaholic behaviors and supported the career transition that allows me to write these words now. At the end of the day, what separates someone who is a workaholic from someone living his or her calling is whether that person feels imprisoned or free.

## WORKAHOLISM IS A FORM OF ADDICTION

Most addictions aren't socially acceptable. We don't pamper those who shoot heroin. Shame and secrecy surround the sex addict. Many of us have a flirtatious relationship with alcohol and sympathize with someone who's crossed the line into alcoholism, but we don't necessarily want to be responsible for getting him or her into treatment. Workaholism can be every bit as devastating as—and even more challenging to treat than—other addictions. After all, most people need to work to survive. So what would the treatment be? "Treatment" for workaholism might mean resting on a Caribbean beach for an extended period. The nonworkaholics reading this may be thinking, "Sign me up!" But for the afflicted, just the thought of going "unplugged" probably evokes a sense of terror (if they even allow themselves to think of it).

In America, we glorify our "gods" of workaholism. Love him or hate him, Donald Trump has made workaholism glamorous. He reveres his father, who "worked eight days a week." Trump admits to working eighty-five hours a week and tells the press he goes to bed at 1 A.M. and awakens at 5 A.M. since it gives him three or four additional hours to one-up his competition. And, he says, he loves the fact that "America is becoming a workaholic nation."

Simply put, addictions are about what we are running from. Quite often, we get intoxicated with something that alters our mood (including work), partly because we feel compelled to run away from emotions or fears that prey upon us. Scratch the emotional surface of any addict, and underneath you'll find some common emotions: a feeling of unworthiness, a feeling of being unlovable, shame, and a host of fears, from fear of intimacy to fear of failing or maybe even fear of succeeding. One of the hallmarks of any Alcoholics Anonymous meeting is the universality of emotions expressed by those in the room, whether a rock star, a homeless man, a single mother, or a newly minted MBA. Everyone is on the same level and realizes that he or she is not alone in suffering.

I stumbled into AA at age twenty-six, a couple of years after graduating from Stanford Business School. I'd spent a little time in the Al-Anon program for friends and family members of alcoholics, but I began to see my own patterns of how I used alcohol as both a social lubricant and a coping mechanism. I went for fifteen years without touching a drop of alcohol while growing my business into my forties. Upon reflection, I realized that I had moved my addiction from alcohol to work, which felt perfectly acceptable for a new entrepreneur trying to make my success in the world. Ultimately, those programs helped me understand and manage my workaholic behaviors and to be comforted by the knowledge that nearly everyone is addicted to something. What are you addicted to?

Though I loved my career in the hotel business and it had many of the meaning-driven qualities of a calling, I can also see that I was running from certain things in my behavior in those early years. My busyness was a means of measuring my self-importance. Sound familiar? Ask yourself the following ten questions with respect to your relationship with your work:

1. Do you often neglect family, friends, your health, and other important elements of your life because you get so wrapped up in your work? Is it impossible to put down your iPhone or BlackBerry?

2. If you created a pie chart of your sense of esteem and confidence as a person, what percentage of that pie would come from your work as opposed to the rest of your life?

3. At social gatherings with non-work-related people, what percentage of your time do you end up talking about work?

4. Are you a bit of a perfectionist and prefer to do the work yourself rather than delegate since delegation is awkward when others won't be able to do the work as well as you would?

5. Are you good at making excuses for why you have to work so hard?

6. Do you believe that money, fame, or professional respect will solve all your other problems in life?

7. Is your sense of self-esteem too reliant on others' opinions of you?

8. Do you have a difficult time sleeping because your mind

races or you feel that there's so much work you could be
doing if you didn't have to bother with sleep? Do you have
a substance addiction to adrenaline (many workaholics
do) or to the "rush" that comes from completing a task or
"saving the day"?

9. Is it easier for you to logically understand emotions than
to allow yourself to feel them? Does the word "intimacy"
send shivers up your spine?

10. Do you know what it feels like to just sit still for ten minutes doing nothing?

Those two last questions sent me off the rails. As a kid, I believed
that I was lovable for what I accomplished. It was so much easier for
me to focus on tasks than to deal with painful feelings. If I had a bad
day at school, my first reaction when I got home was to pull out my
homework and distract myself. My brain was telling me, "If you're
feeling like a loser, you can become lovable if you do well in school."
Using your work to distract yourself from feeling "less than" others
seems like perfectly responsible behavior. And so we're celebrated for
our "nose to the grindstone" mentality.

Workaholism to avoid feelings tends to afflict men more than
women, because women are better able to express their emotions and
discuss relationship conflicts. Workaholic men often use their work
as a shield from difficult family dynamics, thinking that their success
at work may solve their marital woes when, in fact, their workaholism makes their spouse and kids more resentful. Of course, this cycle
just propels the "running from" workaholic deeper into work since
work is something he can control. Executives addicted to success
don't escape their private lives; they simply neglect them.

Questions 9 and 10 above are so profound for me because I've
spent much of my adult life filling my calendar in order not to feel
the pain. The great American male motto is "Do more to feel less." In
my thirties and much of my forties, I thought that the stress I carried

home with me each weekday—that rigidified my rhomboids in my shoulders and upper back and kept my neck stiff—was all about not being able to do more. Then I started to realize that my life of busyness and my insane schedule left no room for the sunlight to find the crevices where creativity and inspiration dwell. My tight shoulders weren't about *doing more;* they were about *feeling less.* I had created a life dedicated to keeping me out of the sun—the light of my feelings and emotions.

Intimacy has been described as meaning "in to me see" (in other words, allowing people to see me transparently for who I am). And that was the last thing I wanted. "Pay no attention to the man behind the curtain!" the Wizard of Oz exclaimed when trying to distract Dorothy from learning the truth about the power behind the throne. I guess I was trying to "wizard" my way through life. If you approved of all my accomplishments, maybe you wouldn't look as closely at that small, fragile man behind the curtain.

## REFOCUSING YOUR ATTENTION ON YOUR LIFE

My five friends and business associates who committed suicide were not workaholics, but for some of them, their sense of identity was so wrapped up in their work that when the economy suddenly downshifted, they became completely disoriented. Tragically, I think they'd forgotten that there's a very powerful bottom half (the denominator) of this equation: "What Are You Living For?"

This abstract question has saved many a life. Just sit with that question for a moment. Pull out a piece of paper and write a few sentences about what's important to you. Then stop and ask the question again. What are you living for? Go a little deeper into how you answer the question. If you're stumped, here are a few follow-up questions: At the end of your life, what will be your legacy? When was the last time you felt true joy in your life (not just the satisfaction of getting something done), and what brought you that joy? If you had twenty-four hours left to live, what would you spend your time doing—or being?

This is an appropriate time to further distinguish between workaholism and a calling. If, after honest reflection, you feel the work you are doing is truly part of your unique reason for being on Earth, let's accept that you may have found your calling. A friend of mine says, "Ambition in the container of mindfulness comes out as aspiration," which means "breathing in" with the right intention. But if you find the above questions difficult to answer because you feel so cut off from anything non-work-related and your work "occupies" you, maybe you have a case of workaholism.

Workaholism, like other addictions, can produce an out-of-body experience or an altered state. Researchers have found the peak performance of work-addicted people to be a form of ecstasy, and the accompanying surge of adrenaline acts like a drug—so workaholism could actually be considered substance abuse. St. Thomas Aquinas believed that, for some people, addiction was a quest for the infinite but that the addicted were looking in the wrong place for the sacred. Could it be that you are "living for" something much bigger than yourself but have somehow gotten distracted into thinking that being perfect at work will put you in high standing with the powers that be? Don't forget that on the seventh day, even God rested.

The average Japanese worker uses less than half of the paid holidays he has available to him. And when many Americans take a vacation, it truly is a time to "vacate"—to escape from life, distract ourselves with sensory pleasures, or take on an avatar-like alternative personality. What if you used one day of your next vacation for reflection, a time when you could take yourself off the work-pleasure-work treadmill to become clear on what you're living for? If you're a workaholic, consider doing this with your spouse; you don't have to figure it out alone, even though I know that's your preferred way of solving problems. The two of you can ask yourselves, "If we were to start over again, based upon what we know is important to us, how could we reimagine our lives?" Or, even more simply and more easily, "What are the smallish delights in our lives that deserve more investment?"

I know it's hard to open up your life to this kind of reflection, given what's been going on in the numerator of your equation—"What Are You Running From?"—and being open to having your spouse join you in this deep dive may be frightening. But first realize that just the act of asking for company in your reflection is a step toward intimacy and toward creating a sense of value in the relationship with you. Plus, it's better to hear from your spouse today about what could be improved than wait till divorce proceedings or your deathbed.

Here's what Abigail Adams wrote about her husband, John Adams, America's first vice president, its second president, and the father of John Quincy Adams, the first son to follow his father into the presidency: "I recollect the untitled man to whom I gave my heart and in the agony of recollection, when time and distance present themselves together, wish he had never been any other. Who shall give me back my time? Who shall compensate to me those years I cannot recall? How dearly have I paid for a titled husband?"—further proof that workaholism has been a family malady since at least colonial days. Did you make a silent vow to your work that's more real to you than the vow you made to your spouse?

## WORKING THROUGH THE EQUATION

$$Workaholism = \frac{\textit{What Are You Running From?}}{\textit{What Are You Living For?}}$$

*If you sense that your relationship with work is out of balance, consider which kind of workaholic profile best describes you.* Researchers have identified three types of workaholics: (1) the compulsive-dependent, (2) the perfectionistic, and (3) the achievement-oriented. (Numbers 2 and 3 probably best describe me.) *Compulsive-dependent workaholics* tend to be focused on staying busy without looking at whether they're being productive or effective. If this profile fits you, consider therapy or some other means of reflection to see what emotional demons are lurking behind your tendency to fill your attention. Your behavior may be making you more stressed, more susceptible to illness, and less creative. *Perfectionistic workaholics* are control-driven and reliant on rules and believe in the mantra that "practice makes perfect." But what if perfection doesn't exist? Are you open to relaxing a little and accepting that your standards may be higher than they need to be and that they are having a negative consequence for you and those around you? *Achievement-oriented workaholics* are generally healthier because their work-obsessed traits tend to be more situational, but they need to be careful about constantly building their self-esteem by being the hero. Are you too reliant on others' opinions of you?

*As with other addictions, reducing the numerator ("What Are You Running From?") will release the stranglehold of your habitual behavior.* It's easy to be in denial about this condition since it's so well sanctioned in our society. Most addicts are in denial: the emaciated, anorexic teenager who looks in the mirror and sees herself as obese; the gambler living in a fleabag Vegas hotel who believes Lady Luck is just about to anoint him with success; the executive who comes home from a social event and obsessively washes the germs from her hands until they are virtually raw. You may see yourself as "above" these folks, but to the rest of the world, your behavior is aberrant as well (ever sneaked some work into your suitcase so that your spouse wouldn't know you'd brought it on your vacation?). Take a step back, and realize that your habit is just an emotional loop you've found yourself in. It's not an indictment of you as a person. But you won't get out of the loop until you're willing to truly see what underlying emotions or unconscious messages in your head are driving your behavior.

*Apply the concept of "opportunity costs" to the denominator of this equation.* Since we're talking about the world of work here, you may be familiar with the expression "opportunity costs" to describe the fact that when you invest time or money in one activity, you won't be able to invest it in other things. There is an opportunity cost to putting money in a bank, which is why we earn interest on it. "What Are You Living For?" is the question that helps you give attention to what your opportunity cost is when you become so focused on your work. Generally, it's easy to lose track of the opportunity costs in life unless you make a list of them and consciously factor them into your decision making. Make a list of the five things you live for most, and put them on your computer screen (as a screen saver or a list next to your monitor). As you take on new work projects, realize that the time you spend on those projects may take you away from these more meaningful elements of your life.

*Explore Workaholics Anonymous.* This free twelve-step program is for people who identify themselves as "powerless over compulsive work, worry, or activity." The WA website (www.workaholics-anonymous.org) provides a collection of helpful resources as well as direction for how to find out if a meeting is happening in your part of the world. The program uses the Twelve Steps and Twelve Traditions of Alcoholics Anonymous as a format, but WA members are free to drink alcohol (just not at meetings). Connecting with others and talking about your common experiences around work and activity addiction will help you identify your feelings and emotions around this issue.

Workaholism isn't an emotion. And quite often, workaholics are disconnected from their emotions. But there's no doubt that using this Emotional Equation to help unlock a problematic relationship with work is highly effective. In some cases, as with Kenichi Uchino, intense social or financial pressures may be driving you to be work-obsessed. Or, if you're like me, it may be that you sometimes attach your sense of identity too closely to your work to distract yourself from feelings of unworthiness. In the early days of my first hotel, The Phoenix, friends would ask me, "How's life, Chip?" I would respond, "The Phoenix is doing well," even when I was pretty nervous that the company might not make it. One day a friend who wasn't satisfied with my answer put her hand on my heart and said softly, "Chip, I didn't ask you how your business is doing, I want to know how you're feeling." For most addicts, our friends and family see our predicament before we acknowledge it. Be open to the feedback. It could save your life.

# 10

$$\text{Flow}^* = \frac{\text{Skill}}{\text{Challenge}}$$

(* With the goal of Flow being equal to 1.0)

I magine what it would feel like to inspire awe, admiration, and respect—while doing your job. Few athletes have achieved the cult status that is afforded basketball's Michael Jordan. This timeless superstar mesmerized us with his ability to turn a game around at a critical juncture; he embodied being "in the zone" (a phrase credited to both baseball's Ted Williams and Wimbledon star Arthur Ashe). When Michael was in the zone on the basketball court, you couldn't take your eyes off of him.

Professional athletes are paid big bucks to be hypercompetitive. But just being determined or aggressive is quite different from tapping into the kind of magic Michael displayed with his play. In psychology, "drive" is synonymous with "arousal," an emotionally charged state that results from a competitive nature. The degree of arousal or drive, up to a certain point, is a key determinant of the quality of performance, whether in sports or business. Beyond that optimal level of arousal, any extra drive can cause performance to decline. This state of optimal performance lasts for only a short time, during which the mind, body, and emotional system are all perfectly aligned. It is a transcendental state in which one is optimally situated between excitement and boredom and between relaxation and anxiety.

A new friend of mine, Mihaly "Mike" Csikszentmihalyi, the author of the landmark book *Flow,* wrote, "Flow is a highly focused state of relaxed concentration that obliterates all else out of consciousness. It is the state of self-actualization or transcendental behavior that is euphoric." Part of the reason we love watching people "in the zone" or full of "flow" is that it's almost like coming into contact with the divine.

The bestselling author Anne Lamott referred to this contact in her book about writing, *Bird by Bird,* in which she noted, "To be engrossed by something outside ourselves is a powerful antidote for the rational mind. . . . There are moments when I am writing when I think that if other people knew how I felt right now, they'd burn me at the stake for feeling so good, so full, so much intense pleasure." But, she warned, "To participate requires self-discipline and trust and courage, because this business of becoming conscious, of being a writer, is ultimately about asking yourself, 'How alive am I willing to be?' . . . So you must risk placing real emotion at the center of your work."

What in Michael Jordan's history created the conditions for him to so finely attune his skill set to meet the challenges of becoming a world-class athlete? On one level he portrayed a casual dignity, but underneath that relaxed demeanor was someone who felt the overriding need to prove himself to the world and also to himself. He recounts being a sophomore in high school in Wilmington, North Carolina, and not making the varsity basketball team. The owner of two Olympic gold medals and ten NBA scoring titles says, "It was embarrassing not making that team. They posted the roster and it was there for a long, long time without my name on it. . . . Whenever I was working out and got tired and figured I ought to stop, I'd close

111

my eyes and see that list in the locker room without my name on it and that usually got me going again."

Although I never had anything like the natural ability of Michael Jordan, I completely relate to his story. As a kid, I practiced basketball incessantly in the alley behind our home. I would practice free throws for hours at a time, but as soon as a few neighborhood kids would show up wanting to play, I would take my ball and go inside because I was so shy. In seventh grade, I surprised all the better-known young athletes by becoming a starter on our championship school basketball team. But in eighth grade—just like Michael Jordan—when I went to look for my name on the list of who'd made the team, I'd been dropped. It was such a shock that I ran out to the car where my mom was waiting for me after school and buried my head in her lap for a good long cry. That evening, I resolved I would work harder at whatever was important to me so that I wouldn't lose again. I've spent the rest of my life honing my skills as an athlete, businessman, writer, speaker, and in all areas of my life.

In August 2010, Mike Csikszentmihalyi invited me to visit his Montana summer home for a few days to discuss what it means to be "in the flow." With no cell phone or Internet service, and in a location near natural hot springs with medicinal qualities, I felt the distinct sense that I'd arrived in a place where I could experience an endorphin high just by walking down the country lane.

One of the most profound things I learned on that trip was that going into a state of flow involves a loss of self-consciousness. This doesn't mean you lose yourself, and of course you don't fall unconscious. It just means that—for a moment—you lose consciousness of yourself. We spend our lives being obsessively aware of ourselves, what's running through our minds, what our body feels like. You know what I'm talking about. But when we get into a state of flow, we temporarily disconnect from this attachment to self, and that allows us to expand our concept of who we are and what we can do in the world. Ironically, taking down the boundaries we apply to ourselves allows us to rise to Michael Jordan–like levels, but that doesn't happen without practice.

## THE RIGHT MIX OF SKILL AND CHALLENGE

My definition of flow will relate to your work life. The Gallup Organization has found that about 15 to 20 percent of adults experience flow on a daily basis, while a similar number never seems to experience this euphoric condition. The other 60 to 70 percent feel the state of flow on occasion—whether it's weekly, monthly, or every couple of years. One of the primary places we can gain access to flow is in the context of our work. Finding flow at work means that you harness your emotions in a single-minded immersion of activity that takes you to peak performance.

Take a look at the two following diagrams that juxtapose skill level on the horizontal axis and challenge level on the vertical axis. The first diagram shows the flow channel, the 45-degree vector that defines when someone feels that his or her skills and the challenge are balanced. The second diagram shows the variety of emotions that occur when a person is out of balance. Do an activity that is relatively easy for your skill level, and you likely feel bored or relaxed. Try something that's above your current skill set, and you may be worried or in the anxiety zone.

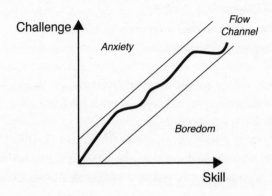

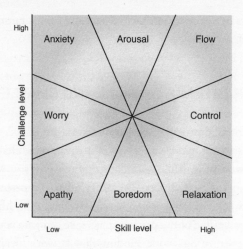

Mike told me that there are three conditions necessary to achieve the flow state:

1. Being involved in an activity that has structure, direction, and a clear goal. That's why games and sports are so well suited to achieving flow, while watching television is not.
2. Having a good balance between the perceived challenge and your perceived skills so that you can imagine being capable of living up to the challenge.
3. Being able to receive clear and immediate feedback about how you're doing, which allows you to adjust your performance to toggle up or down in the challenge level to keep you in the flow zone. Many workplaces do a rotten job of this, as there's very little external feedback to help you understand your objective performance. That's part of the reason why video games can be so addictive, as the feedback is instantaneous.

People who are in the flow use "metacognition." That is, they're aware of their learning behaviors and how they're performing and thus can ratchet themselves to the upper-right-hand part of these diagrams. The "sweet spot" for flow is where the challenge level is about 5 to 10 percent above your skill level, so that as you move from early learning to mastery, you incrementally move your challenge from elementary to world class. For simplicity, this flow equation of skill divided by challenge is supposed to skew toward the number 1.0, yet a more precise equation would have you at just under one, since that would mean you are constantly striving for challenges that are just beyond your skill level.

In the workplace, you may, on occasion, feel as though you're surrounded by Michael Jordans who seem to effortlessly create world-class performance. The reality is that anyone who is tapping into a flow state is naturally pushing the boundary between anxiety and excitement rather than control and relaxation. Think about your work or some other element of your life in which you've broken through a barrier. What was it that motivated you to get to that space? And what confluence of emotions were at play just before you actually started to feel the elevated state of being and awareness that kicked in when you hit your flow? If it's hard to imagine this as an adult, think back to when you were a kid. The process of becoming a flow-driven water skier required me to live in a certain amount of terror and self-consciousness as I pushed my limits. But at some point my excitement started to lessen and I felt a level of comfort that allowed me to stop being so hard on myself. Then I felt in flow.

## MASTERY

Blink your left eye. Now blink your right eye. Now blink both eyes at the same time, three times. You are now a master blinker. The process of learning how to blink left, then right, and then together requires a certain amount of mastery over listening to instructions and controlling your mind and body. (Try to do this after a few glasses of wine, and you'll find it isn't so easy.) Or up the ante and name all fifty of the United States in alphabetical order, after each blink of the eye. Can you do that without making a mistake? Probably not. But if you practiced enough, I bet within a few days you could do it like a master. Frankly, no one would care and it wouldn't get you on *The Tonight Show,* but you would have learned something about learning.

For many people, the realm of the gifted seems like an exclusive club. But mastery isn't reserved for the supertalented or those who have the right genes. Unfortunately, in our culture of instant gratification, we've come to expect that we can become masters in the blink of an eye. We become impatient, and we give up. If you stick with a skill, you start to see some improvement over time until you hit the dreaded plateau when your skill level just seems to coast for a while even though you're pouring energy into improving. Then, all of a sudden, you find that your skill ratchets up to the next level. That's how mastery works. It's not one smooth, upward-facing line of improvement; it happens in fits and starts.

No doubt, some skills are more suited for you than others, and knowing your strengths will help you find the flow zone much more easily. But talent isn't nearly as important as practice if you want to see your skills grow over time. A landmark study by K. Anders Ericsson at Berlin's elite Academy of Music divided the school's violinists into three groups: the stars, those who were merely good, and those who were average at best. All three groups of college-age students had started learning their craft at around age five, practicing a couple hours a week. But by age eight, those who became the stars were practicing substantially more hours than others. By the time Ericsson studied those twenty-year-old students, the stars had practiced around ten thousand hours over the course of their lifetime, while those who were good had practiced about 20 percent less and those who were average had practiced less than half the time the stars had. Since that study in the early 1990s, this marker has been applied to all kinds of other fields to determine who has attained mastery and who hasn't. The equation? Mastery = Ten thousand hours of practice.

You may be thinking "Ouch! Ten thousand hours? That's twenty hours a week for ten years." That's right, mastery builds over many years. In the context of work, it can happen more quickly because you concentrate so much of your time in the workplace. But the reality is that if you want to be a master of giving exceptional performance reviews, for example, you're unlikely to spend a full twenty hours per week on that task, as it's only one of many things you do in your work. In order to become world class and ratchet up your skill set so that you can embrace bigger challenges, you need to be less focused on the outcome or results and more focused on the practice itself. If you are truly energized by what you're doing and feel a sense of "being all you can be" by doing it, I promise you won't notice the number of hours you're investing in it.

## FINDING YOUR MOJO AT WORK

If I'd been told as a shy teenager that as an adult I'd be making my living as a public speaker, I would not have believed it. I lived in my own creative world, but as I became more focused on building relationships in my high school years, I started to get more comfortable in front of a crowd. One of my teachers took me to a Toastmasters class, where I saw adults who were all similarly challenged by the prospect of having to express themselves in front of an audience. I got involved in Student Council, where I had to give the occasional speech, and I was voted student body president my senior year, giving a speech a week to campus groups.

But I found my true voice in college and graduate school, often because we had to speak up and debate a topic in front of a class. With time, I found that my skill was learning how to articulate the emotions I was feeling and translate those into whatever subject was being discussed *and* to do so in a manner that authentically connected me with the people in the room.

After I'd been CEO of Joie de Vivre for nearly ten years, my speaking career really took off. I was incubating a book on being an entrepreneur and sought guidance on how to formulate my thoughts for the sake of the book format. Alan Webber, the cofounder of *Fast Company* magazine, suggested, "If you're going to write a book, start giving speeches on the topic, as great teachers are great learners and the fastest way you'll ever learn a subject is feeling the responsibility of teaching it in front of an audience." So in the late 1990s, I put myself on a path of giving a minimum of three to four speeches a month—outside my company and my comfort zone, whether at the local Rotary Club or at a seniors' center. I wasn't spectacular, but I started to find my rhythm. And on certain occasions, I started to feel as if I were channeling a message that was bigger than me. Then I felt the flow.

Today, I give eighty to a hundred speeches a year all over the world, side by side with some of the most gifted communicators of our time. I don't think I've surpassed the ten-thousand-hour rule yet with respect to my speaking career, but I can instinctively "read" a crowd and tailor my message—on the spot—to just what they need to hear. I also see that, if I coast for too long, giving the same speech to multiple audiences month after month, I end up in the boredom part of the flow diagram earlier in the chapter. So part of my responsibility to myself and to my audience is to take risks with my talks, whether that means giving a speech in my boxer shorts to lighten things up a bit, addressing the sensitive subject of suicide without becoming a bundle of tears, or speaking about a topic that is truly foreign to me. The more I challenge myself, the better I become.

## WORKING THROUGH THE EQUATION

$$\left[\ Flow = \frac{Skill}{Challenge}\ \right]$$

*Calculate your "flow" for different elements of your work.* Let's use the equation to get a sense of whether you're in flow in various components of what dominates your work time. Think of a few things you do regularly. For example, let's assume you work in the HR department of your company. You are leading a project team that meets weekly, focused on compensation levels in your company. And you are the public face of your company at HR conferences, talking about how your company builds its culture. First go back to the diagrams on pages 113–114 and plot where you are on your skill level for both those activities. If you have had considerable experience doing those things and feel you are a master at it, put a dot that matches where you are on that spectrum—from beginner to the left to world class to the right—on the horizontal skill axis. Now let's look at the level of challenge associated with both those activities. Is your compensation project team an aligned group with sufficient authority to make a difference? The more it is, the more you can stretch the group's responsibility and its challenge to make a difference. The higher the opportunity, the higher on the vertical axis you would plot your point. Is your company in the limelight, so that being the public face means you have to be "on your game" all the time at conferences? Based upon where you plot the points, you'll get a sense of which of the eight emotional zones you find yourself in those work activities. Do they feel accurate?

*Take the flow checklist.* Mike Csikszentmihalyi identifies eight factors as accompanying an experience of flow. The first three are conditions that facilitate flow and the last five are experiential indicators of flow. How many of them characterize each component of your work?

1. Clear goals that define success.
2. Direct and immediate feedback so that you can incrementally adjust.
3. A constant balance between your skill level and your challenge.
4. The ability to concentrate and focus exclusively on the activity through completion.
5. A loss of feeling self-conscious when you're merging action and awareness. That may mean you lose awareness of your bodily needs.
6. Often, a loss of sense of time when you're in the midst of doing the work.
7. A sense of personal control over the situation or activity.
8. The activity being intrinsically rewarding, so there is effortlessness of action.

*Be open to change in order to achieve mastery.* George Leonard's little book *Mastery: The Keys to Success and Long-Term Fulfillment* is a legendary teaching on this subject. He writes that one of the biggest challenges of living a life focused on mastery is the unwillingness to change. Here are his five key suggestions for how to facilitate change. First, be aware of the way homeostasis works. Homeostasis is like your thermostat at home. It turns on or off to create a stable, comfortable condition and can keep you from feeling anxiety. Homeostasis is the enemy of change and mastery. Second, be willing to negotiate with your resistance to change. If you are moving two steps forward and one step back, you're on the right path. Any endeavor on the way to mastery will have warning signals to tell you that you've overstepped or are about to overstep a boundary. Take setbacks as positive signals that you can modulate and keep moving forward. Third, develop a support system. Employees and managers often make great progress at off-site management retreats, only to settle back into the day-to-day aloneness of their jobs when they're back in the office. Create a team that is dedicated to change, and help push each other along. An external coach, friends or family, or a supervisor who knows what you want to master can help. Fourth, follow a regular practice. Love what you're doing for the sake of doing it, and you won't even realize that you've racked up the ten thousand hours needed to become a world-class expert. Finally, dedicate yourself to lifelong learning. Mastery isn't a destination; it's a way of living. Also, be aware of what you're mastering in life. The average young American male adult now spends an average of ten thousand hours playing video and online games by the time he's twenty-one. But it's not clear that there's a larger benefit or purpose in this mastery.

*May the force be with you.* The thirteenth-century Zen master Dogen pointed out that in the moments when the world is experienced with the whole of one's body and mind, the senses are joined, the self is opened, and life discloses an intrinsic richness and joy in being that feels at one with the world. Being in flow matches your talents and aspirations with the world's needs. As with "Calling," chapter 8's equation, there is a profound sense that you have found your unique purpose and the reason you are on this planet. But with flow, you also tap into unexplainable forces—whether a muse, a genie, an angel, a savior, or an energy—that help you straddle the skill/challenge tightrope with the expertise of a Cirque du Soleil performer.

Ludwig van Beethoven grew up with a father who was exacting and hard. Beethoven's father would come home after a night of drinking with friends, wake up his son, and force him to practice the piano for the rest of the night. By the time he was sixteen, Beethoven had been discovered by Wolfgang Amadeus Mozart and was seen as a talent that would "astonish the world." But when he was in his twenties, his hearing started to fail, and by his early thirties, he was deaf, suicidal, and despairing. Still, over the next couple of decades, even while facing a series of personal setbacks, he tapped into his passionate talent, not out of a sense of obligation, as it had been with his father, but out of the love of practicing. And just after turning fifty, he composed the ultimate musical contribution to the feeling of flow, "Ode to Joy." Finding flow can happen at any time in your life.

# 11

$$\boxed{\text{Curiosity} = \text{Wonder} + \text{Awe}}$$

I was born in Orange, California, under the influence of, and just five miles from, the Magic Kingdom of Disneyland. My earliest recollections are of walking down Main Street, meeting Mickey Mouse, and being thrilled by the experience of driving a car in Autopia and frightened by the Matterhorn ride. At age five, when I was asked what I wanted to be when I grew up, I answered with a "who," not a "what": Walt Disney. I spent much of my childhood drawing fanciful layouts of my ideal amusement park, which ultimately became my boutique hotels.

At almost fifty years of age, Disney was already a successful film producer, director, and entertainment innovator when he began sketching his vision for Disneyland. Following his calling and working around the clock, he spent five years creating and developing the world's most iconic amusement park. When Disneyland first opened, observers marveled that it was as if a ten-year-old child with a fifty-year-old's wisdom and urban planning skill had created the "happiest place on Earth."

Walt Disney was bigger than life to many people, but he suggested that we could all emulate him: "Somehow I can't believe that there are any heights that can't be scaled by a man who knows the secrets of making dreams come true. This special secret, it seems to me, can be summarized in four Cs. They are curiosity, confidence, courage, and constancy." Disney believed that his drive, stamina, and ability to pick himself up after some pretty big career letdowns came from the first of the four Cs. Albert Einstein had an abiding respect for this emotion as well, writing "I am neither especially clever nor especially gifted. I am only very, very curious."

Creativity tends to get more attention than curiosity, as there's something tangible and actionable associated with the quality. Curiosity typically is an activity without a predetermined purpose. It's the fertilizer of the mind. Yet there's lots of evidence to suggest that it's like blood in our veins, an essential, life-affirming emotion that keeps us forever young. Curiosity can also be the escape hatch for both anxiety and depression. When you are feeling the oppression of either of those emotions, you also likely feel a dimness, narrowness, and declining interest. Being curious is being open: open to learning, open to loving, open to stumbling, open to life. The psychologist Todd Kashdan calls curiosity "the engine of growth."

Warning: Curiosity requires you to admit that you don't know what you don't know. While this may induce some anxiety (we're all so conditioned to have the right answer), this can be a potent launch pad to curiosity. Asking "How do you do that?" or "I don't know—can you show me?" means we let go of having the right answer or being competent. Curiosity allows us to explore with the open mind of a child, without preconceptions, and may very well keep us from growing old too fast. As Satchel Paige asked, "How old would you be if you didn't know how old you were?"

I went to an inner-city high school, and some of my friends used to call me "curious white boy" as a term of endearment. I was fascinated with the mélange of cultures we had at Long Beach Polytechnic High School, famous for being "the home of scholars and champions." At the time, I didn't realize that the label I'd earned was a compliment. Yet we all have a choice: we can avoid asking questions for fear of finding answers that threaten our beliefs and preconceptions and the status quo, or we can face the big questions with a curious heart and mind.

## CURIOSITY FUELS CREATIVITY

Sony founder Akio Morita said, "Curiosity is the key to creativity." I believe it surpasses creativity as the most essential trait of a successful businessperson in the twenty-first century, especially in the global economy. One of the most trusted axioms in business is that a great manager finds the answers, while a great leader discovers the questions. That's particularly true in an era when the world is in a constant state of change. Curiosity has also proven to be a great ingredient in resilience, a trait particularly valuable in an extended economic downturn. Resilient people aren't made of steel; they just provide themselves with more options, and those options come from a curious mind.

Curiosity may have killed the cat, but it helped the most famous business theorist and author of all time, Peter Drucker, live to the age of ninety-five. Drucker was offended whenever he was called a "guru" and throughout his life characterized himself as either a "student" or a "bystander." In fact, the title of his memoir is *Adventures of a Bystander*. He believed that people are meant to "live in more than one world," partly to keep a fresh mind, partly to synthesize ideas across disciplines, and partly because having a diverse life means that when part of your life is askew, you can turn to other parts of your life to help balance it.

Drucker coined the phrase "knowledge workers" to define the role of businesses in the new information age we were entering a generation ago. He wrote, "The leaders of the past knew how to tell. The leaders of

125

the future will know how to ask." He glorified the idea of learning and development as an essential part of the corporate infrastructure and the mind-set of those who would flourish within a company. In his own life, he would pick a new subject to learn every three years, from Japanese art to arcane economics. In his free time, he would study the subject with such ferocity that he was able to teach it to others.

The social psychologist Carol Dweck has done landmark research on how your "mind-set"—more than any other factor—determines whether you will be successful. At one end of a spectrum are those who believe that their success is based upon their innate ability; at the other are those who believe that their learning defines their success. Dweck describes the former as having a "fixed" mind-set, while the latter have a "growth" mind-set.

You may not be aware of your mind-set until you have to deal with failure. People coming from a fixed mind-set dread failure, which they consider a negative reflection of their abilities, so they often aren't willing to risk being curious or risk-taking. People with a growth mind-set see failure as a constructive path toward improvement. Dweck has shown that how we encourage our kids has a lot to do with their capacity to be curious and open to learning. (It's better to say, "Great job, Sally, you worked very hard" than "Great job, Sally, you're very smart.")

How open are you to seeing failure as a positive growth experience? Are your kids more focused on *demonstrating* their competence (proving themselves) rather than *increasing* it (improving themselves)? Do you celebrate your children's fixed, innate qualities or do you help them see the incremental value of hard work and self-improvement?

## ONE PART CHILD, ONE PART SAGE

Curiosity is a curious emotion. A component of curiosity is all about the childlike wonder ("The Wonderful World of Disney") that encourages us to explore our relationship with new discoveries, most of which are relatively simple. Yet Albert Einstein suggested something deeper when he wrote, "The important thing is not to stop questioning. Curiosity has its own reason for existing. One cannot help but be in awe when he contemplates the mysteries of eternity, of life, of the marvelous structure of reality." In its purest form, curiosity mixes the sense of a child seeing the world for the first time with that of the wise elder who realizes that the more she knows, the more she doesn't know—and is delighted and maybe even a little humbled by that realization.

What's sad is the in-between time. Between our wondrous youth and our awe-struck senior years, we choose a narrower path, not by conscious choice but often because life's circumstances necessitate a little more linearity. Ironically, this is the time of our life—midlife—when we tend to report the least amount of happiness. Certainty and structure may create predictability in your life but also lead to apathy and a slow atrophy of your curiosity muscles, as well as your mind and life spirit. In the early stages of Parkinson's and Alzheimer's diseases, one of the first signs that something is wrong is the inability to manage and deal with the curious or novel.

Let's explore these two components of curiosity: wonder and awe. René Descartes proposed that, "Wonder is the first of all the passions." It couples the sense of joyful, innocent surprise with a desire to know more. Surprise is one of the six most universal emotions and it's particularly prevalent in youngsters who haven't yet learned how to mask their sense of wonder about the world.

Adults have a mixed relationship with wonder. When was the last time you marveled at something as if it were the first time you'd ever seen it? As a kid, one of my favorite qualities about Disneyland was the illusion that it physically never ended. Walt, the master, and his architects created a design that didn't allow you to see any exterior walls when you were in the midst of the fantasy world. What subject in the world could give you that boundless, open sense of discovery?

Too often, we lose the wonder when we rise five hundred feet into the air to see Disneyland for what it technically is (an amusement park) as opposed to what it emotionally is (a joyful world of possibility). Is it time for you to put on a "wonder"-ful new pair of glasses?

In *Flow*, Csikszentmihalyi asked highly skilled rock climbers, composers of music, chess players, and others what gives them a similar feeling to the flow they feel when doing their cherished activity. The number one response: "designing or discovering something new," a state that is almost synonymous with wonder. Perhaps joy is not the absence of unhappiness but, more purely, the presence of childlike wonder. Is it possible to regain that sense of wonder we all had before it was "educated out of us"? As the creativity expert Sir Ken Robinson says, "Children are not frightened of being wrong," which allows for creativity to happen. And, he warns, "If you're not prepared to be wrong, you'll never come up with anything original."

Wonder is often compared to awe, but awe implies a certain respect for the unknown, whereas wonder just bathes in joy. Wonder may lead to scientific discoveries. Awe leads to metaphysical or spiritual insights. We feel awe when we are humbled by something bigger than we are. Dacher Keltner devotes a whole glorious chapter to awe in his book *Born to Be Good: The Science of a Meaningful Life* and helps us imagine what John Muir must have felt when he first stumbled upon the Sierra Nevada mountains and Yosemite Valley. Perhaps you remember the awe you felt when the Apollo 11 astronauts projected their view of Earth from the moon, the first time this beautiful image of the entire planet was ever seen. There's a transformative element of awe that puts you into your proper place, connecting you to something grand.

Awe carries an element of humility and sometimes fear, since it truly makes us realize how small we are in the context of the miraculous, untamed world. Enlightenment and Transcendentalist writers wove wondrous words to describe the alchemy of beauty and the sublime that defines our sense of awe. Awe suggests vastness and power beyond what we know or can conceive of, which requires a certain amount of accommodation to that which deserves not just our devotion but also our sense of discovery. Keltner says, "The experience of awe is about finding your place in the larger scheme of things." It can make you feel either small and inconsequential or possibly large and connected with a sense of oneness with all that exists.

Yet awe has taken on some odd connotations today. The United States used a strategy of "shock and awe" during the bombing of Baghdad when trying to oust Saddam Hussein from power. On a lighter note, the word "awesome" has never been the same since Sean Penn hijacked it as his mantra, playing the spacey Jeff Spicoli in the movie *Fast Times at Ridgemont High*.

## CURIOUS TRIBES:
## THE BLENDING OF WONDER AND AWE

Internet communities alone aren't enough. We are naturally social beings who need the occasional hall pass to break us out of our cybercell at home or work so we can connect with our flock. And if there's one experience that can transcendentally unite a flock, it's the experience of wonder and awe in a group setting.

I regularly experience curious joy when among three unique tribes: the annual TED Conference in Long Beach, California; the Sundance Film Festival in Park City, Utah; and Burning Man in the northern Nevada desert, the largest interactive arts festival in the world. Though these three annual events are quite different, they are all immersive. They give me a "contact high" by being able to share my sense of wonder or awe at a mind-blowing lecture, an emotionally intense film, or an ethereal sculpture in the middle of the desert.

I celebrated my fiftieth birthday with more than a hundred friends in a camp we called "Maslowtopia" at Burning Man 2010. Each year, nearly fifty thousand people create a temporary tent city in the normally uninhabited, harsh Black Rock desert. Think *Mad Max* meets *Lawrence of Arabia* meets *Hair.* The mind-altering alchemy of art, spirituality, sexuality, and dancing under the stars is popular with the bobo (bourgeois bohemian) crowd of all economic, gender, and racial backgrounds.

My birthday tribe included folks aged seventeen to seventy. Because we were in a place dedicated to the unexpected, there was a certain amount of caution and anxiety when doctors, lawyers, and teachers packed up their rented RVs, said good-bye to the kids, and hit the open road for this experience. The one thing I said to a couple of my friends who almost chickened out was, "Stay curious" (sort of like the closing of Steve Jobs's famous Stanford commencement address: "Stay hungry, stay foolish.").

Over the course of the few days we were together, we had a transformative experience. We were in a utopian society with no money, not many rules, and an overall feeling that this was summer camp for adults. We also had a healthy dollop of awe. When the sun goes down on your first night at Burning Man, it's like being at Disneyland for the first time. The vastness of the night, the sheer beauty of the electrified art, and the sublime zeitgeist of human transformation all tell you that this is not something you could experience in the confines of your own home.

When I was a kid, a friend and I would catch pollywogs during school recess, wanting to see and understand their metamorphosis. Burning Man induces that sense of wonder and awe for me as a grown-up. When was the last time you went searching for pollywogs?

## WORKING THROUGH THE EQUATION

$$Curiosity = Wonder + Awe$$

*Take a look at your myths about curiosity.* Adam and Eve were banished from Eden because of curiosity. Pandora opened a box, and it released evil, sickness, and unhappiness (with hope, too). Lot's wife was told not to look back on the destruction of the cities of Sodom and Gomorrah, couldn't resist a peek, and turned into a pillar of salt. Thirty years ago, your boss told you, "Don't stick your nose into other people's business." Your wife thinks you have a "morbid curiosity" about your own mortality. Our minds and culture caution us that curiosity taken too far becomes dangerous and obsessive. Has curiosity ever gotten you into trouble? Was it truly curiosity that was at fault? Pure curiosity comes with a deep quality of respect and non-judgmentalism. There's just a sense of wonder and awe. Snooping on your girlfriend's phone calls is not curiosity, it's jealousy.

*Make curiosity a wonder-ful habit.* Curiosity is meant to be fresh and spontaneous, but you may need to retrain yourself to become relentlessly curious. If you have kids and you're spending the whole day with them, play a game with yourself: keep a running count of how many questions your kids ask in one day, and do your best to match them—not necessarily immediately—over the course of that same day. Ask the kind of naive questions your kids ask, such as, "Why does a banana turn from green to yellow to brown?" Also recognize that the two things adults are most curious about are other people's lives and how they themselves tick. So ask all kinds of questions of people, not as if they're on the witness stand but coming from a place of genuine curiosity. There are six simple starting points for your questions: who, what, where, why, when, and how. If you find someone particularly boring or your relationship is lethargic, be curious about why you've fallen into this rut. One of the best ways to address unresolved conflict or apathy in a relationship is for a couple to do something novel together to stoke the fires of curiosity.

*Find awe.* Awe comes in big packages—the grandeur of a mountain vista, an encounter with a higher power, the experience of watching a football game with eighty thousand other crazy fans (even the wave that occasionally travels around the stadium with people standing up and sitting down in synchronicity can produce a little awe). But it can also come in small moments or epiphanies: watching a mother duck tend to her ducklings after a wade into the water and thinking of your mother, listening to your favorite song with the top down in your convertible on a sunny day, or reading a poignant poem that captures exactly what you're feeling. "Awe" was once defined as fear or dread of a divine being, but modern dictionaries have shifted the definition to a "profound reverence in the presence of supreme authority, moral greatness or sublimity, or mysterious sacredness." Awe connects you to something bigger than yourself and in so doing opens you to the bigger questions—where curiosity sprouts.

*Channel Peter Drucker.* Every year, choose a subject to learn; become so expert in it that you can teach it to others. For my first year of doing this exercise, I chose to learn everything about natural hot springs, both academically and experientially—yes, it was a lot of fun. The greatest leadership mind of our time also recommended doing an annual review of what you've learned in the last year. I do this every year between Christmas and New Year's, and I keep track of not just the relevant new data or information but also some of the life lessons that have taught me something. John R. O'Neil, the author of *The Paradox of Success,* evolved this idea into an "annual learning curve checkup" in the context of your work with the intent of reviewing where you're still learning at work and where you're not. If all this sounds too big and bold for you, here are a couple of simple ways you can channel the curiosity of Peter Drucker: alter your habits of how you drive to and from work for five days in a row or be a little more adventurous about what you order at your favorite restaurant. Whether it's the new visuals you'll see on your commute or the broadening of your experience for your taste buds, shifting your senses is another way of opening you up to the emotion of curiosity.

Curiosity is a life-affirming emotion. Curious people are happier, more sociable, and more successful in their work. They live longer, too. This emotion moves us forward. It's the fuel of our creativity and innovation and the essence of how our thinking evolves over time. Most important, in a relentless recession, curiosity is correlated with resilience and inversely correlated with anxiety and depression. So what are you waiting for? Get curious!

# PART IV

# DEFINING
# WHO YOU ARE

*Be who you are and say what you feel, because those who mind don't matter and those who matter don't mind.*
—Dr. Seuss

# 12

$$\boxed{\text{Authenticity} = \text{Self-Awareness} \times \text{Courage}}$$

More than five hundred years ago, Michelangelo perceived that each of his lifelike figures was already living inside the piece of marble he sculpted. He felt he was literally releasing David and the others by chipping away at the stone. Are you encased or trapped in stone or behind some kind of mask? The process of finding yourself—however camouflaged—is the subject of this chapter. More broadly, it is the overall theme of this section of the book: how our identities are formed and the unique alchemy that makes us who we are.

Oprah Winfrey is an improbable billionaire. Born into poverty in rural Mississippi to a teenage single mother, she was originally named "Orpah" after a biblical character from the Book of Ruth. She spent her earliest years raised by her grandmother Hattie Mae, who made her granddaughter's dresses out of potato sacks. Hattie Mae taught Oprah how to read before the age of three and had her reciting verses in church, which earned her the nickname "The Preacher." After age six, Oprah moved north and reunited with her mother. Life got harder. She was molested by a couple of family members at age nine, ran away at thirteen, and got pregnant at fourteen (her son died in infancy).

In spite of those painful beginnings, Oprah went on to blossom in high school. Voted Most Popular Girl, she was an honors student who won an oratory contest and ultimately the beauty pageant title Miss Black Tennessee. She studied communications and leveraged that to become the youngest TV news anchor in Nashville. She credits Hattie Mae, who encouraged her to speak in public and "gave me a positive sense of myself."

Phil Donahue may have pioneered the daytime TV format that highlighted ordinary people, but Oprah Winfrey transformed it. Phil talked to his audience. Oprah listened. But she didn't just listen; she empathized. She gave people, especially women, a comfortable and safe place to talk intimately and reveal themselves. Oprah was the ultimate role model. Telling her own stories and bringing them out of others, she introduced real emotions to a time of day when TV was full of artifice (soap operas and tabloid talk shows). She has said that the secret of a successful talk show is finding "the thread of authenticity" in yourself and others. This confessional approach created awkward moments of TMI (too much information) and symbolized an era in which private lives are no longer private. But the sincerity of Oprah's quest for authenticity and her ability to use that vulnerability as a means of connecting with others changed everything—including how we choose our presidents (Bill Clinton used "Oprah-style" debates to beat his competitors in 1992). And it is why Oprah is the richest self-made woman in U.S. history.

Does that mean the fastest way to get rich is to get real? No, but it does suggest that knowing where you come from (your roots) will help you know who you are (authenticity) and where you're going (your calling). In junior high school, I did all I could to imitate the "normal" people around me because being different felt dangerous. It finally took going to school in a dangerous part of town, surrounded by all kinds of folks who didn't look or act anything like me, to feel the liberation of exploring who I really was. I finally came out as a gay man at age twenty-two. My diverse teenage roots helped me to feel good about being different. Years later, after I'd grown my company to nearly a thousand employees, I wrote a book called *The Rebel Rules* with a subtitle that defines what has helped me to find success in my adult years: *Daring to Be Yourself in Business.*

## THE QUEST FOR AUTHENTICITY STARTS EARLY

Infants begin to gain self-awareness between eighteen and twenty-four months of age when they start becoming conscious of their own thoughts, feelings, and sensations and how they are separate from other people and objects. From that time on, we struggle to fulfill Oscar Wilde's famous advice "Be yourself; everyone else is already taken."

The process of growing up can be one big exercise in stepping into other people's expectations for you, rather than becoming conscious of and comfortable with your own dreams. One of the words drilled into us as teens is "responsibility," the ability to respond appropriately to situations and life. But that word loses its meaning if we tend to be more reactionary. Something happens, and we react immediately without taking time to consider our response. A number of influences define how we react: our parents, the rules in our community, our most prevalent emotions, and, of course, our growing ego.

Though there are a few folks who need to completely change who they are—their family name, their religion, their physical body and even their sex—in order to feel authentic, most of us simply manage a slight twinge of self-betrayal. But we know or feel when we're somehow out of alignment, and a thin veil of dissatisfaction arises when we give ourselves time to acknowledge it. As our identity becomes more fixed—or secure—in our young adulthood, we build a life around it. And of course, the more we invest in that identity, the more painful it may be in the future if we realize that, in fact, we are far off our authentic path. For many people, it's easier to conform and pretend than to make a big shift. Who has the time or the skill set to pound rock all day looking for that hidden self? Psychologists have shown that authenticity is not simply an aspect of or precursor to well-being but the very essence of well-being and healthy functioning. Living a fulfilled life is living an authentic life.

## YOUR TOOLS: SELF-AWARENESS AND COURAGE

In the next chapter, on narcissism, we'll explore how we rigidify our self-image in order to portray a certain identity to the world, which is one of the key impediments to authenticity. But for now, let's recognize that you'll need two primary tools to start sculpting yourself out of that rock: self-awareness and courage. They're both vital. Self-awareness without courage means that you know who you are but the rest of the world doesn't. Courage without self-awareness can lead to macho posturing. So this is a multiplication equation, because the alchemy of those emotions—not just their addition—creates authenticity.

Self-awareness means that you're an expert at emotional hide-and-go-seek. In our youth, when we tried to fit in, our sense of self may have gone undercover, or we may have defined our identity based primarily upon the groups we were a part of—whether a sports team, cheerleading squad, theater group, or no group at all. We became so attuned to listening to our external antennae that we neglected the internal antennae. We got so obsessed with looking good that we forgot what it means to be real.

I've come to understand this "inner me" by seeing it as an archaeological dig into layers of rock and sediment built up over the years. In my teens, my achievements made me feel worthy, which reinforced my goal-oriented behavior. In my midtwenties, I started digging with the help of a therapist and discovered some spacious, miraculous caverns where a sense of understanding about who I was existed under all those layers—no matter what was going on in the surface world. Still, the older I got, the more I had to break through in order to get to the core: a sense of my authentic truth.

Carl Jung suggested that, at some point during our middle years, "the glowing coals of consciousness buried deep within the personality begin to break into flames. When this occurs, hitherto repressed and hidden aspects of the self may seem to overwhelm the conscious self, initiating a difficult period of disorganization of the personality." That is what we call a "midlife crisis." The most important challenge might be in finding the willingness to give up who you think you are in order to find out who you might become. That is the path to authenticity.

So how can you open yourself up to self-exploration and awareness without the help of a guru, therapist, or hard hat (for excavations)? First, if you're going to do this on your own, you will need a certain amount of objectivity in order to "witness" yourself. The patterns in which you think and behave every day can be difficult to discern and take responsibility for. Moving toward self-awareness requires you to see yourself in an unvarnished way and, as much as possible, without being judgmental, since a harsh critic will shut down the archaeological dig.

Try these four sets of questions as a means of starting to develop the objectivity necessary to be self-aware:

1. Who knows you best? Would they describe you more accurately than how the rest of the world sees you? When you're in their presence, do you show up differently than you do in the rest of your life? What are a couple of emotions that you feel in their presence, and what's the source of those emotions?

2. What's the biggest masquerade in your life today? In other words, when do you feel the largest disconnect between who you are and what you're doing? What were, or are, the circumstances that led you into this situation? How do you cope with or compensate for this feeling of disconnection? And how do you think it affects the people and relationships in your life?

3. These are my favorite interview questions to ask execs who want to join my company: How are you most frequently misperceived in the workplace (or at home), and why? What's the "real you," and why is it that others don't see that as much as you'd like them to? What's been your biggest mistake in your career, and what did you learn from it? It takes a certain amount of self-awareness and courage to answer that one.

4. If an objective observer, someone who doesn't know you, watched you twenty-four hours a day for a month, what do you think he or she would list as your three greatest strengths *and* your three greatest weaknesses? How do you feel about each of those six qualities?

Courage can be a natural result of spending sufficient time getting comfortable with your center. In fact, the Latin root of the word comes from the center of your physical being: your heart. Courage takes great heart. After years of blending in socially, a self-aware person can feel a certain pride when he starts marching to his own internal drummer. Feeling that elevation or liberation creates a momentum that brings courage along with it and empowers you to be your authentic self. Once you start moving in that positive direction, there's a self-sustaining ripple effect that gives you even more courage to be authentic. Self-awareness feels good.

The book *Character Strengths and Virtues: A Handbook and Classification* by Christopher Peterson and Martin Seligman outlines six fundamental human strengths, courage being one of them. Courage can be broken down into four main subcategories: bravery, perseverance, honesty, and zest. Let's do a little inventory of how courage shows up in your life today:

1. Bravery: When was the last time you stood up for something that felt right in a difficult situation? Ernest Hemingway defined courage as "grace under pressure." It may require an ability to withstand both physical and psychological assaults and being unpopular and/or out of the mainstream.

2. Perseverance: Think of a time when you stayed committed to an idea, goal, or relationship long after others would have quit. Was this a form of courage or stupidity? If it was the former, how did it feel when the perseverance paid off? Did it give you more courage?

3. Honesty: Can you think of a time when you had to tell the truth—even risking potential dire consequences associated with coming forward? Living with integrity is something we all aspire to, but it can take great courage to do so in certain circumstances, such as being a whistle-blower in your company or the family member who shines the light on the "elephant in the room."

4. Zest: Have you and others ever been faced with long odds, but your general positivity or zest for life was what kept the group calm and courageous in a really difficult situation? Courage can be contagious when even one person has a certain confidence that everything will work out.


## "I AM WHAT I AM"

Mastering fear describes my "coming out" process. My identity while growing up was as the junior version of my former marine captain

143

father. I was Stephen, Jr. (a "chip" off the old block). My dad was our baseball coach. I was the star pitcher. My dad was our Boy Scout leader and had been an Eagle Scout himself. I became an Eagle Scout. I went to the same high school as my dad and, like him, started on the varsity water polo team. I was recruited to play collegiate water polo at Stanford. My parents met at Stanford and I thought I'd meet my future wife there, too, until I started experiencing little cracks in my armor. I joined a fraternity, but I pledged a different one from my dad. I studied economics as my father had, but while I was studying overseas (something my father had never done), I started playing the guitar, wearing my hair long and shaggy, and hanging out in cafés, wondering why I felt so disconnected from myself.

Between my first and second years at Stanford Business School, I worked for the summer in the New York office of the conservative investment bank Morgan Stanley. Wearing suspenders, smoking the occasional cigar, and acting like a "master of the universe" (typical of 1980s investment bankers), I was truly a fish out of water. On Independence Day 1983, I walked from my apartment at 86th and Riverside to Greenwich Village with the intent of liberating myself. At age twenty-two, I stepped into my first gay bar, met a nice young man, and entered into a summer romance. My double life of straight investment banker by day and openly gay man by night was not always easy. But fortunately, my partner, who'd come out from a very religious family, really helped me with my self-awareness that summer.

When I went back to California, I felt an enormous sense of relief in seeing myself for who I really was. Yet I was still expected to find a wife, have a few kids, and live a better version of my parents' existence. My self-awareness grew, and I realized that I needed to tell Dad and the rest of the family, my fraternity brothers, my athletic buddies, and all the other folks who saw me as something quite different from who I was. The idea of telling Dad had me the most frightened. It took all my courage to take him for a walk after dinner and let him know that Stephen, Jr., was going to be departing from his path in a big way.

After a few very rocky months, my dad once again became my biggest supporter. And more than anything, when he invested in my first business—and we had some rollicking fights about the concept and strategy of that first hotel—he recognized that my openness about my sexuality allowed me to be more authentic in all of my life, especially with my instincts about how to create a very cool hotel. If we'd left it up to my dad's taste, that first hotel would have had all the sexiness of a Sears showroom! In the end, I believe I'm a more emotionally intelligent leader as a result of that deep dive into self-awareness and courage, which was necessary for me to open up to my authentic self.

In what parts of your life is it time for you to "come out"?

## WORKING THROUGH THE EQUATION

$$\text{Authenticity = Self-Awareness} \times \text{Courage}$$

*Create a "to-be" list.* We're all familiar with "to-do" lists, and some of us feel lost without them. But when was the last time you created a "to-be" list? What is it that you authentically want to be when you grow up? This could be a series of identities such as being a mother or being a leader at work or in your community. Or it could be a series of qualities that you aspire to, such as being lighthearted and humorous no matter what's going on or being a source of wisdom within your extended family. Just be careful not to let any of the "doing" elements get in the way of your "being." When in doubt, ask the question "Who do I need to be—not what do I need to do—to represent my authentic self in the world?"

*Your shadow: What's it teaching you?* Sometimes self-awareness emerges as a result of seeing your dark side in someone else. Think of a couple of people who frustrate the heck out of you. Which of their qualities grate on you the most? Let's say someone you know loves to snoop and gossip about others and it drives you crazy. Do you do the same but excuse your own behavior? Are you motivated by the need for attention, approval, or position? Self-awareness may come in the context of seeing yourself in others, not just those you admire and want to emulate but also those who are meant to be mirrors.

*What would Herb do?* For years I had Southwest Airlines cofounder and former CEO Herb Kelleher's photo sitting behind my desk—a reminder that, when I was most flummoxed by a business challenge that required some rebellious, courageous thinking, I would channel Herb. When we're on self-awareness low ground, most of us tend to react rather than respond to challenges. We let our habits do the talking, which means we crowd out the opportunity to allow courage to take a stand. Think of somebody in your life who is naturally courageous and exhibits one or more of its four qualities: bravery, perseverance, honesty, zest. The next time you're faced with a serious challenge—one that you would normally react to without summoning courage—picture your courageous role model sitting on your shoulder, giving you advice.

*Prepare to dig.* Draw a circle on a piece of paper and write the words "The authentic me" in the center of the circle. Then draw a series of circles around that first, core circle. The more you feel disconnected from your self, the more circles you draw. Start with the first circle outside the core. When did this sedimentary rock form around your authentic self? What's not real or not part of you? Move out to the next circle, all the way out to the self you show the world today. You may find that you've shored up some unstable walls that you simply need to dismantle or let fall.

Relief will come once you're able to dig down to that core and tap into some of the authenticity that is the real you.

If you have glossed over this chapter because you feel a little above all this silly talk about authenticity—which is clearly meant only for other people—for you there is the next chapter: Narcissism.

# 13

$$\left[ \text{Narcissism} = (\text{Self-Esteem})^2 \times \text{Entitlement} \right]$$

mage is everything." Remember the Canon ads with the flamboyant tennis star Andre Agassi sneering at the camera and spouting this ultimate narcissistic mantra? Agassi was one of the game's most successful athletes. But he was also a pop culture phenom who married an equally famous cultural icon—Brooke Shields—while an army of paparazzi helicopters whirled above their coastal California wedding.

Agassi always seemed to be mugging for the world, clamoring for attention with his wigs, Vegas fashion, and in-your-face antics that fueled a rock star–like reputation. His story is a common modern fable of how athletically gifted children grow up to become self-absorbed, entitled adults—like fellow phenom Tiger Woods and Serena Williams. Agassi's drill sergeant father subjected all four of his children to an abusive regimen of tennis training, but Andre was the only one who made it through.

By the time Andre hit the pro tennis circuit, his soul had been wired to believe that he was the best, which fueled a public bravado that made him both loved and loathed. It's as if the mind of a superathlete has to believe all of the hype and is somehow mobilized to live up to the glorified image that has been created around him. A superathlete is often surrounded by sycophants who feed that self-absorbed image, including multinational corporations that become part of the star's brand.

In his tell-all memoir, *Open,* Agassi recounted this modern narcissistic treadmill existence. Of winning and losing he wrote, "A win doesn't feel as good as a loss feels bad, and the good feeling doesn't last as long as the bad. Not even close." Winning is very important to the narcissist.

Agassi is now retired. He shaves his head and has admitted that he is a recovering drug addict. He is happily married to fellow tennis star Steffi Graf, is the proud father of two, and has perhaps found a kind of antidote to his image affliction by giving back to less advantaged youth in his hometown of Las Vegas. Through humor and humility, Agassi seems to have concluded, after a certain amount of pain and suffering, that image isn't everything.

Can you guess who *New York Times* columnist David Brooks was referring to when he wrote, "The narcissistic person is marked by a grandiose self-image, a constant need for admiration, and a general lack of empathy for others. He is the keeper of a sacred flame, which is the flame he holds to celebrate himself." He was talking about Mel Gibson, whose belligerent tirades tarnished his hero image forever. Yet in this Warholian era, when there are so many vehicles to become a star—from the plebian YouTube to the premium *American Idol*—it isn't just celebrities who suffer from this collision of self-absorbed emotions. At every turn, we've been told that we are special. And this national inflation of self-esteem has created monsters.

Narcissism isn't an emotion, but it is a condition—like workaholism—that stands at the intersection of many other emotions, some well regarded (confidence and magnetic optimism) and some derided (vanity and aggressiveness). The mythological source of this modern condition comes from Narcissus, a handsome Greek youth, who, when he saw his own image for the first time in the reflection off the surface of a pond, fell in love with it. Unable to leave the pond and lose sight of himself, Narcissus died from a lack of sustenance.

I have to admit that this ancient story cuts deep. As a child, I was sort of scared of my own image, but once I became more self-assured, I became an extroverted accomplishment junkie. People said I blossomed during that time, but I now think that the blossom was a narcissus (the small daffodil that sprouted where the mythological Narcissus died) as I started to believe my own hype. Underneath it all, I felt like a nervous fake, a tightrope walker without a net. One day I actually taped a piece of wisdom by the poet David Ignatow to my bathroom mirror to remind me about the risk of too much self-love: "I should be content to look at a mountain for what it is and not as a comment on my life." But of course, taping a warning to a narcissist's mirror can be a futile act.

## NORMALIZING NARCISSISM

Historically, narcissism was judged on a spectrum, with those at the far end of the continuum being considered unhealthy. Yet in an era when self-promotion is rewarded and self-confidence seen as desirable for everyone, narcissism no longer seems quite so aberrant. If pop culture is today's religion, narcissism is its primary dogma. In the 1950s, thousands of teenagers were asked if they considered themselves an "important person" and 12 percent said yes. In the late 1980s, the same question was asked and nearly 80 percent of the kids said yes. Is this a good or a bad thing? Have we taken self-esteem too far?

Whether it's an official disorder or not, narcissism needs to be addressed. In this chapter, we will look at "garden variety" narcissism. Many clinicians refer to a "healthy narcissist" as someone who has realistic self-interest and a strong desire to achieve. Freud even argued that healthy narcissism was an essential part of normal development. Michael Maccoby, the author of *The Productive Narcissist: The Promise and Peril of Visionary Leadership,* suggests that many great business leaders possess a single-minded rejection of the status quo and a compelling vision that allow their narcissistic qualities to have a positive impact on their organization. But when does confidence become grandiosity or image savvy become venality? Is Richard Branson a narcissist? Should we just accept it, given his immense talents? A narcissist's charisma, creativity with their big dreams, flattery of those who serve them, physical attractiveness, and extreme confidence can be alluring. Extreme narcissism, however, is destructive, not just to the narcissist but to everyone around him.

Here are some of the common qualities and emotions of narcissists:

- Obviously self-focused in interpersonal exchanges (they can't stop talking about themselves)
- Feeling superior (they consider themselves better than others, sometimes because they exaggerate their talents or achievements)
- Preoccupied with fantasies that focus on unlimited success, power, intelligence, beauty, or love
- Envious (they often envy others or believe that others are envious of them and are acutely aware of how they stack up in the pecking order of whatever group they're in)
- Feeling entitled (they believe they are entitled to special treatment and will sometimes bend the rules to obtain it)
- Overly sensitive (they can be easily hurt but don't readily show it or even consciously feel it, yet can have a tendency toward rage when they sense danger to their carefully constructed facade and world)

- Lacking empathy (and/or having a fear of intimacy and problems in sustaining satisfying relationships as a result)
- Unwilling to take responsibility (for their role in an unfortunate situation; very adept at shifting blame)
- Vulnerable to shame (more than guilt because they are more outer-directed than inner-directed, but it takes quite a bit to get them to the point of shame)

Few of us would readily admit to narcissism. Sure, we may occasionally have an inflated ego, but we're certainly not as much of an egomaniac as that blowhard client or that self-centered trainer at the gym. Yet true narcissists don't have the self-awareness to see those qualities in themselves. Or, as I've done myself, they rationalize why they occasionally need to act this way. Yet a productive habit soon becomes an ingrained behavior, and the next thing they know, they're living in a house of mirrors.

## TAKING SELF-ESTEEM TO THE EXTREME

Ever since William James coined the term "self-esteem" in 1890, its meaning has been debated. Is it something we strive for, or is it the by-product of skills, competency, and a well-lived life? I'd always bought into the belief that more was better, until I read *The Narcissism Epidemic: Living in the Age of Entitlement* by the social psychologist Jean Twenge and W. Keith Campbell. That's when I changed one of the ingredients of this equation from Self-Absorption to (Self-Esteem)². The authors make the persuasive argument that the 1970s (the "Me Decade"), which spawned the self-esteem movement in child rearing, has overshot its value and left us with an entitled culture. Believing that high self-esteem will help inspire young people to greatness has created a society of people who are fundamentally imbalanced. A person with authentic self-esteem cares for others, while narcissists are so focused on themselves that they've completely lost touch with everyone else around them—except from the perspective of how they view or serve them.

This is the only equation in this book that uses an exponent to make its point. Exponents are shorthand for repeated multiplication of the same thing by itself. For instance, the shorthand for multiplying five three times is shown at the right of the equals sign in $(5)(5)(5) = 5^3$. It's fitting that narcissism would use an exponent, a number multiplied by itself, to make the point that self-esteem taken to the extreme can be dangerous. It is also fitting that self-esteem squared (which is what we call a number with an exponent of 2) is parenthetically separated from the world. The parentheses are mirrors on either side of the self, staring each other down. Narcissism is the ultimate form of loneliness. When one feels such an inflated sense of self, there's little room left onstage—or in one's life—for anyone else.

Self-esteem multiplied by itself leads to a feeling of entitlement and usually disappointment. When you create a story in your head that you are unique, you naturally believe that you are entitled to special treatment. This kind of thinking leads to the kind of pursuit of instant gratification that created the financial and residential real estate meltdown of the past few years. People believed they were entitled to their "no-down-payment" monster homes. And the bankers, rather than preach financial responsibility, played along with the deception. One of the most prevalent emotions today in the Sunbelt communities where foreclosures have been rampant is "punctured pride." It wasn't just the real estate bubble that burst, it was also the bubble of entitlement.

A feeling of entitlement is an extreme version of expectation, and disappointment is the natural result of badly managed expectations. It's almost as though a feeling of entitlement is expectation squared, so you know that on the other side is the potential for a big, disappointing fall. Yet we see people at work who seem to have no concern for anyone around them. We see them cutting us off on the road and in line at the store. And we see them pontificating on all kinds of websites.

## SELF-ABSORPTION IN THE "FAKEBOOK" ERA

Since 1927, *Time* magazine has chosen a man, woman, or idea that "for better or worse, has most influenced events in the preceding year." Charles Lindbergh, Franklin D. Roosevelt, Corazon Aquino, Mikhail Gorbachev, and, in 2010, Facebook's Mark Zuckerberg have all won this prestigious honor. But in 2006, *Time* gave this distinction in the era of Web 2.0 to "You," along with a mirror on the cover to remind you just how important *you* are. Tony Long, in *Wired* magazine, has asked, "What is the Internet, if not a narcissist's dream come true?"

Welcome to the age of mass narcissism. You have the opportunity to "broadcast yourself" on YouTube or "tweet" to your heart's delight about the minutiae of your day on Twitter. With the grand slam of you-focused-ness—Facebook—you can create endless lists of friends or fans to view your photos and personal data. Facebook can feel like a competition of who can "outmug" others—an "I" for an "I." Or you can choose an anonymous persona or avatar personality on Second Life, where you can essentially live out your fantasy vision of yourself.

Back in the pre–Web 2.0 era, I felt comfortable confiding in friends, looking for their advice or counsel with the knowledge that, as true friends, they would keep the conversation private. I didn't have to worry about who might overhear our chat or that our conversation might be retained in digital eternity. I also didn't feel that I had to be "on": I could just show up as myself without considering the audience.

But today, everyone who plays in the Facebook world has an audience. This new era has ushered in a level of self-consciousness that may be shaping how we construct our identities. When we're constantly on display or in performance, do we all become poodles mugging for "Best in Show"? There's even a new social phenomenon called FOMO ("fear of missing out") that refers to the anxiety and loneliness that come from skimming through other people's Facebook pages and reading about their glorious exploits—things you perhaps could do yourself if you weren't constantly surfing Facebook.

I recently had a conversation with a friend's daughter. For the full two hours I was visiting their home, she was on her MySpace page, primping her profile and proud to show me how she was presenting herself to the world (ironically, she did this—horrors—in pajamas with no makeup). When I asked her to tell me the main reason she spent time on this site, her answer was revealing: "I don't have anywhere else to go, and this is where I meet everyone." MySpace has replaced the mall. And the mall is now open twenty-four hours a day.

Peggy Orenstein wrote an insightful piece in *The New York Times* entitled "I Tweet, Therefore I Am," in which she laments the emotional effect of this "packaged self" culture we're creating. The emotion of empathy, for instance, has largely declined among college students during the past thirty years; the steepest part of this decline occurred about the time social media started taking off. So vigilant are we in presenting ourselves to the world that we forget about others—and, ironically, may even forget about what's really going on inside us. Orenstein quotes a professor from MIT who suggests that "Twitter is outer-directedness cubed" (love those math equations).

## THROW AWAY THE MIRRORS

This was a hard chapter for me to tackle. Of course, developing an Emotional Equation, doing the research on it, and then reflecting on how I myself experience this equation is profoundly foreign to someone with narcissistic tendencies. It's asking someone with a fear of heights to wash the windows of a hundred-story building. Fortunately, I had the safety device of knowing you weren't going to see my first draft. Yet narcissists live their lives as if they're one big first draft on display: imperfect, flawed, and not ready for primetime. Their biggest fear is that they'll be "found out" and will experience humiliation through social comparison with others.

Because of a propensity to internalize failure, the narcissist's emotional response to failure is to feel shame—not guilt, which is what most people might feel. Guilt is when you feel you did something wrong. Shame is when you feel you *are* wrong—to your core. In order to avoid this painful emotion, the narcissist externalizes blame for things that go wrong. If you are in the company of a narcissist during difficult times, be prepared to shovel shit or have it flung at you.

A few years ago, when my company was in one of its fastest growth periods, I was going through an emotional meltdown. My need for control and my desire to put on a public face of success was so intense that I numbed myself out much of the time (a common trait of narcissists). We had a well-regarded travel writer stay at one of our newer hotels, and it was a debacle from the start. All I could imagine was the story this writer would tell about having been checked into a room with people already sleeping in the bed and finding hair in the bathtub. Though I don't exhibit the rage you see in extreme narcissists, I did let my managers have it, as I was deeply upset by this.

Then one of our senior execs, whom I considered both a friend and a very capable work ally, pointed out to me—in the most delicate and private way—that I had forgotten to pass along the travel writer's reservation to the hotel. So the hotel team had been given no notice to prepare for his visit. This was a moment of truth for someone with narcissistic tendencies. Would I allow my inflated self-esteem to "right-size" itself, and could I, as the founder and CEO of the company, get over the entitlement of the office I held and admit my mistake to both the travel writer and the hotel staff?

I did apologize to the hotel management team for my mistake and how I'd put them into this awkward situation. I took the travel writer out for a meal, not to distract him with narcissistic BS but to build a relationship and to say I was sorry for how his stay with us had started. Then I sat down with that same senior exec who'd broken the news to me and asked him for advice (something a narcissist rarely does). I asked how I could be a better leader, as I felt both shame and guilt. He told me that I was most powerful when I exhibited "purposeful humility," and he gave me a few examples of when I'd shown that quality—and when I hadn't.

When he left the room, I just sat there, feeling partially deflated and partially curious about how I could live my life differently. Embracing vulnerability takes courage. I decided to shift my world from feeling alone in a house of mirrors to a vista from the one hundredth floor of that building, standing side by side with my colleagues and working together to live up to a shared vision. I hope that the people in my life—and my company—have benefited as a result of this conscious choice.

## WORKING THROUGH THE EQUATION

$$Narcissism = (Self\text{-}Esteem)^2 \times Entitlement$$

*Dilute your self-esteem so that it's not "squared."* Some psychologists believe that narcissism is no more curable than personality is disposable. But you can "dial back" on some of your habitual self-absorption. First, take an inventory of where it is getting you into trouble. Does your spouse feel unappreciated and forgotten? Do those who work with you think you're an egomaniac, seeing things only from your own perspective? Have you lost most of your friends (I don't mean acquaintances, but true friends)? Start with the part of your life that's most challenged. Consider getting a 360-degree evaluation by those who are close to you. At work, that could mean an anonymous survey given to your coworkers. At home, it might mean an in-depth "listening exercise" in which your spouse tells you how your self-absorption affects the rest of the family. To be able to change, you need first to see that your way of being can often be counterproductive. Hopefully you'll learn some examples of self-absorbed behaviors that are working against you—such as not listening to others, championing only your own ideas, or losing the trust of others because you occasionally mess with the truth. Choose one behavior that you feel is within your control to change. Make it your highest priority on a daily basis to start making that shift, and see how those around you respond to this new, less self-absorbed you.

*Replace bravado and entitlement with humility and compassion.* Want to get over narcissism? Spend a day with a narcissist who is more haughtily entitled than you. Is she coming from a place of serving (others) or deserving (for herself)? Now think of someone you truly admire. What qualities about him or her draw you? What's most magnetic about other people on a one-on-one basis is their humanity, not their "superhuman" qualities. Although we can envy those at times, when we're thinking about who has made us feel good in our lives, it's probably someone who has exhibited humility and compassion. How can you surround yourself with people who will give you positive feedback when you're showing your humanity?

*Change your environment and open your eyes to others.* It may be hard for people to change their nature, but changing your situation can be one step in the right direction. Narcissists tend to create a safe bubble, a house of mirrors that gives them a sense of security. This carefully constructed habitat must be disrupted for the habits of a narcissist to start diminishing. This is also true of your work. Have you chosen a career path that requires constant admiration from fans or followers? I have a friend who is a politician, and he's constantly blaming his narcissistic qualities on the demands of the job (and his adoring public). You have to change either the job or your relationship with it. As I've asked this friend, "Have you ever considered whether the fawning electorate might like you more if you were just truly authentic?" Or maybe you need to change your relationship. Are you married to someone who cannot see you or to someone who can't speak for herself? Before you change the relationship, explore whether you and your partner can shift how you relate to each other. Make a commitment that at dinner you will spend half of the meal listening for a change. And rather than spacing out, make sure you ask at least two or three thoughtful and compassionate questions that show you care and are genuinely interested—for no other reason than you love him or her. The psychologist Jean Twenge suggested that I add "minus caring for others" to the end of this equation, because true narcissists have a blind spot for everyone but themselves.

*Look for something bigger than you.* Love. Nature. Religion. A purposeful venture. Parenthood. Contact with a transformative experience that is beyond you is one step toward healing for the self-absorbed person. Most narcissists turn a blind eye to self-help books, but others become spiritual narcissists, seeing self-love as the end goal. My friend Rabbi Alan Lurie says, "Spirituality to the ego-self is an object of attainment much like fame, wealth, an expensive car, and a sexy body." Spiritual one-upmanship ("I'm more evolved than you") is a risk for the narcissist in recovery. You know you're healing when you can have a sense of humor about the old habits that don't want to die. If you feel very small as you wake up to the vastness of nature or religion, you're still confining yourself with parentheses. Liberate yourself from your self-esteem squared so that you can feel the oneness that comes with that which is miraculous.

The philosopher Martin Buber, author of *I and Thou,* wrote, "When two people relate to each other authentically and humanly, God is the electricity that surges between them." You are not God. If you feel you are, I promise you that you are wearing a mask and you're stuck in a web of deceit. And sometimes that web is actually the Web. It's important to remember that living online is not really living.

I do see the value of social media, and I play on all kinds of sites, at times, with a voracious appetite. But these forums are merely spices on my communication menu, not the main meal. I like to think of Twitter as a scrapbook of odd thoughts and articles that I want to keep track of and others might appreciate. I do my best not to use it as a pulpit or as a means of getting constant attention. As for Facebook, I take it with a grain of salt. The efficiency and immediacy of electronic stimuli will never replace the joy of human contact.

# 14

[ **Integrity = Authenticity × Invisibility × Reliability** ]

One man's integrity can be another's obstinacy. The novelist, academic, and Christian theologian C. S. Lewis wrote, "Integrity is doing the right thing even when no one is watching." Integrity does not require an audience. Even so, Lewis built quite an audience over the past century through his books, including *The Chronicles of Narnia, Surprised by Joy,* and *Mere Christianity,* which was arguably the most influential Christian book of the twentieth century.

Until about age thirty, Lewis was an atheist in British academia. After his conversion he was called "The Apostle to the Skeptics" because of his questioning of the rationale of Christianity. A legend to believers and nonbelievers alike, Lewis lived out his faith in an aggressively secular scholastic environment. Oxford was generally not welcoming to the concept of faith. During World War II, Lewis became the second most recognized voice in England after that of Winston Churchill for his BBC radio lectures, which eventually turned into *Mere Christianity.*

Being a public messenger of Christian theology hurt Lewis's academic career, and he was denied a full professorship for many years. His views were also different from other Christians, for instance those of the physician and theologian Albert Schweitzer, the medical missionary to Africa. Schweitzer's views made him an occasional outcast, too—on both the European and African continents—but Schweitzer received a Nobel Peace Prize for his work. Both men operated in complete accordance with their ethical belief system no matter where they lived and worked, no matter who the audience.

Integrity is the number one quality we look for in our business leaders today. Most businesspeople strive to follow a moral compass and adhere to ethics that can withstand the expedient, transactional nature of life. I once felt that integrity was a tall peak to climb and that I needed a spiritual Sherpa to assist me to those heights where the "air" is rarefied. I've come to believe that integrity can be distilled down to the simple acronym AIR (authenticity, invisibility, reliability). Schweitzer wrote, "A man does not have to be an angel in order to be a saint." You can have integrity and still be a flawed—and very human—being.

The word "integrity" stems from the Latin adjective *integer,* which means "whole" or "complete." In this context, integrity is the inner sense of "wholeness," the feeling that all parts of our identity are integrated into one. Appropriately, we're addressing integration right after talking about the narcissistic world of the Internet in the last chapter. Albert Schweitzer was a husband, father, musician, theologian, physician, philanthropist, and philosopher. Today, all your identities may be made more complicated by the fact that you're showing up on LinkedIn, Facebook, Twitter, and a variety of other Internet sites where you can portray yourself to the world in a variety of ways. Never before has the integration of our multiple selves been more important and challenging than now.

I use the metaphor of scaffolding as the image for how we create various identities for various relationships. When among the members of my Young Presidents' Organization, I was a CEO, and the scaffolding of my identity was ambition, curiosity, and sociability. As the founder of my company, I have a parental role and am hyper-responsible about what is good for my "family." In my Spiritual Salon, a group of a dozen folks of various faiths who share an existential curiosity, I am an inquiring student of life. Having different roles for different habitats can be confusing, and at times the world seems just to want the surface from me. When in doubt, I try to connect with my essential and integral core in all these different environments. Usually my company's mantra, "Create joy," also defines my role in these groups. I'm not the best organizer, but I do seem to create joy by connecting people with one another and, more deeply, with themselves.

Take a look at your various identities, and ask yourself whether you've been able to integrate them around a particular way of being, philosophy, or mantra. Are you consistent in being the responsible one? The hero? The joker? The mediator? If this seems a little foreign to you, do an Internet search for archetypes (usually you'll find six to twelve different archetypes profiled) to determine which one feels most real to you. That real you is the pathway to integrating your identity no matter what environment you're in. Years ago, a wise therapist told me that she defined dysfunction as the distance between your public image and your private reality. A friend of mine calls this the "integrity gap."

## INTEGRITY IS IN THE AIR

Let's do some math. I believe there are three emotional variables—authenticity, invisibility, and reliability—that, when taken together, add up to integrity. Taken alone, none of these three lives up to the full-fledged definition of integrity. Since they add up to the acronym AIR, let's think of integrity as being as essential (yet often underappreciated) as the air we breathe. It's not until our air or integrity is at risk that we recognize how vital it is.

In chapter 12, authenticity was defined as the merger of self-awareness and courage, so think of those two qualities as integrity's "kissing cousins." You can be a pain in the rear, scrupulously honest, and open about who you are and what opinions you hold, but that can seem as if you're grandstanding. Think of someone—maybe a political commentator you don't like a whole lot—who is authentic in what he communicates but whom you wouldn't characterize as full of integrity. There are some missing parts.

Invisibility is the second ingredient, and it's a subtle one. Mahatma Gandhi said, "My life is an invisible whole and all my activities run into one another . . . my life is my message." As C. S. Lewis noted, the value of integrity comes from doing what we do and being who we are when there's no audience watching. This is essential in the narcissistic world we live in: a lack of self-consciousness and a desire for creating good without the need for receiving credit. There is a strong hint of humility in the quality of invisibility.

Reliability involves consistency, faithfulness, and living up to your words and deeds. Integrity is being responsibly aligned with your values no matter what circumstances you're facing. If you think of someone who embodies integrity for you, it's likely that he or she has a devoted commitment to a way of living and being that you admire.

The integrity gap occurs when at least one of these three qualities is lacking. It often happens when you're in a foreign environment and your role of the moment is not as well connected to your integrity as usual. Somehow you aren't quite as honest or open in what you communicate (lack of authenticity). Or you communicate in a way that suggests that you are image-driven or selfish (lack of invisibility). Or you may come across as authentic and pure in your intentions (invisible), but you can't "deliver the goods" consistently (lack of reliability).

## INTEGRATING YOUR IDENTITY

We change costumes to suit the different environments we find our-selves in. This can present a problem when one role collides with an-other. After attending Burning Man one year, I posted a few photos of the event on my Facebook page, as many friends had asked to see pictures of this visually captivating experience. I didn't think much of the photos when I posted them, as Burning Man is one big cos-tume party, and, as a guy who was born on Halloween, I don't think twice about going to masquerade balls or wearing silly clothes. A couple of the photos showed me wearing a tutu and an Asian sarong.

What I hadn't considered was that a number of my employees are also my Facebook friends. A few weeks after I posted the photos, the number two exec in my company told me that the pictures were mak-ing the rounds through company computers and a couple of employ-ees were a little shocked by them because I was shirtless. Initially, I felt a little embarrassed, but when it was suggested that I take the photos down, I had to ask myself, "Which is truer to my identity: keeping the photos up or taking them down?" Given the eclectic, fun-loving nature of the company and how tame the photos were, I chose to leave them up. A journalist who got wind of the controversy asked me to coauthor a blog on the topic of identity from the viewpoint of a CEO in the Internet age. Unexpectedly, tens of thousands of people read the blog and we received hundreds of comments, about 20 percent of which were negative, seeing me as an errant, irresponsible CEO. My identity as the face of the company, even though it's a progressive and quirky organization, ultimately trumped my ability to be myself.

You may have faced a similar situation in which your vision of who you are was at odds with the rest of the world. Psychologists describe the various domains of the self as being: (1) the *actual* self (either as you perceive it or as others perceive you); (2) the *ideal* self, which is your representation of the attributes that someone (your-self or another person) would like you to possess; and (3) the *ought* self, the attributes that someone (you or another person) believes you ought to possess. A modern example of this conflict between the ideal self and the ought self could be when a happy professional woman without kids approaches forty and ponders whether to continue her career path (ideal self) or pursue motherhood (ought self). Or, depending on the person, motherhood could be in the ideal position and the career in the ought position.

These sorts of self-discrepancies create a great deal of discomfort. When our actual self and ideal self are at odds, we feel disappointment with, or regret about, ourselves. When our actual self is at odds with someone else's idealized vision of us, we can feel shame or embarrassment. When there's a rift between our actual self and what we think we ought to be, it can lead to guilt or self-contempt. And when there's a gap between our actual self and what others think we ought to be, it tends to create fear or a sense of feeling threatened. In sum, the greater the discrepancy between our actual self and any of the other areas, the greater the intensity of discomfort.

No one ever said that achieving integrity was easy. It's hard enough to coalesce all those selves into a whole, but it gets even more complicated when you have others' expectations weighing on you, too. If someone falls in love with your mask, you have two choices: either you wear the mask and risk creating a division between your private self and your public image, or you remove the mask and risk losing the relationship. One of the reasons that many people in their fifties start to become happier is that they've finally decided to stop wearing so many masks.

## WHAT MASKS ARE YOU WEARING THAT ARE WEARING YOU OUT?

For every actual suicide in the United States, there are nearly twenty attempts, which means that almost one million people try to take their own lives each year. For men, one of the leading influences in such rampant internalized rage may be that they feel a lack of identity integrity. And they have few places where they can remove their masks and share their pain. In the San Francisco Bay Area, there's a "Men of Tears" support group that's dedicated to helping men find a safe space to tap into their emotions, from which they may have disassociated since childhood. Women are a quarter as likely to commit suicide and five times as likely to cry as men. Holding back emotions has been found to amp up cardiovascular stress, produce anxiety, kill brain cells, and impair memory. As I've found in my own life, the more you restrain sad feelings, the harder it is to gain access to the rest of your emotions. So whether you like the current U.S. house speaker John Boehner or not, the fact that his tear ducts are on regular public display is probably good role modeling for all men.

The masks men choose to wear—or not—have a social impact. The one and only time my company ever conducted a formal focus group was when we were conceiving and designing Costanoa, the luxury campground I mentioned in chapter 4. Since it was a new concept, we chose to do two focus groups. One group had a facilitator with seven male participants, and the second group had a facilitator with seven female members. The purpose was to introduce the idea of Costanoa in both words and images. The focus groups had twenty minutes to discuss and read the materials we gave them about the campground, without the facilitator in the room, but during the twenty minutes, our development team sat silently behind a mirror watching both groups, who were unaware that they were being observed.

In the male group, when the facilitator left the room, six of the seven men leaned back in their chairs, away from the group, while they read the printed materials. The seventh guy kept looking at the others, as if he wanted to start a conversation, but the other six all ignored him. During that twenty-minute period, no one uttered a word. It wasn't that the men weren't engaged. More than half were making notes to themselves, but the social mask of being strong and independent seemed to stifle any interaction. In the female focus group, the exact opposite experience ensued. All of the women put down their materials, introduced themselves to one another, talked about their lives, and then started collaboratively brainstorming about their idealized version of Costanoa. The women ended up turning Costanoa into a luxury spa based upon their collective wishes, while the men individually created more than fifty questions in the form of "Have you thought of this or that?" The focus group leaders said this was normal, as men have a much harder time integrating who they really are with the mask of who they feel they need to be with other men (too much "mask-ulinity").

Nonetheless, men do have a great capacity to connect with one another. The most unlikely place in which I observed the profound power of men taking off their masks was San Quentin State Prison. I had been invited to observe a nonprofit group, the Insight Prison Project (IPP), work with a collection of twenty-five lifers (men in prison for life, mostly for murder) who met on a regular basis. Given that I'd had a family member wrongfully incarcerated in San Quentin for a number of months, I'd heard just how savage life in this infamous institution could be. Yet as I witnessed those gentlemen (and that's what they were) enter the room—and look me directly in the eyes when they introduced themselves—I knew something different was at play.

Due to the phenomenal skills of the IPP team, that group of hardened criminals wasn't so hard after all. There was a remarkable softness in the way they spoke as each introduced himself by saying his name, the name of his victim, and the crime he had committed. It was as if the masculine mask had melted away to show a vulnerable little boy behind it. The men shed tears and told profound stories of how they'd hurt people and how it made them feel now. The whole room was spellbound. Toward the end, when a spider showed up in the middle of our circle, one of the men pointed to it with a little fear, and another man calmly moved it out of the room to safety. Killing it was not an option.

Our environment has an enormous effect on what side of us shows up—one of our masks or our true self. Additionally, the prison group helped me see the tenderness and beauty that masks can hide. The key is to liberate yourself from your masks and to be authentic and reliable, no matter who is watching.

## WORKING THROUGH THE EQUATION

$$Integrity = Authenticity \times Invisibility \times Reliability$$

*Do your own integrity audit.* Viktor Frankl advised, "Listen to what your conscience commands you to do." When do you give yourself the time and space to listen to your conscience? Do you have bags under your eyes because your conscience is trying to speak to you at 2 a.m.? If you're having difficulty tapping into your conscience, here are three simple questions to ask yourself, addressing each of the three ingredients of this equation:

- What tools and resources—including candid friends—do you regularly use to help make you more self-aware and clearer about your authentic self?
- When was the last time you did something momentous that took lots of effort but for which you didn't require or expect any personal credit (and you didn't resent the fact that you didn't receive any attention for what you did)?
- How would you rank the various identities of your life— as a parent, as a romantic partner, as an employee, or as an employer—based upon the question "Where do you 'walk

your talk' most consistently?" Is there any correlation between where you're consistent and which identities are working best for you these days?

*Make integrity a foundational part of your work life.* One of the places we most experience the disconnection between our private reality and our public image is at work. Dee Hock, who started Visa International, the company that created the Visa credit card, says that integrity is the most important ingredient in creating a healthy workplace. When hiring someone, he suggests, "Hire and promote first on the basis of integrity; second, motivation; third, capacity; fourth, understanding; fifth, knowledge; and last and least, experience. Without integrity, motivation is dangerous; without motivation, capacity is impotent; without capacity, understanding is limited; without understanding, knowledge is meaningless; without knowledge, experience is blind." When I'm interviewing someone, I ask, "Tell me a time when your own value system collided with your work or with some group you were a part of. What did you do about it?" You can ask yourself this, too.

*Watch the MTV show "If You Really Knew Me."* Yvonne and Rich Dutra-St. John created the nonprofit Challenge Day as a means of helping teens to feel comfortable being themselves amid the intense pressure to "fit in" during their adolescent years. MTV turned their work into a TV series in which each episode takes us to a different high school, where we see the caustic effects of wearing image-driven masks, whether it's being a jock, a cheerleader, an "emo" (dramatic or highly emotional student), a "stoner," a leader, a "band geek," or a "God Squader." We often spend our adult emotional lives comparing our tender insides with other people's more composed outsides, rather than connecting with people heart to heart. I promise you that watching an episode or two will give you the incentive to start your next off-site work retreat with a one-on-one exercise: completing the sentence "If you really knew me, you would know that . . ."

*Become clear about your actual self, your ideal self, and your ought self.* Take a dozen old magazines and put them on a table. Take three pieces of paper, one for each of your three selves, and mark the first "My Actual," the second "My Ideal," and the third "My Ought" at the top. Start with thinking about your actual self, your ideal self, and your ought self with respect to your work or your home life, whichever feels more emotionally potent at the moment to you. Cut out photos from the magazines and paste them on each of the corresponding three pieces of paper based upon what feels right to you. Once you've finished, take three other pieces of paper and mark one of them "Others' Actual," another "Others' Ideal," and the last "Others' Ought." Now imagine for a moment how other people see you in all three ways: how they actually see you, how they ideally would like to see you or have you be, and how they believe you ought to be. If this is difficult or abstract, just imagine one person in particular whose opinions are very important to you. Now tear into those magazines and start pasting images that line up with how that person imagines your actual, your ideal, and your ought self. When you're done, you'll have six pieces of paper, three representing your own images of yourself and three representing someone else's perspective on you. How congruent are the images, and where is the biggest divide? Are you currently trying to integrate your various identities? What can you do to find more congruence?

George Eliot is often cited to have said, "It is never too late to be what you might have been." And William Shakespeare counseled, "To thine own self be true"—good advice for any of us struggling with juggling our various identities. Integrity isn't just about being moral and ethical; it's about allowing your truest self to show up in all of the in-person and online landscapes of your life. People who are best able to live in a place of integrity don't just integrate their various identities, they learn to disintegrate all of their identities so that what remains is their essence. When you are in the presence of someone living his or her essence, you can feel the purity, innocence, and wisdom of what we're all meant to be.

# PART V

# FINDING CONTENTMENT

### Ancient Contentment

*Contentment is natural wealth; luxury is artificial poverty.*

—Socrates

### Historic Contentment

*Contentment makes poor men rich;*
*discontentment makes rich men poor.*

—Benjamin Franklin

### Modern Contentment

*To accept what you are is to be content,*
*and contentment is the greatest wealth.*

—Vimala McClure

# 15

$$\text{Happiness} = \frac{\text{Wanting What You Have}}{\text{Having What You Want}}$$

Deaf and blind before her second birthday, Helen Keller was an unlikely model for happiness. Born on a plantation in Alabama in 1880, she learned how to walk and talk faster than most. But at just nineteen months old, she became ill with what might have been meningitis or scarlet fever, which robbed her of sight and hearing for the rest of her life.

Helen Keller could have spent her life in isolation with no understanding of happiness. But with the help of her devoted teacher and later companion, Anne Sullivan, she pushed through disabilities that could have kept her apart from the world and became the first American deaf blind person to receive a college degree. She became a prolific writer and speaker and a role model for all of us, not just people with physical challenges.

If anyone had the right to be bitter and complain about the cards that fate dealt her, it was Helen Keller. But she expressed gratitude that her infirmities had given her the means to find her calling. And she's one of the more profound commentators on the nature of happiness: "Many persons have a wrong idea of what constitutes true happiness. It is not attained through self-gratification but through fidelity to a worthy purpose." She also wrote, "When one door of happiness closes, another opens; but often we look so long at the closed door that we do not see the one which has opened for us."

A physical or medical setback can lead you to open another door in your life or to appreciate your life more fully. I have a friend who temporarily lost his sense of smell, which made him appreciate the rest of his senses, and his health, that much more. Whether it's been breaking my hand playing basketball or having serious intestinal parasites after traveling to a primitive part of the world, I've found that my greatest health challenges have been a wake-up call for becoming more conscious about my overall well-being and happiness.

Happiness wears many costumes. In his book *Delivering Happiness: A Path to Profits, Passion, and Purpose,* Zappos' CEO Tony Hsieh suggests that you can fit most versions of happiness into one of three categories: pleasure, passion, or purpose. There's the transitory, party-girl or rock-star version that is playful, fun, and full of indulgent pleasure. Yet pleasure can often be driven by external stimuli, so one can be constantly chasing the next high. Then there's the passion-driven form of happiness, when you feel engaged and enthused with the flow of life. Finally, there's happiness that takes the form of serenity or purposeful bliss that seems to come from a source that's bigger than you when you move beyond your own personal needs.

Happiness has become a goal of both business and political leaders. A number of countries are creating gross national happiness (GNH) indexes for their citizens to supplement their gross domestic product (GDP) financial indicator. The lovely little Himalayan country of Bhutan measures the conditions for how happiness occurs with four pillars, nine indicators, and seventy-two metrics to measure the conditions of how happiness occurs. But though Bhutan gets credit for starting the happiness movement in governments, the crown for the happiest place on the planet tends to go back and forth between Scandinavia and Costa Rica. Facebook even has an application that gauges worldwide happiness (http://apps.facebook.com/gnh_index/). We may all aspire to happiness, but its meaning and practice can be difficult to pin down.

I think the best way to describe happiness comes from Rabbi Hyman Schachtel's 1954 book, *The Real Enjoyment of Living*, in which he produced this piece of wisdom: "Happiness is not having what you want but wanting what you have." The good rabbi may have taken his lead from the ancient Jewish Talmud, which declares, "Who is rich? He who is contented with his lot." Or he may have been revising a quote from Socrates: "He who is not contented with what he has would not be contented with what he would like to have." Many religious leaders have suggested that to want what you have is to think, act, and feel as if ordinary existence is sacred. This suggests that wanting what you have is actually a profound form of worship.

Do you tend to regard happiness as a destination or an object—or as having as many objects as possible? We often believe that if we gratify our instincts or desires, we will achieve happiness. And why shouldn't we? Isn't the pursuit of happiness in America's Declaration of Independence and in our DNA? One dictionary defines "pursue" as to "chase with hostility." Do you pursue happiness with a spirit of hostility? We do get great pleasure out of pursuing goals and acquiring things. But quite often, the idea of something or the process of trying to attain it brings more happiness than the actual attainment of it.

## WANTING VERSUS HAVING

This equation is a bit of a mind twister. What's the difference between "wanting what you have" and "having what you want"? (Some of my friends prefer to distill this equation down to "Having" divided by "Wanting.") Researchers from the University of Pennsylvania and Stanford University examined 12 million personal blogs to determine the shifting meaning of happiness and what other feelings tend to coexist with happiness. Number one on the list was "contentment," and, in fact, the majority of the list of concurrent emotions related to feeling appreciative, peaceful, or glad about one's state in life—all states that would fit into the "wanting what you have" camp. A small number, such as being excited or aspirationally hopeful, fit into the "having what you want" category. Younger people tend to associate happiness more with excitement and the future, while older people tend to associate happiness with peacefulness in the present.

This may also be part of the explanation for why there's a "U-Bend" (as *The Economist* called it in a 2010 cover story) in self-reported well-being. The height of happiness for adults is at eighteen to twenty-one years of age, after which it declines until we hit bottom at around age forty-six to fifty, when anxiety and disappointment peak. Then, surprisingly, with each passing decade, our levels of happiness improve so that, in our eighties, we're actually happier than we were at age twenty. Hey, we have something to look forward to!

As is true of any division equation, the way to increase happiness is to grow what's in the numerator and shrink what's in the denominator. For this particular equation, there are some Buddhist principles in play. The elimination of attachment to having things (the denominator) could lead this equation toward infinite happiness. But some of the happiest people I know take the opposite approach: they have a voracious appetite for pursuing things, but they have learned to balance it with a healthy numerator of appreciating what they have.

Maybe success should be defined as "having what you want" and happiness as "wanting what you have." Success and happiness are often mistaken for twins, but success is more of a maximization or optimization strategy while happiness has more to do with satisfaction and appreciation. Psychologists have proven in clinical studies that an extremely important element of happiness is expressing and feeling gratitude. They've also shown that people who are "maximizers" (success motivated) tend to be less happy than those who are "satisficers." Happy people focus on the "good life," not the "better life."

So maybe an alternative Emotional Equation would be:

$$Happiness = \frac{Gratitude}{Gratification}$$

When you regard the gift of happiness as something that naturally evaporates, you are more apt to feel gratitude for it in the moment. Happy people do not feel entitled, as do narcissists. They see life as a bowl of ice cream in the midday sun: it's better to enjoy what you have rather than go searching for the chocolate sauce. Too many of us end up missing out on the good stuff as we're plotting our strategy to maximize our multitasking lives. Or, as John Lennon once said, "Life is what happens to you while you're busy making other plans."

## HAVES, HAVE-NOTS, WANTS, AND NEEDS

Some people have staked their lives on the belief that having a few extra dollars in their pocket will make them happier. That's true, but only up to what's comparable to about $75,000 in annual income for an American family. Being a "have-not" is stressful, and although researchers have found that lower income in itself doesn't cause sadness, it does create a series of problems that people with money don't have to worry about as much.

But according to a Princeton University study, if you earn

above $75,000 annually, your individual temperament and life circumstances have more of an influence on your sense of contentment than money does. Only about 10 percent of your happiness comes from your life circumstances (including how much money you make), while 40 percent is due to your intentional activities or way of thinking. Remarkably, 50 percent of your happiness is considered an innate biological set point, much like your familial tendency toward height or weight.

The Princeton researchers did find one other positive by-product of making more money: the more people make, the better they feel their life is going. Studies show that the vast majority of people would prefer making less money as long as they are making more than their neighbors across the street. Positional consumption—how we feel we rank in relation to others—has become our litmus test for how we feel about ourselves. Which would you prefer, making $100,000 in an environment where most of the people around you make $150,000, or $75,000 where those around you made $50,000? That's the choice many aging Americans consider when they retire and move to a developing country. (And it's part of the reason why we're going to continue to see beachfront real estate values in Mexico, Costa Rica, and Panama skyrocket.)

We jump on the aspiration treadmill as our means of pursuing happiness. We chase a moving target, keeping one eye on how everyone else is doing and the other on our own growing wants. Alas, the more we make happiness a target, the more widely we miss it. Somehow, along the way, we mix up our insatiable wants with our actual needs.

At the root of this pursuit of happiness is "if-then" thinking. There's almost an equation behind the belief that *if* we attain what we want, *then* we will automatically feel happier, richer, or more beautiful. Think about a time when you became so focused on something that you truly believed it would make a big difference in your happiness. Was the pursuit worth it? Sometimes it is, often it's not. Ask the lottery winners who made the fortune of their dreams overnight. Typically, within a couple of years, their level of happiness has settled back down to where it was before they won, after a whole new set of decisions, challenges, and wants invaded their lives. One study that surveyed people over a thirty-six-year period to determine what a family of four would need to get along found that the estimate of how much income was necessary for getting along increased almost to the same degree that their actual income increased. Some call this the "Rule of Two," as we seem to habitually want about twice as much as we have. This is part of the reason why the modern world is no happier today than fifty years ago even though there's been real income growth in most countries.

According to the conservative pundit George Will, a need "is defined, in contemporary America, as a 48-hour-old want." The result is a "blurring of needs and wants," which leads to a "tyranny of the unnecessary." There will always be something—a want—that you don't have. What are the things in your life that you truly need? Get out a piece of paper, settle into a quiet corner, and just ponder for a moment: "What are the ten most essential needs in my life?" I'll give you the first four answers, which form the base of Abraham Maslow's hierarchy of needs: water, food, sleep, and air. If you're missing one of those physiological needs for more than a short period of time, you won't live. Imagine having one of those cut off—or imagine losing two of your five senses, as Helen Keller did—and you'll realize what a true need it is in your life. Now that we've identified four basic needs, fill in the six other needs. Does it feel at all liberating to realize that your needs can be this simple?

Next, make a list of your ten favorite "wants" of the moment. They might include shedding twenty pounds. A new car. A bigger home. Or maybe just a little more love from your spouse. Wants are perfectly fine, but in many cases, wants can never be completely satisfied. So just when you attain what you wanted, you realize that your neighbor is thinner, richer, or getting more loving at home.

That's the game we play in our minds—and we've been doing so for years.

It's time we played a different game. The English essayist John Lubbock wrote, "Happiness is a thing to be practiced, like the violin." What if the secret of happiness is to practice this emotion rather than pursue it?

$$Happiness = \frac{Practice}{Pursuit}$$

How can we practice happiness? The first step is simply being conscious or aware of what you're looking for. Just as you can practice a golf swing, you can practice happiness. In *The How of Happiness: A Scientific Approach to Getting the Life You Want*, Sonja Lyubomirsky outlines a set of practices that you can incorporate into your life. Some of her suggestions include expressing gratitude regularly, practicing optimism when imagining your future, savoring life's little pleasures in the moment, being deeply committed to lifelong goals and ambitions, and nurturing relationships as if they're the oxygen in your life.

## LEARNING THIS EQUATION THE HARD WAY

As I mentioned in chapter 8, life—and almost death—happened to me on August 19, 2008—while I was chasing what I wanted. I took the experience of going "flatline" as a clear example of divine intervention—the "powers that be" reminding me to appreciate a little more what I already had in my life and to get off the gratification treadmill.

Heeding the message, I realized that I was a little bottom-heavy in this equation. So I took three steps to improve the numerator.

First, I handed over the role as president of my company (which I held for a time in addition to that of CEO) to our very able COO. Second, I made a list of obligations and "must-dos" that were no longer serving my life. In one case, it meant stepping down from a nonprofit board; in another, it meant giving up the cable TV sports package that allowed me to watch every Sunday NFL football game. It also meant spending less time—or no time—with people who didn't bring joy to my life.

That freed up a good chunk of my life and helped me to make time for the things that I love to do and be—and that I hadn't had enough time to experience. I spent more time with my son and his three delightful kids. I gave more space to my meditation and yoga practice. I became more conscious of which friendships I was investing in and chose to spend more one-on-one time with each of my four closest friends. I also reestablished my quarterly practice of doing a three-day juice fast. Sometimes the best way to appreciate what you have is to take it away. I feel so high at the end of those fasts, partly because I feel so light in spirit, that they continue to teach me about how little I really need to be happy.

## WORKING THROUGH THE EQUATION

$$Happiness = \frac{Wanting\ What\ You\ Have}{Having\ What\ You\ Want}$$

*Do an annual "wanting what you have" checkup.* Martin Seligman, the positive psychologist and author of the groundbreaking *Authentic Happiness: Using the New Positive Psychology to Realize Your Potential for Lasting Fulfillment,* suggests an annual practice called a "January retrospective." Shortly after New Year's Day, he spends part of a day focused exclusively on rating his life satisfaction in each of the following domains: love, profession, finances, play, friends, health, generativity, and overall. He then chooses one more category, "trajectory," that scrutinizes the year-by-year changes across domains. I add the categories of family and spirituality to the mix when I do my annual review, and I also spend a few moments savoring one element per category and imagining what life would be like without it. For example, you might consider your relationship with your community or spiritual organization. Close your eyes and ask yourself, "What would life be like without this relationship?" If absence makes the heart grow fonder, using this annual checkup to appreciate the fact that you have such gifts in your life can also be a means of inspiration and appreciation.

*Experience happiness with happy people.* What if *Forbes* magazine followed up its annual issue of the 400 Richest People in the World with the 400 Happiest People in the World? Maybe it's time for us to start measuring something that's more worthwhile. What if you were to list the four friends, business associates, or family members—anywhere in the world—who are the happiest people you know? If you can, spend a little time with them, and you'll witness how they give more attention to the top half of this equation than to the bottom half. Think of one key lesson you can learn from each of those four people, and start practicing that lesson and evaluating its impact in your life. Eric Hoffer has written, "When people are free to do as they please, they usually imitate each other." Happiness has also been proven to be contagious. Harvard's Nicholas Christakis has shown that your friend's friend's friend has more effect on your happiness than an extra $5,000 in your pocket. In fact, if your friend is happy, there's a 15 percent greater likelihood that you're going to be happy, and with each further degree of separation, there's only a 5 percent declining effect. We know that yawning and giggling can be contagious, but now you know that happiness is infectious as well.

*Create the right happiness habitat.* In *Choosing the Right Pond:*

*Human Behavior and the Quest for Status,* the economist Robert Frank recommends that we be very careful about what pond we choose to live in, as our reference group will have a big impact on our perception of wants and needs. Surrounding yourself with friends or work colleagues who are forever chasing shiny new objects may cause you to feel deficient unless you're constantly pursuing one thing or another. I know that surrounding myself with other type A CEOs isn't usually my doorway to happiness. Many of my friends are artists, who are often money-starved. I'm often time-starved. Spending an afternoon with one of them always helps me realize that the real scarcity in life is time, not money, since when we die it's not because we're penniless but because we're out of time. They also help me see that when you spend your money on experiences rather than possessions you're less likely to constantly size yourself up against your neighbors, since experiences are harder to measure and compare. Plus you share experiences with others, so those emotional connections—and the memories that last—also positively affect your happiness.

*Grow your gratitude.* If positive psychologists are correct in suggesting that gratitude is the most essential ingredient in your happiness cake, you should start mixing the batter. But, the happiness researcher Sonja Lyubomirsky counsels, don't put too much gratitude into the recipe, as that's like a cake with too much sugar. Creating a gratitude journal tends to increase your happiness by making you conscious of appreciating what you have. But spending quality time with the people you love is more meaningful than trying to habitually make time for documenting gratitude three times a week or more. Even better, if you make a weekly gratitude entry in your journal, make a point of expressing some gratitude within the next week to those you've mentioned there. Gratitude is the most effective means of reminding you to "want what you have."

It feels as if this chapter needs a warning label: "Beware of Chasing Happiness." Happiness ensues, so be careful of pursuing. Take the advice of the French novelist Colette, who wrote, "What a wonderful life I had! I only wish I had realized it sooner." Happiness surrounds you even when it eludes you. It's only a matter of seeing it for what it is: recognition that your life is full of precious gifts whose value is often neglected until they're gone.

# 16

$$\boxed{\text{Joy} = \text{Love} - \text{Fear}}$$

Expected to die at birth, Sean Stephenson has beaten the odds all his life. By the age of eighteen, a rare genetic condition—osteogenesis imperfecta, or glass bone disease—had led to more than two hundred broken bones, which left Sean standing barely three feet tall. In a world where a strong sneeze or a simple fall might cause a major injury, Sean could have spent his life in a bubble, protected from all who might potentially harm him. Instead, he became one of the world's most popular motivational speakers, as well as a clinical psychotherapist, writer, marketing consultant, and member of President Bill Clinton's White House administration.

How did this *little* man (in the vertically challenged sense only), confined to a wheelchair his whole life, create such a magnetic world filled with joy? (If you haven't seen his dance videos, you should definitely search for Sean on YouTube to see the joyful spirit of this very *big* man, now in his thirties.) Simply, Sean believes that love and fear can't coexist at the same time. He says that most of us wear "fear goggles" to protect ourselves from a world that has wounded us. Yet this scarcity-based approach to living doesn't allow space for the abundance of love to enter into one's life. Sean has told me, "I stayed alive because I've developed my heart muscle. I developed a habit of love. We don't grow by just loving the people who are good to us. We grow by learning to love those who are less lovable, those who are pumped with fear in their lives. No one ever conquered fear with more fear. When I make a decision coming from a place of love, I never regret it. When I make a decision from fear, I almost always regret it."

Sean could have lived a life in which fear motivated his relationship with his health, his wealth, and his relationships. But instead he's become a successful entrepreneur, including working with Miss Fitness Universe and her bodybuilder husband to create a fitness video together. Many people with Sean's challenges have given up hope for a successful life. Not Sean. In addition to his career successes, he's in a glorious relationship with a smart, beautiful, "able-bodied" woman, Mindie Kniss. Theirs is a model for how great partnerships can be made. Sean says, "Living a life coming from a place of love creates positive movement. It is like joy bubbling over or wanting to skip down the street. Joy is the most enduring and powerful emotion in life because it's synonymous with love."

Joy is an attitude of the heart. The irony is, if we are willing to give up the search for happiness, we just might find joy. It's an incredibly meaningful word for me since I named my company Joie de Vivre. What drew me to joy is the graceful, hard-to-pinpoint state of elation that comes with this life-affirming emotion. Winning the lottery may bring you happiness, but watching the birth of a child will bring you joy. J. D. Salinger wrote, "The most singular difference between happiness and joy is that happiness is a solid and joy is a liquid."

Happiness may help you smile, but joy feels more like a "full-body-contact" emotion. There's a spontaneous yet enduring quality to this emotion. We often say that someone couldn't "contain her joy" or was "overflowing with joy." Though happiness may be the result of happenstance—both of which share the same root—joy seems to bubble up from a well deep inside us. Happiness is epidermal (on the skin). Joy is internal.

## "THERE IS NO FEAR IN LOVE, BUT PERFECT LOVE CASTS OUT FEAR"

This quote from the Bible defines what I call "the love bubble of life." Think of a pie chart. There are only two slices of the pie: love and fear. One crowds out the other. These are the two motivating forces in the world. Many scientists believe that all other emotions we feel are direct descendents of these two emotions. The author Gregg Braden suggests, "Emotion is the power source that drives us forward in life. Love or fear is the driving force that propels us through the walls of resistance and catapults us beyond the barriers that keep us from our goals, dreams, and desires." My hero the psychologist Abraham Maslow suggested that at any given moment we have two options: to step forward into growth or to step back into safety.

Imagine some issue in your life, one that requires you to make a choice. It could be the decision to leave your job to pursue a new career. Or to give a friend advice when you know she may not want to hear your candor. What would it feel like to make this choice from a place of love instead of fear? What happens to your body when you imagine each path? It's easy to take the path of fear because we often associate something in the present with a painful past experience or an outdated belief. Whenever you feel a clenching up or some kind of armor arising, you are in the state of defensiveness we call fear. It's where most people spend their lives. No wonder our bodies become more fragile and inflexible over time.

The biologist Bruce Lipton suggests that from an evolutionary perspective we are always faced with two choices: growth or protection. Billions of cells in our bodies wear out every day. The biological mechanisms that support growth and protection cannot operate optimally and simultaneously. Fear triggers more than 1,400 known physical and chemical responses and activates more than 30 different hormones and neurotransmitters in our bodies. With so much going on, it's hard for the body to focus on growth (or love) at the same time as defense. Fear is an aggressive predator of joy.

The pressures of modern life keep us in a perennial state of fight or flight. Being in a sustained state of self-protection motivated by fear inhibits the creation of life-sustaining energy.

If you are obsessed with your work life—often to the detriment of your personal life—you may be tempted to skip this chapter. That would be a mistake. This equation has just as much relevance in the context of a company.

Fear is the most prevalent and contagious emotion in most companies, especially in bad economic times. Fear is a demotivator, and it has a corrosive effect on creativity and innovation. If we were to transfer this equation into the corporate world, it might be:

$$\textit{Innovation} = \textit{Creativity} - \textit{Cynicism}$$

Innovation is joy. Creativity is love. And cynicism, which breeds conformity, comes from fear. Companies that fall into a fear cycle aren't able to develop the creativity that fuels an innovative organization primed to adapt to our evolving world. These dinosaur companies, stuck in fear, will become extinct in the twenty-first century. So joy, love, and fear are just as relevant to your work life as your love life.

## FEAR MASQUERADING AS LOVE

Falling for someone can feel like a love/fear frappé. We initially feel the expansiveness that comes with opening our hearts, and, as a result, we are filled with a joyful spirit. Then come the jolts of fear that threaten us. Maybe we're not good enough for our love interest. Maybe he or she isn't trustworthy. Falling in love can be a tasty and terrifying blend of joy and fear. There are countless examples of married couples who met each other during the most vulnerable times of their lives—the perfect condition for a love/fear frappé.

One well-known study of love and fear is known as "Love on a Suspension Bridge." The study was done using two bridges in British Columbia: one that was safe and relatively easy to cross—low, across a quiet river; the other a bridge that was made for the adventurous—230 feet above rocks and rapids, a rickety wooden structure that swayed in the wind and put your heart into your throat.

An attractive female member of the experiment team was tasked to approach men who were crossing either of the two bridges about halfway across. She would introduce herself as a psychology researcher and ask the men to take part in her study by writing an imaginative story in response to a photograph she showed them of a woman with one hand covering her face and the other outstretched. The supposed intent was to gauge the effect of natural beauty on one's creativity. For the men who chose to participate by developing a short story at the middle of either bridge, the female researcher would then give them her name and phone number—in case they wanted to find out more about the study's results.

The researchers found that men on the less safe-looking bridge were more stimulated by the height of the bridge and were likely to confuse that feeling with being "love-struck." They were thus much more likely to call her back (half of the men versus just one-eighth of the men on the safe bridge), potentially for amorous reasons. Whenever our emotions are heightened—whether due to love or fear—we can often confuse what's at play. Our nervous system registers a physiological response—a faster heartbeat, a jump in adrenaline, a sense of heightened awareness, breaking a little sweat, and maybe queasiness in the stomach—and chalks it up to love, even though we may actually be in a state of fear. Maybe that's why we *fall* in love. It's the delicious confusion that can prove to be the enigma of our lifetime. Have you ever mistaken fear for love or love for fear?

## THE FEAR AND JOY OF BEING AN ENTREPRENEUR

All of the physical symptoms mentioned in the last paragraph— feeling adrenalized, sweaty, and worked up—are what I felt in 1986, when I was pondering the idea of starting my own company. I'd been on the fast track since my teens, completing my undergraduate degree at Stanford and then being accepted into the university's desirable business school. While getting my MBA, I was president of the Real Estate Club, and I received some phenomenal job offers from the best institutional real estate companies in the country. But I chose to work for a maverick real estate developer in San Francisco— at one-third the pay I had been offered for the other jobs. My logic was that I wanted to be a creative, entrepreneurial real estate developer when I "grew up," and the best way to learn that trade was from a master in the field. I endeavored to get my hands dirty.

But a year into that post-MBA job, it became clear to me that I didn't love what I was doing. It came as a shock, as I was certain I'd taken the right path—giving up the riches and prestige for the choice of operating out of a basement to manage the challenging renovation of a large historic building. At twenty-four, I felt lost. If you're not finding your calling at work, you usually look elsewhere. For me, that meant studying how to write screenplays and training to be a massage therapist at the Esalen Institute in Big Sur. I was the only Stanford MBA who was going to be a massage therapist when he "grew up."

As I approached my twenty-sixth birthday, I decided to take one last shot at transitioning my fledgling real estate career into an industry that felt less transactional, more hospitable, and definitely more creative. I decided that I would start a boutique hotel company, and my first purchase, with the hope of raising $1 million from investors, was going to be a "no-tell motel" in the heart of San Francisco's infamous Tenderloin District—as far from glamorous as you could get. Of course, most of my logical Stanford Business School friends thought I was nuts. I had no experience in the hotel industry. I'd never been a CEO. The hotel was in bankruptcy and foreclosure, and its biggest corporate account was "Vinnie and his girls." Let's just say the place was very popular during lunch hour—and it didn't have a restaurant. One of my closest friends laid it on the line when he said, "Chip, I don't know if you're fearless or just stupid, but let me just warn you that this will be a disaster for your résumé."

The root of all fear is attachment. When we fear something, we tend to be attached to an outcome that we want or don't want to happen. Our fear may be directly proportional to how important we think the outcome will affect our lives. I'd spent all of my adult life preparing to be a successful businessperson, yet now my friends and advisers were telling me that I was about to ruin my life or, worse (as it seemed at the time), my résumé.

I had a conversation with Art Norkus, a cantankerous bandleader who owned the motel I was about to buy. He wasn't necessarily as schooled or trustworthy as many of the folks who were stoking my fear, and, of course, he had a vested interest in trying to convince me to take the awful property off his hands. He sat in the gaudy suite of the motel nursing his 3 P.M. gin and tonic and unleashed this question on me: "What's your biggest fear in life?" I fumbled for an answer and blurted out, "I guess being a failure." Art shook his head and gave me a sly smile. "Then go get yourself a corporate job, sonny. You'll feel like a success until you're about fifty, when you'll divorce your wife, get a young girlfriend, buy a sports car, and don a toupee. You'll show the world you're a success, but inside you'll feel like a failure because you took the safe path. That's why all those midlife corporate execs buy Harleys. It makes them feel like they didn't sell out."

I didn't know what to say, but I completely resonated with his message. Then he asked me, "So what's *really* your biggest fear in life?" I asked his bartender wife to stir up a gin and tonic for me, too. As I sipped some courage, the following words tripped out of my mouth: "I guess my biggest fear is that I'll disappoint myself—that I won't pursue my dreams—that I will suffocate trying to live up to others' expectations of me." Art smiled and counseled, "Chip, drop your fears, and you'll be shocked at how it will liberate you, and on the other side, you'll likely find the love of your life—whatever that's meant to be."

It was that afternoon that I decided to finally, once and for all, drop my attachment to being the Stanford MBA who was supposed to be a corporate CEO someday. I was going to be a motelier (not even a hotelier) because, quite frankly, I loved the property and got joyful goose bumps every time I walked into the courtyard and imagined what it could be. And as I felt the fear dissipate, just as Art had predicted, what rushed into its place was a love of this new wacky venture. Right behind that was "joie de vivre."

## WORKING THROUGH THE EQUATION

$$Joy = Love - Fear$$

*Write a field guide for how to live in fear—one subject at a time.* Sometimes the best way to combat fear is to show—taken to its extreme—how illogical it can be. Let's imagine that your "Joy" equation is weak because your fear of financial insecurity is paralyzing you. Develop a series of training steps that would help someone else understand how you obsess about financial issues. A friend of mine developed this training list because he found that financial fear was crowding out love in his life. Try these on for size, and ask yourself how many are relevant to you:

1. First, paint a bleak picture of your future.
2. Imagine each possible financial issue out to its worst conclusion.
3. Assume you are powerless to affect the outcome.
4. Believe you are doomed to failure.
5. Continue to add more financial responsibilities in the midst of your fear.
6. Imagine giving up all the things and freedoms you have when the moment of collapse hits.
7. Assume that your family can't get along without you and will resent you if you ask them to make some sacrifices.
8. Practice telling your family that you have been wiped out.
9. Make sure to remember and relive this process any time you are about to make some progress.

Once my friend shone the light of day on the mental loop he was in, he realized what a recipe for stress and torture it was. He also saw that most of the points in the training manual were either false or hilariously exaggerated. The only way to shift a fear pattern is first to see it for what it is.

*Take a page from FDR.* In early 1933, after being elected president in the midst of the Great Depression, Franklin D. Roosevelt addressed the nation, saying "Only a foolish optimist can deny the dark realities of the moment." He also touched on happiness and joy: "Happiness lies not in the mere possession of money; it lies in the joy of achievement, in the thrill of creative effort. The joy and moral stimulation of work no longer must be forgotten in the mad chase of evanescent profits." And, of course, he said, "The only thing we have to fear is fear itself—nameless, unreasoning, unjustified terror which paralyzes needed efforts to convert retreat into advance." What's the lesson in this? In difficult times, be a realist but don't let fear overtake you. When in doubt, focus your attention on what brings you joy, as this, most likely, will be your path toward replacing fear with love. The question I ask myself when I'm most in a place of fear and darkness is "Where is the love in all of this?" It's an odd question to ask when you're on your knees, but just remembering the fact that love can prevail will help you throw off the thick blanket of fear that envelops and stunts your growth.

*Practice the Law of Attraction.* Fear begets fear, and love begets love. Millions of people have found that just shifting their mind shifted their life. For both individuals and organizations, a momentum is created by emotions. Sporting teams can go on a winning or losing streak based upon the collective thinking of the group. If you embrace love as the primary currency that connects you with others, you have the potential to create a winning streak in your life that may be unimaginable for someone mired in fear. Check out Esther and Jerry Hicks's book *The Law of Attraction: The Basics of the Teachings of Abraham* for some helpful advice on how to mirror love in the world. If you want love, learn to give love. If you want attention and appreciation, give attention and appreciation. Energy flows or stagnates. The word "affluence" comes from the Latin word *affluere,* which means "to flow to." Open the love channel in your life, and you'll find an affluent gusher of joy right behind it.

*Do something just for the joy of it.* The way this equation works, when you reduce fear to zero, joy equals love. Searching for love can be futile, but finding joy can be your doorway to love. A few years ago, my company was celebrating our twentieth anniversary and I decided to throw a Joy party. We invited ten thousand women from around California—all with the name "Joy"—to a party at our luxury Hotel Vitale on San Francisco's waterfront. The first twenty-five who gave us an affirmative RSVP were given a free hotel room for the night of the party so they could have a Joy slumber party.

When I first suggested this to some on my executive team, they were skeptical. Why spend money on a group of people who weren't even our customers? Yet our company had spent two decades appreciating the significance and responsibility of having a name associated with this positive emotion. We ended up with a roomful of joy (and Joys), 125 women sharing the same name, along with their husbands, significant others, friends, and children. What was miraculous was how those strangers bonded so quickly through their stories of "being Joy," as if they were long-lost friends. There were lots of Joy-full tears. It was one big love bubble, not just for the Joys and their families but also for our employees, who realized the significance of our company name and our mission of creating joy in the world. And with a little "Law of Attraction" proof, that hotel received a large new piece of business, a corporate retreat that more than paid *for* the party, due to the word of mouth *from* the party. That night I went home with a heart full of love and not a fear in the world. How can you be careless when you're embracing joy? You may just find love on the other side.

Back in the late 1970s, Dr. Gerald Jampolsky wrote the seminal self-help book on this topic, *Love Is Letting Go of Fear.* Using the self-study curriculum for spiritual transformation *A Course in Miracles* as a basis, Dr. Jampolsky premised that we spend much of our life imagining the outside world as the cause and ourselves as the victimized effect. Once we see that letting go of all the historical influences that take us in the direction of fear leaves us not empty but in a state of love, we are more apt to start changing our habits, choosing love over fear. Love is like electricity: it's an energy we can choose to turn off or on based upon whether we want to be in the darkness of fear or not. Once we live in that place of love, the overflowing emotion of joy emerges.

# 17

$$\text{Thriving*} = \frac{\text{Frequency of Positive}}{\text{Frequency of Negative}}$$

(*Thriving being equal to 3.0 or more)

At his defense trial in April 1964, Nelson Mandela declared, "During my lifetime I have dedicated myself to this struggle of the African people. I have fought against white domination, and I have fought against black domination. I have cherished the ideal of a democratic and free society in which all persons live together in harmony and with equal opportunities. It is an ideal which I hope to live for and to achieve. But if needs be, it is an ideal for which I am prepared to die." The South African judge spared Mandela when he sentenced him to life imprisonment instead of death, which was his prerogative as punishment for treason. Mandela would spend the next twenty-seven years in prison, eighteen doomed to hard labor and life in a tiny cell with no toilet or running water—hardly a motivation for thriving or positivity. Yet Mandela is perhaps the most visible icon of optimism we have today.

Cultivating positivity is a conscious choice. And Mandela would be the last man to place himself on a pedestal when reflecting on how he wrestled with it. But rather than languishing in self-pity, regret, resentment, or a host of other emotions, he became the embodiment of positivity. During his years at the prison on Robben Island, he would model self-respect, respect for others, compassion, and a steadfast confidence that inspired all who knew him. His resilience and attitude transformed life for all of his fellow prisoners. While becoming a legend among the African people, he quietly shifted his daily reality from captive to captivating, taking on the role of teacher, mentor, leader, and friend to prisoner and jailer alike.

Following his release and after receiving the Nobel Peace Prize, Mandela set up the Truth and Reconciliation Commission (TRC) in 1995 to bring about transparency to, and forgiveness for, the crimes and atrocities perpetrated by both blacks and whites. As South Africa's new president, Mandela appointed Archbishop Desmond Tutu to run the commission, which investigated human rights abuses and held public hearings in which victims were allowed to tell their stories and receive rehabilitation and reparations, and abusers could stand accountable for their crimes and receive amnesty instead of incarceration. Groundbreaking and controversial, the TRC was not universally accepted. But this revolutionary application of positivity to the wounds of a nation, a people, and individuals stands as a benchmark of what is possible in the face of impossible pain and suffering.

The celebrated poet Maya Angelou wrote most eloquently about how to thrive in her own life: "I've learned that no matter what happens, or how bad it seems today, life does go on, and it will be better tomorrow. I've learned that you can tell a lot about a person by the way he/she handles these three things: a rainy day, lost luggage, and tangled Christmas tree lights. . . . I've learned that every day you should reach out and touch someone. . . . I've learned that people will forget what you said, people will forget what you did, but people will never forget how you made them feel."

Isn't that the truth? So often we evaluate our lives based upon the extreme highs or lows of the unique cards we're dealt. Yet it's the mundane details of life and how we experience them that season the flavors of our existence on this earth. At the end of the day, how we relate to our daily slog through the perpetual rush-hour traffic may have a greater influence on our life than how we respond to that once-in-a-lifetime health scare that traumatized us for a couple of months.

There's a medical condition called failure to thrive, or FTT, that refers to infants that aren't growing at a normal pace due to external or internal factors. Failure to thrive can also define corporate cultures that are like stagnant ponds that stink due to a lack of fresh water coming into the system. A 2010 Gallup survey found that there was a significant correlation between the U.S. states that were thriving economically and those that had residents who expressed positivity or optimism about their lives. Though this equation is defined as "Thriving," it could have easily been called "Positivity."

A number of researchers have simultaneously discovered the importance of positivity ratios. This is a relatively new phenomenon, as psychologists have mostly focused on what's wrong with people rather than what's right.

In 1998, the psychologist Barbara Fredrickson wrote a paper called "What Good Are Positive Emotions?" that led her to writing the book *Positivity: Groundbreaking Research Reveals How to Embrace the Hidden Strength of Positive Emotions, Overcome Negativity, and Thrive.* Historically, negative emotions were seen to have evolutionary benefits, helping humans survive. The benefits of positive emotions were less obvious, except for perhaps their influence on the desire to procreate.

Fredrickson showed that positive emotions create a "broaden-and-build" impact in which a positive emotion leads to a desired state. (The ten she focuses on are joy, gratitude, serenity, interest, hope, pride, amusement, inspiration, awe, and love.) For example, joy sparks the urge to play and be creative. Interest—or curiosity—sparks the urge to explore and learn, while serenity gives us a sense of savoring our current circumstances and integrating them into a new view of ourselves and of the world. So rather than narrowing our focus, as negative emotions do, positive emotions give us a greater sense of possibility and allow us to tap into the deep well of our other traits or talents.

This research has been reinforced by evidence from the business world. Management theorists have been able to show empirically that positivity influences productivity in the workplace, as it creates an "upward spiral" of momentum. We see it in sports, we see it in our romantic lives, and we see it in our relationship with ourselves. Positive emotions are the key to a strong sense of resilience.

## THE MERGING OF EMOTIONS AND EQUATIONS

The more Fredrickson learned about the influence of positivity, the more she wanted to create a tool that would help define the value of positive emotions. Fortunately, she connected with Marcial Losada, who had developed a mathematical model that helped define why some business teams flourished while others didn't. Losada observed teams and tracked key variables in their meetings, such as whether people's statements were positive or negative, self-focused or other-focused, or based on asking questions (inquiry) or defending a point of view (advocacy). After cataloguing a large number of organizations, Losada came to the conclusion that the tipping point for the ratio of positive to negative influences for a successful team is about three to one. Once a work group had that kind of positive reinforcing environment, it was easy to track its influence on employee satisfaction, customer satisfaction, and profitability.

Fredrickson's work, which was grounded in evolutionary theory and experiments, came to the same conclusion. When we have about three times as many positive emotions or influences in our lives as the negative ones, a domino or cascading effect starts to emerge that leads to what I call a "momentum of victory," when good things ripple into more good things.

John Gottman, one of the world's leading marriage psychologists, has found similar results amongst romantic couples. His book *The Mathematics of Marriage: Dynamic Nonlinear Models* shows that stable couples have a five-to-one ratio of positive to negative affects (affects can be defined as observable expressions of emotion), while couples heading for divorce have a 0.8-to-one ratio. Just watching a fifteen-minute video of a couple talking with each other, Gottman can predict with 90 to 95 percent certainty the likelihood that the marriage will last or will deconstruct in the next few years, based on the ratio of positivity to negativity. One way to understand this equation is to estimate the ratio in your marriage—between laughter and smiles versus arguments and frowns.

The psychologist Dacher Keltner has created the Jen Ratio in honor of the Confucian concept of *jen*, which refers to a multilayered mixture of humanity, benevolence, and kindness. Someone displaying *jen* is able to bring the good things out of themselves, others, and life. Thus the Jen Ratio includes in its numerator the number of times during a particular period when we've acted benevolently, so that we had a positive effect on others, while in the denominator are the number of times we've been selfish or malevolent.

Finally, Daniel Kahneman and Amos Tversky's landmark psychological research backs up all of this by showing that losses or negative experiences in our life have two to four times as great an impact on us as similar positive experiences. Negative experiences are far more destructive to our psyche than positive ones are constructive. That's why our math needs to skew positively in the three-to-one to five-to-one range, as one zinger of a negative can cancel out a bushelful of positives.

Let's apply this to your work environment. For every moment of anguish you feel due to the combination of anxiety and frustration that comes with working in a fear-based workplace, it's healthy to find at least three positives that you can point to that negate the anguish. These could include having a productive lunch with your boss, getting two hours of uninterrupted time to work on your favorite project, or reading some positive customer reviews that help you feel confident that you and your team are on the right track. That sounds easy, but according to Barbara Fredrickson's research, at least 80 percent of the population falls short of the three-to-one ratio. Still, just setting this goal can make a difference.

## POSITIVITY IS NOT LIVING IN DENIAL

Now that you know the Holy Grail for positivity rests on this three-to-one ratio, you may be tempted to bend the rules. You're thinking "All I need to do is think positively and ignore all the negative stuff that crops up in my life." But there's a reason I chose Nelson Mandela, instead of a positive-thinking icon such as Norman Vincent Peale, as the profile to start this chapter. Mandela faced seemingly insurmountable challenges, but as a peacemaker and world leader he welcomed depth over surfaces and awareness over denial. In fact, he used his own negative circumstances as a means of embracing the positive in his life.

Let's distinguish between positive thinking and positive emotions. Positive thinking can lead to positive emotions, but there's no guarantee of that. In fact, positive thinking in the form of unrealistic expectations can be corrosive. Disappointment can be directly proportional to your level of expectations. Barbara Fredrickson acknowledges that insincere positive thinking, such as telling yourself you feel good when you really don't, can lead to false positive emotions and be toxic. The skeptic Barbara Ehrenreich, author of *Bright-Sided: How the Relentless Promotion of Positive Thinking Has Undermined America,* believes that the delusional nature of Americans' positivity has become so pervasive in business, religion, psychology, health care, and the like that we're on the verge of becoming an Orwellian state (à la *1984*).

Blind optimism, fake cheeriness, and self-directed pep talks are not what we're talking about. Critical thinking is not antithetical to thriving. In fact, being able to recognize the risks that you face, imagine the means to adapt to those risks, and assess whether your path is wise can help reduce anxiety without necessarily taking you into a downward negativity spiral. One only wishes that the designers and operators of the "unsinkable ship" *Titanic,* which sank on its maiden voyage a hundred years ago (in 1912), had implemented a little more critical thinking. They had installed only enough lifeboats for half the people aboard because a disaster was unthinkable; yet this kind of thinking led to an unthinkable disaster.

Denying the unthinkable doesn't work, but neither does dwelling on it. Living a thriving life takes a collection of actions, practices, and conditions to create lasting benefit, not a simplistic belief that your mind alone can shift you into positive emotions. This can be most apparent during a crisis.

Think of a time when you felt paralyzed by some bad news or a catastrophic event. Negative thoughts and feelings pour over you and can be overwhelming. Combating negative thinking with positive thinking typically doesn't have enough of an effect. When your mind is spinning out of control in one direction, getting it to spin in the other direction just through mental energy is virtually impossible. More often than not, the equation that comes from this type of thinking-only behavior is Fear + Rumination = Anxiety Attack.

Instead, you can take a step back and imagine how your actions can help stimulate positive emotions related to giving and love—as did the relief groups that immediately started volunteering and making a difference after the massive Japanese earthquake and tsunami of 2011. Similarly, cultivating practices that evoke positive emotions during normal times, such as prayer or regular expressions of gratitude, can be like depositing money into your emotional bank account, so that you are better prepared for the worst of times.

# CHANGING HABITS CAN CHANGE EMOTIONS

If you change the "psycho-hygiene" of your organization, you might change the world. I learned this odd hyphenated word from Abraham Maslow's diaries, and I think it accurately describes the cultural and psychological intangible that exists in every organization. Does a company know how to bathe and rejuvenate itself when faced with difficult times? Or does the psychological sweat from the pores of everyone in a metaphorical workplace fire just stink up the place?

Back in 2002, at the depth of the dot-com crash in the San Francisco Bay Area, I focused on our company's psycho-hygiene by shifting how we ended our executive committee (EC) meetings each week. Those two-hour sweat-a-thons were brutal. We were doing everything we could to avert employee layoffs, but we were also freaking out because it was difficult to make payroll at our numerous properties, and with each passing month the regional hotel revenues just got worse and worse. We were on the verge of an FTT (failure to thrive) diagnosis.

I came up with something to shift the negative focus—and the energy in the room. Any of the fifteen committee members could recognize an employee in the field who deserved some extra credit. It might be that the VP of operations would highlight Joe, the bellman at the Hotel Rex, because he had worked two sixteen-hour days in a row when the hotel's only elevator had to have emergency repairs and all the hotel guests had to carry their baggage up as many as seven flights of stairs. Joe had provided this additional coverage during a time when he had family visiting from out of town. So though he had earned some overtime pay for doing the extra work, he had also given up valuable time with his family.

Initially, our leaders in the weekly EC meeting were a little shy about bringing up examples of valor and virtue. But with time they got the hang of it, and the meetings would end on a high note that was really valuable to our psycho-hygiene during a time when our sweat glands were on overdrive. Three elements of positivity came out of this. First, it helped remind our senior leaders that amid the economic wreckage we were sorting through, there were still meaningful examples of employees exhibiting our mission statement to "create joy" on a daily basis. So as painful as the times were, there was one ripple of positivity that gave us the hope that we weren't idiots—and that our work wasn't futile.

A second ripple of positivity exuded from Joe, a guy who might have been surprised that the manager of his hotel had even noticed that he'd worked 32 hours in two days. After Joe received a "shout-out" in the EC meeting, one of our members reached out to him directly to give a personal thanks, which resulted in Joe exuding a positive attitude for days to come. And everyone around him—his coworkers, our hotel guests, and his family—was able to see and feel the effect on him. Because we recommended that the thank-you come from someone outside Joe's Operations Department (for example, the VP of Marketing), we created a positive ripple between two departments. The reality is that in a recession a lot of finger-pointing goes on. Operations blames Marketing. Marketing blames Sales. Sales blames IT. IT blames Accounting. And we all blame HR. This simple exercise in cross-departmental recognition broke down the silos that had risen during fast growth and anxious times.

Positivity doesn't have to be momentous, but implementing sustained new habits in your own life or in an organization can have a "butterfly effect" by sending positive ripples out into the world. On a personal level, the higher you are in a company hierarchy, the greater the lasting, profound effect of your exhibiting positivity within the organization.

## WORKING THROUGH THE EQUATION

$$Thriving = \frac{Frequency\ of\ Positive}{Frequency\ of\ Negative}$$

*Take the positivity self-test and check out other resources at www .positivityratio.com.* Barbara Fredrickson has created this website with a simple twenty-question test that will help you measure your positivity ratio. As with any test, this is a representation of where you and your emotions are at the moment, so it's advisable to take it several times over the course of a few weeks. The ten primary positive emotions that stimulate positivity are joy, gratitude, serenity, interest, hope, pride, amusement, inspiration, awe, and love. The ten primary negative emotions that take you in the opposite direction are anger, shame, contempt, disgust, embarrassment, guilt, hate, sadness, fear, and stress. The first time I took this test, I was disappointed to find that I scored below the three-to-one ratio that defines when someone is in the upward spiral of positivity. But in reviewing my scores, I came to realize how potent the denominator (negative emotions) was in ruining a fine day. So I've found that when I'm in a frenzied space and feel almost numb about my overall emotional state and the individual emotional components that are creating it, I take this litmus test and it wakes me up to what's going on inside me pretty quickly.

*Spend a day doing a positivity and negativity inventory.* Start the day with at least thirty rubber bands in your pocket. As you go through the day, each time you get into a way of thinking or being that feels decidedly positive or negative, take out a rubber band and put it around either your left (positive) or right (negative) wrist. There's no need to chastise or call attention to yourself for this. Just quietly make the note by putting on another rubber band. Then move on with your day, as the exercise won't work if you're overly self-conscious. What's an example? Your friend may call to tell you about the big promotion she won at work. Assuming you have a moderate to large reaction, if your resulting emotion was appreciation and love for her, put a rubber band on your left wrist. If instead you felt more than a little envious, put a rubber band on your right wrist. At the end of the day, tally up the bands on your left wrist versus your right. Are you even close to a three-to-one ratio? Were there times in the day that were more positive or negative than others? Were there particular experiences that felt as though they deserved more than one rubber band? More likely than not, you will be surprised by how hard it is to get to a three-to-one ratio. One thing that has helped me to reduce my negativity is moving from a reaction to an inquiry. Rather than immediately going to envy, I try to be curious about why the emotion is arising in me. Curiosity allows me to have a sense of humor at my habitual reactivity, and it may save me from having to add another rubber band to my right wrist.

*Identify one particular negative element in your life and apply genuine positivity to it.* If you hate your commute, how could you introduce an experience that would shift the energy? Is it time to learn a new language by listening to an audio program? Can you express gratitude to two friends by (hands-free) phone each time you do your thirty-minute commute? Think of the positive ripples that would create in your life. Or maybe you find the holidays depressing because you end up spending too much money and most of your time with family members you either don't know or don't like. Go back to that list of ten positive emotions and pick out two that you will deeply explore on your next year-end family vacation. What if you took a much greater *interest* in your mother-in-law's family history or your uncle's collection of beer mugs? Are you creative enough to come up with a few genuine questions that might help you get underneath the surface of how you know them? Maybe the second emotion you focus on could be *gratitude*. How many ways can you show gratitude during this family time without looking like a lunatic? Try it; you'll be surprised by what kind of thriving may emerge.

*Apply John Gottman's learning to your relationship.* John Gottman has found that lasting effects of behavioral marital therapy usually come from one of three strategies, with the first two increasing the numerator and the third reducing the denominator: (1) increasing your positive affect during times when the two of you are not in conflict; (2) increasing your positive affect during a conflict; in other words, looking for positive ways to connect when you're in the midst of a disagreement or difficult time; or (3) reducing the negative affect during conflict resolution; in other words, not saying something that you will regret later. A friend and his wife have a little ritual they do each evening to honor Gottman's five-to-one love code for relationships. Before they go to bed, they tell each other five things that they really appreciated about the other that day or something more general about the other's positive qualities. Exercising your positivity love muscle before going to sleep can prolong your relationship. And if you have, or plan to have, children, know that this is all the more important because, as Gottman discovered when working with his mathematicians, marital conflicts increase by a staggering factor of nine after the arrival of the first baby. So you may want to do this in the morning, too, after a night of lost sleep.

Dr. Rick Hanson has suggested that our brains are "Velcro for negativity and Teflon for positivity." In other words, negative influences tend to stick to us while positive ones slip away like water off a duck's back. So often it comes down to what perspective you choose to take. Even in the worst of times, I try to ask myself, "What if there were no such thing as a mistake in my life? What if some positive lesson is supposed to come out of this negative experience?" This takes me back to the original equation: Despair = Suffering – Meaning. When in doubt, know that finding meaning is a shortcut to tapping into positivity. And this, appropriately, brings us to our next equation: Faith.

# 18

$$\left[ \text{Faith} = \frac{\text{Belief}}{\text{Intellect}} \right]$$

When in doubt, seek guidance from someone wiser than you. I would not have attempted this exploration of faith or tried to distill such a profound subject into an equation without first consulting an expert. Fortunately, in October 2010, I was lucky enough to spend two days with the Dalai Lama during his visit with researchers at the Center for Compassion and Altruism Research and Education at Stanford University. On one of those days, a small group of about twenty-five of us was invited to ask him questions.

Recognized as the reincarnated Dalai Lama at age fifteen, Tenzin Gyatso had headed the Tibetan people for less than a decade before, in 1959, fleeing from the invading Chinese to India, where he established a government in exile. His Holiness has spent the past half century advocating for Tibetan rights and exploring and teaching Tibetan Buddhism to the world. He has taken an active interest in neuroscience, trying to understand how meditation can alter brain functions.

I asked His Holiness whether faith and reason were incompatible.

First, he said that any religious leader who believes that you have to turn off your mind completely to find faith is on the wrong path. He reminded me that the Buddha told his followers, "Don't be devoted to me purely out of faith, as it is best to investigate." But whenever we become too attached to our intellect, we can lose a connection to the wisdom of our heart. Faith mines the wisdom of the heart. Intellect taps into the reason of the mind. Belief is the intersection where heart and mind meet.

Being mindful and heart-skilled is the path to being faithful. Unfortunately, most of us have afflictions of the heart or mind because we rely too much on blind faith or rational reason. To the Dalai Lama, exploring the spirit—which is what religions are meant to do—means discovering new capacities of the mind and the heart.

Is it possible that the simultaneous rise of fundamentalism and atheism is just a reaction to each other: one focused overly on faith and the other on reason, intellect, or doubt? For me, faith and doubt live across the street from each other. Faith seems to always be smiling, but the neighbors wonder if she's got all her marbles. Doubt scowls too often, seemingly always deep in cold, rational thought. Faith surrenders. Doubt struggles. The balance of faith and doubt somehow keeps me from going too far down the path of naiveté or cynicism. They're twin companions. For me, the war between believers and nonbelievers is a passion play about mystery. How much certainty do we want to fill our cup with? Between those who are certain of the literal, fundamental truths of their religion and those who are certain that God does not exist lies the majority of people.

This equation deserves a multiple-volume set, not just a short chapter. So in the context of this section on contentment, I'll just give you my own personal perspective on faith. It may or may not work for you. For me, it brings contentment as well as elevation to both my heart and mind. Some may believe, as Jean-Paul Sartre did, that I'm just filling a "God-shaped hole" that is my defense against the inexplicable, the ill timed, and my own human frailty. I don't see faith as a weak attempt to mask the meaningless in life. Quite the opposite; I see it as an embracing of what's truly meaningful in life.

## GETTING OUR DEFINITIONS STRAIGHT

Let's define our terms before we start arguing, although language can be limiting when talking about these basic elements of life. Faith and belief are often thought to be synonymous, but the former rests on a certain trust for which there may be little obvious proof, while the latter mixes in empirical evidence. Atheists such as Richard Dawkins suggest that faith is "belief without evidence." The motivational teacher Gregg Braden defines belief as "the certainty that comes from accepting what we think is true in our minds, coupled with what we feel is true in our hearts."

When listening to music, we can use logic to read the lyrics or, if we can read the musical notes, understand the score. But knowledge alone doesn't create the elevation of spirit that fills our hearts when a particular piece of music touches us. The Greeks called this insight *noesis,* the ability to sense something immediately. Belief feels as though it comes from a place that is beyond heart or mind, as it takes into account all of our senses, including the sixth sense of intuition.

The social scientist George Vaillant suggests that faith comes from the emotion of trust, while belief—which may come from the six senses—is really a cognition. We all have faith or trust in something, even atheists, who have faith in their mind, in nature, in the universe, in all kinds of things. We tend to associate faith with religious discussions, but there are all kinds of ways to distinguish between faith and belief. For example, I might stand at the bottom of a rock-climbing wall and tell someone, "I believe in the rock-climbing techniques I've just been taught." But when I'm fifty feet up that wall, I may be thinking (if not saying), "I have faith in these rock-climbing techniques." Maybe faith is belief with "skin in the game."

Depending upon how we use our intellect, we may never climb the wall at all.

A simple question you might ask yourself is "What do I have faith in?" And, to make it more interesting, "How does that compare with what you believe in?" I have faith that the electricity in my little writing cottage in the backyard is safe and reliable even though I am the last person you'd ever want to hire as an electrician. I believe that the electricians I did hire are reliable and that the city building inspectors checked their work thoroughly before issuing a certificate of occupancy for the cottage. In a less industrialized country, I might not have that faith due to my shakiness in my beliefs about others' competency.

Our faith in something can be influenced when our beliefs shift. I've seen friends, including some doctors, shift their faith in medicine from the Western surgical model to the Eastern holistic approach based upon a shift in their belief system about the body. The more you see the body as a machine, the more you might gravitate to having faith in Western medicine. Those who see the body as an energy system may resonate with acupuncture and other Eastern modalities that are a natural outgrowth of that belief system. Think about some deeply held faith you have in your life, and you'll see the link to a belief system that is supporting that faith.

The world religions scholar Karen Armstrong cautions in her powerful book *The Case for God* that faith (and religion) was "never supposed to provide answers that lie within the competence of human reason." That is the job of intellect. The Greeks believed that there were two ways of looking at life: through *mythos* and through *logos*. Both were perceived as essential, but *mythos* (myth) was used to give metaphorical explanation to that which was hard to fathom or explain and, in many cases, the intangible in life. *Logos* created the logic of life and how we typically operate from day to day. Yet, today we live in a world full of *logos*, where a myth is typically thought of as just not true. We've merged the worlds of *logos* and *mythos* and thrown them into a mud-wrestling ring with the odds stacked for the brawny intellect and against the ethereal faith.

Faith and belief became intertwined as if they were one and the same, yet they're cousins, not twins. That shift has also changed our perspective on belief. Rather than seeing scripture as a meta-phorical story, with the purpose of speaking to universal archetypes and bringing meaning to our lives, many fundamentalists now use creedal doctrines as a litmus test of belief. In some religious quarters, either you logically have to believe all the doctrines or you are not a person of faith.

That messes with the equation. Let's look at the math for a moment. If you believe that belief is a mixture of heart and mind and give heart (defining faith as heart) a value of 3 and mind (defining intellect as mind) a value of 4, the equation would have the following value: $3 = 3 \times 4 \div 4$ or $3 = 12 \div 4$. But if we get rid of intellect (the 4s in the left equation), we're left with $3 = 3$ or faith = belief. That's how many atheists see religious folks, as people of faith without intellect. That's not to say there aren't plenty of religious scholars and intellectual believers. I've always admired the quantum scientists who have dual philosophy and physics degrees, which is a tacit acknowledgment that one does not exist without the other. The fact that intellect is in the bottom of the equation doesn't mean that someone who is smart can't be full of faith. Each of the equation's components represents a "predilection toward" faith, belief, or intellect. Someone who has an inordinate reliance on his intellect may be less likely to live in a place of faith, but that doesn't mean smart people can't be faithful and it doesn't mean that faithful people can't have high IQs.

Albert Einstein once said, "The most beautiful emotion we can experience is the mystical. It is the sower of all true art and science. He to whom this emotion is a stranger . . . is as good as dead. To know that what is impenetrable to us really exists, manifesting itself to us as the highest wisdom and the most radiant beauty, which our dull faculties can comprehend only in their most primitive forms—this knowledge, this feeling is at the center of all true religiousness. In this sense, and in this sense only, I belong to the ranks of devoutly religious men." Modern faith needs to recapture this sense of wonder.

An era in which *logos* always trumps *mythos* also messes with the equation. That's like sending an equation to someone on Valentine's Day. There are more transcendent ways to express your love.

## WHAT FAITH OFFERS

There are limits to faith, just as there are limits to reason. Martin Luther, using an old definition of faith that doesn't jibe with the fundamentalist version, explained that "Faith does not require information, knowledge and certainty but a free surrender and joyful bet on his unfelt, untried and unknown goodness." Faith may not give us all the answers, and at times it may be blissfully ignorant of the questions. But even an atheist like Sam Harris acknowledges, "Faith enables many of us to endure life's difficulties with an equanimity that would be scarcely conceivable in a world lit only by reason." How do you deal with the unreasonable in life? Do you call upon your own sense of faith? If so, faith in what?

Science can help us understand that we have a disease, and it might help cure that disease. It can instruct us as to why we feel the emotions we do. It can help us understand our behavior in the midst of crisis. It may reduce our anxiety by reducing uncertainty, but it doesn't give the comfort that a deeper meaning may arise from this challenge.

As we learned in chapter 5 on regret, humans overvalue the need for certainty by creating a risk-averse life dedicated to reducing our potential losses. Faith gives us a certain level of confidence that if we've truly tapped into the full sensual (as in six senses) nature of belief, we can take down the guardrails and experience our life with more freedom based upon the knowledge that no matter what's happening to us, there's a divine inspiration infused.

There's plenty of evidence that medical placebos work quite well in certain situations, partly due to the faith that comes from the belief that we're being given something that will help cure us. Researchers have shown that just the attention we receive and, in some cases, a doctor's level of enthusiasm for a particular treatment that he or she gives us may predispose us to a more positive health outcome. Faith can work wonders in our lives, but there are times when you want more than a placebo.

What doesn't faith offer? Science and religion cover different domains, one dealing with facts, the other with values. If scientific research shows that my heart condition has a ten times better chance of being solved by surgery than by a placebo, I think my intellect will pull rank in that decision. I want to be sure that the airline mechanics fixing an elderly commercial plane have a logical, intelligent checklist for all the safety procedures *before* we head down the runway. I don't just want to have faith that my bank is holding all my retirement savings in its vaults; I want my trust backed up by my belief in the banking laws that govern our country.

The Pew Research Center's Forum on Religion & Public Life does regular surveys on Americans' religious knowledge. Logic would suggest that those who are most knowledgeable about the core teachings, facts, and history of religion would be the most religious among us. But as further evidence that intellect is in the denominator of the "Faith" equation, the groups that score highest on religious knowledge are atheists and agnostics, who score 20 percent higher than even evangelical Protestants. Though some may be troubled that I'm suggesting that intellect is inversely proportional to faith, these data seem to suggest that that's the case.

# FAITH CURES OBSESSION

Have you ever found yourself in an endless mind loop about a troubling situation? It may relate to a decision you made that you regretted or a difficult conversation that keeps replaying in your head. You're likely hanging out in the denominator of this equation, possibly on a subject that is meant not for *logos* but for *mythos*. As a dedicated, hyper-responsible CEO, I can get carried away with believing that I can solve almost any problem with reason, logic, and my own actions. But when I see an issue fester into an obsession, I have to realize that worship needs to replace worry, even though they're polar opposites.

One early Sunday morning in November 2009, I'd memorized every line in the ceiling of my bedroom, having slept just a few winks the past few nights. It felt as though my life was crumbling around me. My company was on financial life support, running out of cash as we approached the slower winter season. My efforts to find a suitable financial partner for the past year had been scuttled by the deepening recession. I felt imprisoned by the CEO identity that no longer suited me but felt deeply responsible for finding a solution for my company that would satisfy our employees and our investors.

Elisabeth Kübler-Ross wrote, "People are like stained-glass windows. They sparkle and shine when the sun is out, but when the darkness sets in, their true beauty is revealed only if there is a light from within." My octogenarian meditation teacher, Salliji, helped me see the light within me first by quieting my obsessive mind that was possessed with finding a solution, especially at three fifteen in the morning. She reminded me that I'm not the sum total of my achievements or my emotions, and she helped me see that intellect alone wasn't going to solve all my problems. Most important, Salliji—through meditation training and wise advice—helped me to reconnect with a belief system that reminded me that I wasn't at the center of the solar system. My petty grievances and run of bad luck were painful, no doubt, but she helped me see that joy comes from wanting others to be happy and all suffering in this world comes from wanting only oneself to be happy.

So on this particular morning, I knew it was time to connect with a wider, loving community. I got dressed and showed up at Glide Memorial Church, a San Francisco Methodist church that I'd been on the board of for nearly a decade. Glide's Reverend Cecil Williams is quite famous as an inner-city religious leader who has made a profound difference in his Tenderloin neighborhood (where I launched my company with our first hotel) by serving a million meals a year to the hungry and offering nearly a hundred different social programs to those in need. I love Glide, yet, as is true of so many of us, I hadn't been willing to reach out and receive that kind of community support for many months. Suffering alone was familiar territory.

Two miraculous things happened that particular morning. First, as I was entering the church, a frail woman gave me a scuffed-up flyer. I looked at the headline: "Tenderloin Activist Steve Conley Has Died." She looked me straight in the eyes and said, "He would have learned so much from you." Freaky! My legal name is Stephen Conley. So, given the state I was in, it felt as if she was telling me that I'd died and I was supposed to learn something from myself. Then, at the end of the service (which is called a "celebration"), Reverend Williams and his wife, Jan, asked me to join them privately in their chambers for some advice from me regarding the church. As I left, Jan gave me a reassuring hug and told me that she felt things were just about to get better in my life, even though we hadn't spoken a word about what I was struggling with. The author Eckhart Tolle suggests, "Life will give you whatever experience is most helpful for the evolution of your consciousness." As I left the church, I had the feeling that serendipity might work wonders in my life, even if I have no control over the script.

As an adult, when I've been struggling with an obsession or something is eating away at my conscience, I've employed two emotions in equal parts. First, I get curious about what I'm supposed to learn from this. If it's taking such a toll on my brain and soul, I have to believe that there's a big lesson involved. Being curious takes me from being reactive or emotionally full of turmoil toward imagining that there's something bigger for me to learn. Second, I mix the curiosity with some faith. Curiosity alone may lessen the mind loop, but it keeps me in my mind. Faith gives me some breathing room. It says to me, "Chip, trust that this is not a punishment, but a gift instead. Don't try to open the package too early." So when I'm most in doubt or full of obsession, my equation is Curiosity + Faith = Peace.

## WORKING THROUGH THE EQUATION

$$Faith = \frac{Belief}{Intellect}$$

*Calibrate your heart and mind through your relationship with belief.* Belief is the linchpin of the faith equation, and it's based upon balancing what your heart is whispering to you and what your mind is logically telling you. Notice how you use the word "believe." When you say, "I believe *that*," you are typically speaking from the mind, based upon your knowledge. When you say, "I believe *in*," you are more likely speaking from a place of knowing that comes from your heart rather than external evidence. The Nicene Creed, the most widely used Christian expression of faith, starts with "We believe in . . . ," and the origin of the word "credo" is a combination of two ancient words for "give" and "heart." In other words, the Nicene Creed is about giving your heart to your faith. How often do you "believe that" versus "believe in"? If you have a healthy mix of "that" and "in," it means you're probably doing a masterful job straddling the divide between faith and intellect.

*Douse doubt with faith.* The author and poet Madeleine L'Engle was once asked, "Do you believe in God without any doubts?" Her response was, "I believe in God with all my doubts." As mentioned earlier in the chapter, faith and doubt have a symbiotic relationship, just like our heart and mind. I worry about people who end up too far on the extreme in either direction for any length of time. Doubt is part of the human condition, and it's admirable in how it creates humility, especially when compared to the pious TV "faith" evangelists who proclaim with absolute certainty that some natural disaster was caused by the sins of that community. Those evangelists know a lot about Heaven and Hell but not much about any place in between. Give me doubt over that kind of judgmental faith any day. But sometimes our doubt becomes an endless merry-go-round that isn't so merry. At such times, we need to surrender our doubt to a faith in something bigger than ourselves, whether that's trust in the divine, belief in the value of love and the human spirit, or just the objectivity of fate. Sometimes the worry is worse than the fate.

*Practice, don't preach.* In Hebrew and Latin, faith is a verb, not something we possess. We *do* faith; we do not *have* faith. That's because faith is indistinguishable from trust. The faithful I most admire use religion as a means of behaving differently. For them, understanding their faith is synonymous with living their faith. Actions do speak louder than words. One of the commonalities of all organized religion is a deep respect for compassion that in some ways comes from the Golden Rule, which dates back to Confucius, five centuries before Christ. A winner of the prestigious TED Prize, Karen Armstrong, has created the "Charter for Compassion," which can be found at www.charterforcompassion.org. If you want to apply faith in action, read the charter and the stories and commitments about how people are actualizing compassion in the world.

*Find enchantment.* Ralph Waldo Emerson, the Transcendentalist poet, wrote, "Our faith comes in moments; our vice is habitual. Yet there is a depth in those moments which constrains us to ascribe more reality to them than to all other experiences. . . . I am constrained every moment to acknowledge a higher origin than the will I call mine." Emerson would often find those moments in nature. As we discussed in the "Curiosity" chapter, awe is a doorway to seeing something bigger than ourselves and having faith that the divine— even if the divine is just the majesty of nature—exists beyond our grubby, oversaturated lives. Celtic Christians called the moments Emerson refers to as "thin places," where the veil between reality and the divine can more easily break through to us. Where does that happen in your life? Where are your thin places? Whether that faith is God-given or a more secular faith that contains purity and beauty, there's great comfort in knowing that a force much bigger than ourselves exists.

One of the "thin places" in modern life has, oddly, been the sports stadium. In *All Things Shining,* Hubert Dreyfus and Sean Dorrance Kelly suggest that the most real things in life take us over with an experience they call "whooshing up"; this happens often when we're in a group, as the group dynamic adds an exclamation point. It is in such moments that our faith in something greater than ourselves is most profound.

Bill Moyers hosted a documentary film on the hymn "Amazing Grace" that included footage from a scene at Wembley Stadium in London, the site of many booze-inspired post–soccer game brawls. Moyers interviewed the opera star Jessye Norman backstage, discussing "Amazing Grace" while, for twelve hours, rock 'n' roll groups had been raging on stage. The dichotomy of chaos and grace was palpable. Then it was her turn to take the stage in what seemed like a cruel hoax. Drunken fans' voices pierced the darkness and silence as she glided to center stage by herself with no backup band. A cappella, she slowly started to sing "Amazing grace, how sweet the sound . . ." As she continued, the crowd of seventy thousand people—most of whom were unaware who this songstress was—quieted, held spellbound by the grace of the moment. As she moved into the third verse, the crowd started to sing along, somehow recollecting the words they'd heard long before. Frenzy left the stadium, and out of chaos came grace.

Somehow, amidst all of the turmoil and troubles in our lives, underneath it all there's a quiet faith you can tap into—whether you are religious or not—that can soothe your soul and help you feel less alone in the world. Whatever our different myths, metaphors, or rituals, faith is something beyond ourselves that creates a sense of compassion in the universe.

# 19

$$\left[ \text{Wisdom} = \sqrt{\text{Experience}} \right]$$

You may be looking at this equation, Wisdom is the square root of Experience, with some fear, thinking "This one's too complex." Trust me. Read this chapter. You can take comfort in knowing that Katharine Graham, the owner and publisher of *The Washington Post* (and the queen of D.C. society) for nearly three decades felt much the same way when she was abruptly placed in her seat of power without training. Her Pulitzer Prize–winning book *Personal History* used the expression "paralyzed by fear" numerous times. Katharine's friend and colleague Meg Greenfield, who was the paper's editorial page editor, gave Katharine the same advice I'll give you as you read this chapter: "You can give up. You are in control of that decision. And keeping that in mind can help you stay in as long as you want."

Katharine Graham was born into a wealthy entrepreneurial family and ostensibly never needed to work. Her husband, Philip, took over the family business but suffered from manic depression. In the early 1960s, he told Katharine that he was having an affair with a *Newsweek* reporter; later he was committed to a mental health facility and ultimately took his own life. In the midst of this emotional tempest, Katharine Graham assumed the reins of the company and became the highest-profile female executive in the United States at a time when there were no other women at the same level in business or publishing.

Less than a decade into her reign at the *Post*, the paper took a lead role in investigating corruption in the White House related to the Vietnam War and Watergate, which tested her personal resolve as well as her decision making. In her memoir and in interviews, she admitted that she was often full of self-doubt and insecurity, but she seemed to find the right answers and courage deep inside herself, even when it meant "staring down a president" in the paper, which led to Richard Nixon's resignation.

Graham was an astute observer of life. She said, "No one can avoid aging, but aging productively is something else." Her memoir is a candid portrayal of finding wisdom through experiences.

In a biblical story, Wisdom is a woman who has built her house on a hill and prepared a feast for all to experience: "Come, eat my food and drink the wine I have mixed. Leave your simple ways and you will live; walk in the way of insight." The light that illuminates our lives, wisdom is an essential quality that arrives without notice or fanfare. Wisdom may shock, as King Solomon did when resolving a dispute between two women who both claimed to be the mother of a child. By suggesting that he divide the child by sword and give one half to each woman, he saw through the conflict to the truth that motherhood is self-sacrifice.

Wisdom is searching for truth and insight and applying that knowledge to the attainment of a common good. Plato called it "the highest of human things," and Aristotle defined it as the knowledge of causes or why things exist in a particular fashion. In *Practical Wisdom: The Right Way to Do the Right Thing*, Barry Schwartz and Kenneth Sharpe outline Aristotle's prescription for a good life, which, if it were an equation, would likely combine our individual experience with empathy, intellect, and moral virtue. Unfortunately, many of the rules and laws of modern life constrain us from doing the right thing and we scarcely have time for the deliberation we need to determine the wisest course of action.

Though we tend to think that wisdom is reserved for aging philosophers or, hopefully, your best friend when you're in an emotional jam, Aristotle believed that practical wisdom was available to all of us and that it was the master virtue for individuals and society. To quote Schwartz, "The central quest for Aristotle was not the general debate over whether anger was good or bad, or the abstract question about what the nature of the 'good' in fact was. It was the particular and concrete issue of what to do in a *particular* circumstance: who to be angry at, for how long, in what way, and for what purpose. . . . It depended on our ability to *perceive* the situation, to have the appropriate *feelings* or desires about it, to *deliberate* about what was appropriate in these circumstances, and to *act*."

After pondering this essential quality of wisdom and conversing with two good friends of mine, Dr. Dan Russell and Sandeep Sood, both of whom are better mathematicians than I am, I came to realize that wisdom is, fundamentally, a subtractive virtue, not an additive one. Wise men filter insights when others get lost in piles and piles of knowledge. T. S. Eliot wrote, "Where is the wisdom we have lost in knowledge? Where is the knowledge we have lost in information?" He wrote that a half century before the "knowledge era" descended upon us, long before we commonly referred to ours as an age of "information overload."

## SIMPLIFYING WISDOM

Most American twelve-year-olds today have more scientific knowledge than the most famous philosophers of two thousand years ago. Heck, we now know the world is round and the earth revolves around the sun, which is more than Aristotle knew. But wise men have always had a knack for seeing patterns and distilling them down to universal truths. The psychologist Paul Ekman, who has specialized in understanding the universality of facial expressions (his work inspired the TV crime-solving drama *Lie to Me*), can take a look at any person and immediately know what emotions that person is feeling. John Gottman can watch a married couple interact for fifteen minutes and predict with remarkable accuracy the likelihood that they'll divorce and how soon.

Some of this is what we call gut instinct, since our enteric nervous system, located in the tissue lining of our digestive system, contains more than 100 million neurons. We've all had experiences when our mind is telling us one thing, based upon logic, but our gut is screaming something else, based upon something as ephemeral as our intuition. Researchers have identified a wide variety of influences that can affect the gut instinct, but one of the most commonly cited is one's level of experience with similar situations. In other words, we learn to create our own simple pattern recognition that we apply—almost unconsciously—to people we meet and situations we face.

Wisdom is all about distilling down the complexity of life, with all its distractions, to what's at its core. That's true in both our personal and work lives. Your company doesn't become a customer service laggard because of a single customer service error with an important client. It is the series of repeated actions or issues that remain unresolved that creates a pattern of behavior and thinking that leads to a weakening service culture. The fact that you may be thirty pounds overweight isn't due to the dozen donuts you ate one morning; it's a function of hundreds of decisions you've made about what to ingest and how to exercise your body over months or years. That's why we hire consultants and coaches; they aren't necessarily any wiser than we are, but they're more objective in seeing the patterns.

So the equation for wisdom isn't about adding intuition plus experience plus awareness plus altruism plus five other positive qualities. The beauty of wisdom is its simplicity. The one quality that most consistently shows up in researchers' observations on wisdom is experience. That's why we consider those who have a few decades under their belts more likely to be wise than younger people.

What if wisdom *is* the square root of experience? It sure sounds good. Let's define square root for a moment with an example: 3 times 3 equals 9. To look at it another way, 3 is the square root of 9 (by "squaring" 3, or multiplying it by itself, you get 9). Square 9, and you get 81. Do it again with 81, and you get 6,561. As you can see, the numbers escalate pretty quickly. But at the root of all this is the simplicity of 3, since, after a bunch of square roots, 6,561 becomes 3— just as there is some simple truth at the root of some messy situation in your life, whether it's your CEO cutting back on the investment in service training, which leads to unhappy customers and less revenue, or your feeling bad about yourself, which leads to less discipline with your diet and nutrition and ultimately weight gain and health issues. Life experience is the result of thousands or millions of tiny actions, each of which contributes to the larger whole. But wisdom seeks the core truth at the center.

Wisdom is being able to see that the complex in our lives (the 9)—the sum of our experiences—is at its heart due to something that is central to our existence (the 3) and the way we approach our experiences. To use a Hollywood example, it's being able to see through *The Matrix* and grasp the root of what makes us, and everything around us, tick. Unfortunately, many people aren't willing to wear the pair of glasses that will help them see the root cause of their experience. We may feel that when faced with a series of challenges, we just have to work harder. Our equation for life is one long series of additions. But the "Wisdom" equation suggests quite the opposite: when we're faced with the greatest odds against us, often we need to edit rather than add.

If we are wise enough to contemplate our own experiences, we can figure out the square root—what's at the core—so that we can be not only wise but also heroic in using wisdom to take the right action to make fundamental changes in our lives.

My friend Sandeep reminded me of the parable of a rich man, fond of felines, who asked a famous Zen ink painter to draw him a cat. The master agreed and asked the man to come back in three months. When the man returned, he was put off, again and again, until a year had passed. Finally, at the man's request, the master drew out a brush, and with grace and ease, in a single fluid motion, drew a picture of a cat, the most marvelous image the man had ever seen. First he was astonished. Then he grew angry. "That drawing took you only thirty seconds! Why did you make me wait a year?" he demanded. Without a word, the master opened a cabinet, and out fell thousands of good, bad, and ugly drawings of cats. How can you become the Zen master who cracks the code of your life?

## THE SERENDIPITY OF INSIGHT

This equation actually does require another ingredient, but I didn't want to scare you by including it at the start of the chapter. As you can see from the equation, as experience gets larger, wisdom keeps increasing but in slower increments. There's some truth to this, as many of us have a quick learning curve and start to plateau in midlife, but then there are those who have read chapter 10 of this book and tapped into the mastery and flow of life. For those folks, wisdom isn't something that necessarily grows at a decreasing rate, but there are occasional bursts or jumps and jags associated with new lessons or insights.

Based on these facts, the "Wisdom" equation—though good—is incomplete. To truly capture the nature of how wisdom works for those who are on a path of learning, the following graph shows our age on the horizontal axis and our level of wisdom on the vertical axis. There are points in life when we are struck by an "aha" experience (which comes from the German expression *Aha-Erlebnis,* another

226

way of describing an epiphany). Such insights appear at infrequent intervals, and they have the effect of boosting our wisdom with sudden, essentially instantaneous transformative breakthroughs. This means that wisdom isn't just some quality that is a function of how we leverage our experience, it's also a function of how we cultivate the ability to create insights.

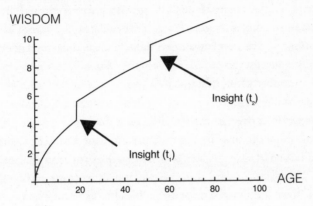

For the mathematicians in the crowd, this means that $W = \sqrt{E}$ + Insight $(t_i)$. Making the insight comes at $t_i$, giving you one big insight or many smaller ones. The graph shows two big insights, but you could instead have many smaller ones. Though to keep things simple I haven't included this in our overall equation for the chapter, it does express the idea that rapid improvements in all kinds of disciplines don't necessarily happen smoothly and predictably into eternity. In biology, they call this "punctuated equilibrium," when a species makes huge leaps in its evolution—leaps that are unpredictable and revolutionary.

Beyond the math, the question to ask is, How does one create a hothouse for insight so that wisdom will grow like roses in a greenhouse? First, let's recognize that insights tend to arise by combining data or disparate people or situations into some kind of link that previously had been unimaginable. This may be what Reed Hastings experienced when he imagined the idea of starting Netflix, with its DVD-by-mail approach, as an alternative to the retail DVD-rental store Blockbuster. His insight came from realizing how idiotic it was that he was paying a $40 late charge for a $10 DVD that had been sitting around the house for a couple of weeks unreturned.

My friend Dr. Dan Russell's insight about adding "Insight" to the equation came when he was hiking with a friend in the hills overlooking the ocean. Nature is a great stimulator of insights. For me, running on the beach seems to be encouragement for endorphin-inspired insights to pop into my brain. Water is a popular medium for a number of my friends, too, who give a puzzle "shower time" when they're looking for some intuitive, insightful guidance. Many companies encourage their managers to take field trips to the zoo, to the museum, to any place that can stimulate another part of their brain, usually the right side, which often doesn't get much exercise in the workplace. And for some people, the ultimate means of quieting their lives and brains (and gaining insights) is to do silent or *vipassana* ("insight" in Pali) meditation.

## HOW WISDOM HELPED ME FIND
## A NEW PATH IN LIFE

We entrepreneurs often think of our businesses as if they're our children, and in some cases (like mine), we never cut the umbilical cord, so we unconsciously feel like we're constantly feeding the baby. I imagined I'd be running Joie de Vivre until I was seventy-five years old, not unlike what Sam Walton did with Wal-Mart, and for years I felt glorified by the thought. But in the midst of the torturous downturn that took the worldwide hotel industry by surprise, it was clear that I needed to once again put on my armor for battle—just as I'd done after the dot-com crash a few years earlier.

What was different about this second downturn in the first decade of the new millennium was that my company was in the midst of launching fifteen hotels in a twenty-one-month period—just as U.S. metropolitan hotel revenues were dropping by 25 percent a year. The traveling and stress associated with the company's growth at such a time were taking a huge toll on me.

So in 2009, I started talking with a variety of "white knights"— secretly, so as not to upset the executives in my company—hoping that I could find an equity investor or a merger partner who could provide sufficient working capital to get through these stormy seas, as well as growth capital that would allow us to prosper in the future. Beyond trying to solve for this adversity and opportunity, I knew that I was ready to change my career. Being a CEO was no longer my calling. The times called for a gladiator who could lead the company much as I had through the previous bust. This was a difficult realization to come to and took a certain amount of internal gut wisdom, but, as is true with any essential insight, I knew it was correct for me and for my company.

But just because I had the insight, it didn't mean I was flush with solutions. During the economic debacle, I kept hearing that savvy hotel investors were looking for either trophies or train wrecks. Though Joie de Vivre (JdV) was a successful company, it wasn't a national brand. We had virtually no net income because we'd been growing like gangbusters—so we were no trophy. And we weren't willing to be considered a train wreck by the vulture investors looking to feast on the carcasses of dead hotels or companies they could buy cheap. I didn't have a lot of choices. Those I did have meant either that the company would virtually evaporate in a merger, leading to extreme layoffs and potentially the end of the company name and legacy or that I would have to sign a five-year employment agreement as CEO to satisfy investors that their bet on JdV was worthwhile. Though more than two decades of being a CEO gave me the experience to find a partner, what was missing was some insight to help me sort through those awful alternatives.

My insight came on a hike with my friend Vanda, who is also an executive coach. As I lamented my situation and the huge responsibility I felt with more than three thousand employees at risk, she helped me see that the various possibilities involved solving for either JdV's needs (finding a private equity investor) or my needs (doing a merger that would allow me to leave my CEO post). None of the options solved for both. She gave me a homework assignment to make a list of the five most important qualities that would be good in a partner but to do it from two perspectives: what would be good for the company and what would be good for me. Then I was to create a five-by-five grid that had those qualities on two axes so I could evaluate each of the potential partner opportunities based upon how they were solving for those qualities. The resulting grid helped me see how disparate the choices were, as I was either going to release myself but gut my company or save the company but make a five-year commitment to doing something that I no longer loved and kept me from my new calling—essentially gutting myself.

Some blind faith (and an awful lot of emotional support from my father) made me believe that I would find an investor who could solve for both JdV's needs and my own. Yet the clock was ticking, and we were running out of cash. Then, out of the blue, I received a call from a business associate who'd heard we were entertaining offers to sell the company or a majority share. Though I'd never met his boss, the billionaire John Pritzker, whose father had started Hyatt more than a half century earlier, I'd heard great things about him and his humane, intuitive, and humorous approach to business and life. Though Pritzker's Geolo Capital came to the dance very late, the fact that wisdom and insight had led me to creating the grid just a few weeks earlier helped me get to the stage of saying "yes" to their advances virtually overnight. And though a complex transaction like this could have taken a half year or longer to consummate, by focusing on what was most important, we were able to make it happen relatively quickly. By June 2010, I had a new partner, and the day the deal was announced I was on the podium of the New York Stock Exchange during the ringing of the opening bell.

My CEO experience and the lessons I'd learned gave me the wisdom to know that I had to sell my company or bring in a majority partner after owning it virtually by myself since its founding two decades earlier. But it was the insight of realizing that I needed to find a solution—one that solved both my needs and the company's needs—that helped me evaluate the golden opportunity when it (serendipitously) came along. Given that Geolo Capital wasn't as high profile or obvious a partner as some of the others we had been talking to, I might have dismissed the opportunity had Vanda not given me the insightful pair of glasses I needed to see through the matrix and evaluate John Pritzker's proposal.

## WORKING THROUGH THE EQUATION

$$Wisdom = \sqrt{Experience}$$

*Use the Serenity Prayer as a daily practice.* Reinhold Niebuhr was one of the preeminent American theologians of the twentieth century, and his enigmatic, outside-the-box appeal is evidenced by the fact that both Barack Obama and John McCain name him as one of their favorite religious philosophers. Niebuhr is credited with creating the Serenity Prayer: "God, grant me the serenity to accept the things I cannot change, the courage to change the things I can, and the wisdom to know the difference." As Frankl taught us in the first equation in this book, serenity comes from accepting the constants in life and challenging the variables. It takes wisdom to see what's a constant and what's a variable. Innovation in business and life comes from the wisdom of challenging what most people think is a constant, when, in fact, it is a variable. I say this prayer every morning and, on difficult days, throughout the day.

*Explore your experience.* The fact that "experience" and "experiment" share the same linguistic root is not happenstance. The wisest people I know are able to survey their lives like a laboratory and see the series of experiments they've encountered as a means of creating wisdom. Take out a piece of paper and make a list of the ten most profound experiences or experiments in your life. What was the lesson to be learned from each one? What wisdom has it created in your life that you can leverage today? I know—on a gut level—just how engaged I was as a CEO during the San Francisco Bay Area dot-com downturn. My level of engagement and the way it energized all those around me in the company allowed Joie de Vivre to almost triple in size during that difficult time. That experience made me realize just a few years later that I didn't have the enthusiasm to do it again and that without making adjustments to the company I could put JdV at great risk.

*Fix situations, not people.* The square root of experience usually means that we are able to see beyond personalities. As a business leader, I've often been faced with a problematic situation that is being blamed on one person or the interaction of a few people. Too often, we blame a mess on the people involved without having the wisdom to take a step back and see the untenable situation that is fostering it. Situations, more than individuals, produce most difficulties. Whether in clarifying roles and responsibilities, creating alignment regarding short-term goals, providing tools for people to be successful, or defining a company's culture and operating rules well enough, everyone understands what defines effectiveness and success—circumstances are powerful determinants of behavior. Create the right situation, and you'll find that the right people show up. Nobody smokes in church.

*Understand what activities most prompt your insight.* Experience fuels wisdom, and insight is what allows your wisdom to create a quantum leap on occasion. Ponder when you've had an insight pop into your head or gut within the past couple of years. What were you doing at the time? Quite often, you were out of the "laboratory" and your subconscious was being given the time and space—and maybe the outside perspective—to age like a fine wine in a wooden cask. Earlier in the chapter, I mentioned a few different environments that were ripe for promoting insight. Once you've identified your ideal habitat (a space that is relatively easy for you to be in or get to), reserve—and revere—that space for when you really need it. In my new writing cottage in the backyard, I do my best to concentrate on creative activities. I rarely watch football there.

I saved the most "elegant" equation for last. In a world awash in quick fixes, lowest-common-denominator thinking, and the pursuit of efficiency if not happiness, wisdom is our sanctuary of sanity. Wisdom is the ultimate editor of our lives. It sees the wheat and discards the chaff. This is particularly important as we age, since our brain cells die, our memory starts to fade, we tire more quickly, and our mind moves a little more slowly. The antidote to this decline is that we gain wisdom with time. We can still have brilliant insights even into our eighties or nineties. The magic of life is not in computing more but in learning to make sense with less.

# PART VI

# DIY (DO IT YOURSELF)

# 20

[
Creating Your Own Emotional Equations
]

The poet Rainer Maria Rilke once wrote, "No feeling is final." Our emotions can be riddles. Wikipedia defines a riddle as "a statement or question or phrase having a double or veiled meaning, put forth as a puzzle to be solved." Some require ingenuity to solve. When I'm in a difficult emotional state, I often find that interpreting something symbolically helps me gain objectivity.

One of my favorite metaphorical tales about emotions and the ego comes from ancient times. The story describes a human being as made up of four parts: a coach, horses, a coachman, and a Master being carried inside the coach. The coach represents the body, which carries you through life. The horses represent your emotions and passions, pulling energetically in different directions unless properly harnessed. The coachman is the ego, and while the Master is asleep, it is the coachman who decides where to go. The Master represents the real Self, the higher Self, and cannot play any role in the journey through life until awakened. Once awakened, it is the Master's role to take charge of the coachman, to tell him where to go and what to pay attention to.

In the context of your Emotional Equations, one of the fundamental questions you need to ask is "Who is taming and directing the passionate, emotional horses in my life?" Is it the never-sleeping, external coachman (the ego)? Or is it the Master, the evolved or divinely inspired part of you, that is too often napping in the coach?

The ego is not necessarily bad, and, as the coachman, it can be expert at managing our passions and body for maximum short-term gain. But I know the coachman is in charge when my emotions have a racing, pulsing nature to them—whether I'm feeling happy or unhappy.

The ego reacts. The soul responds. An experience or thought creates a reaction that leads to an emotion, all in the blink of an eye. And if the thought is a long-held belief such as "the world is dangerous and I need to protect myself" (which leads to fear and anxiety) or "I am fabulous and everyone wants me" (which leads to narcissism), the reaction is so habitual that we don't even notice we've become emotional robots. When the Master is at the helm, my emotions aren't reactions, they're responses to my state of being. When I respond from a state of being, I am less focused on the short-term outcome and what's in it for me.

Philip Yancey, an author who has explored the nature of faith, suggests that in a crisis, "The force of my emotional response gives a strong clue as to the grip the world has on me. . . . A crisis helps to unearth the foundation on which I construct my life." So know that if your ego is at play in constructing your Emotional Equations, you'll typically find that you are like a weathervane that shifts with the wind. Marcus Aurelius advised, "Try to see, before it is too late, that you have within you something higher and more godlike than mere instincts which move your emotions and twitch you like a puppet." Keep that in mind as you imagine how you'll craft your own Emotional Equation that can become your mantra through good times and bad.

# FINDING YOUR EQUATION

The equations that will be most resonant and longlasting for you will be those that come from a purity of intention—from a desire to create a more authentic awareness of yourself and how you can express your gifts. The best equations feel like simple, time-tested truths.

You are welcome to create equations for making money, making yourself physically beautiful, or making yourself famous, but the most effective will be less focused on what you're getting and more focused on what you're becoming. If you're going to go to the trouble of developing your own equations, you might as well create some that can serve you for decades to come.

A word of caution: don't use your Emotional Equations as a means of turning off your emotional spigot. You are not Mr. Spock on *Star Trek*. Sometimes stewing in your own emotional pot can create something amazing. Think of the caterpillar's metamorphosis into the butterfly—it's not pretty at the start—midway through this transformation, life is just a bunch of goo. So don't be frightened or repelled by the emotional experiences you're trying to solve. They're serving as a means of getting to know yourself better and could lead to your own metamorphosis.

To create your own Emotional Equations, start by asking yourself two questions, preferably in a place where you won't be distracted. Close your eyes for about a minute and just observe your breath coming in and going out. Slow yourself down enough that you can get into that observer place to see your coach, your horses, your coachman, and your Master.

1. Do a mental scan of your body. How do you feel overall? Are there areas that feel particularly good or bad? Consider what you've been struggling with lately and where that has settled in your body. I find that when I'm stressed or really tired, my vocal cords and voice get raspy. It's as though my

throat is the referee of the tug-of-war between my head and my heart. When this happens, I can usually tell that I'm feeling conflicted between logic and sentiment. Maybe your body feels sluggish and lacking in energy. What emotion is hiding behind that lethargy? Is it sadness? If your shoulders are like rocks, is anxiety weighing them down? Your physical feelings are a window into your emotional feelings. Write down a few body feelings and what emotions may be underneath them. Louise Hay's *Heal Your Body* is a great guide to understanding the connections among your body, your emotions, and potential illnesses.

2. What's emotionally alive in you at this moment? Did any of the feelings you listed define a resonant emotion for you? Are you able to "feel" for the root cause of your emotion instead of taking it at surface value? Name three to five emotions that you've felt consistently in the past two or three days. Write them down along with what circumstances led to each. Then pick the one that's predominant and circle it. It can be either an emotion you want to eradicate from your life or one that you want to amplify.

Hopefully, you now have one emotion that you can explore in more depth. Let's explore three different emotions and how you can create a helpful equation that can become a mantra to benefit your life. (Note: these case studies do not use real names and are composites based on several people's feedback on how they created their own Emotional Equation.)

## CASE STUDY 1: RESISTANCE

Joan is a forty-five-year-old woman who has been married twenty years and has three kids. She has spent most of her life doing her best to get by and has provided for her family as a working mom for the last decade. Right now, she's the only wage earner in the household. Since Joan graduated from college, she has gained about two pounds per year, which has turned into fifty pounds of extra weight. She also smokes, which she tries and fails to give up every other year, ballooning her weight further. So more often than not, given the complexities and stressors of her life, she has gotten comfortable with the status quo. When her husband and kids try to get her to change her unhealthy habits, she finds herself in full-scale resistance to their pleas, taking on the victim role because she's the person holding the family together financially.

As Joan looked at the two sets of questions we just reviewed, she felt disconnected from her body. She didn't have feelings, and that sort of scared her. But then, as she breathed into the exercise, she started feeling as though she were the rock of Gibraltar: sturdy, unmovable, and reliable. At the same time, she felt a little emotionally dead inside and disappointed in herself that she wasn't able to make any progress in changing her unhealthy habits. The emotional word that seemed to resonate for her most was "resistance." She was fortunate to tap into this, as, for many people, being resistant is an almost unconscious reaction. So what should Joan do with her resistance?

Assuming that she wants to lower or get rid of her resistance, the first thing Joan could do is look up the antonym (opposite) of resistance, which is "surrender" or "acceptance." Joan looks at those words and feels a little cautious as she thinks, "I want to lower my resistance, but I'm not sure I want to surrender completely because I have to be strong." The natural reaction to moving out of your comfort zone is to imagine a change that is traumatic and disruptive. So how can Joan make change into a positive, something to which she aspires?

Rather than focusing on surrender, Joan decides to use "acceptance" or "change." She can imagine what her life will look like as a result of improving her diet, losing some weight, and giving up smoking. She visualizes herself in a year, incorporating those changes and not resisting them. She writes down the words "healthy growth" as the result of making those changes in her life, feeling as though she's growing and improving physically, mentally, and emotionally. Now we have three potential ingredients: resistance, change, and healthy growth. How do they fit together? (If you need to, go back to chapter 2 to reread the underlying reasons to use addition, multiplication, subtraction, or division.)

As Joan looks at her three variables, she writes them down in two columns: one marked "Healthy" and one marked "Unhealthy." She puts change and growth into the Healthy column and resistance in the Unhealthy column. Change seems synonymous with growth, but somehow resistance is misaligned. Sounds as if a subtraction equation may be forming. What if . . .

$$Growth = Change - Resistance$$

Joan could translate this in the following way. She knows she wants to grow in healthy ways, and in order to do so, she has to be willing to change her habits and reduce her resistance. She can now use this Emotional Equation as a reminder each time she finds herself resisting some of her healthy new habits.

How could you use this equation in your life? This equation is relevant to organizations as well. How many companies do you know that have gotten stale because they were focused more on resistance than on change?

## CASE STUDY 2: HUMILIATION

Russell is a sixty-year-old bank vice president. He has worked with the bank for two decades, but the last few years of the recession have been a struggle. He's worried about being laid off and has seen many other longtime employees shown the door. Russell tends not to express himself for fear that he'll be sacked if he speaks up. On some fundamental level, he chose this "safe" job with the bank as a means of providing financial security for himself and his family even though the work has never been his passion. Now his security feels threatened.

Due to the company's reorganization, Russell is now reporting to a similarly titled vice president, Justin, a tech whiz kid who is twenty years Russell's junior. Justin decides to test all eight of his direct reports on their knowledge of the bank's information technology systems in order to learn how best to deploy them as managers. Rather than giving the test results back privately, he decides to share them in a group meeting with his direct reports. Russell is embarrassed, as he scores the lowest of the eight, but in the moment, he's able to chalk it up to the fact that he's ten years older than most of the other managers and thus not as tech savvy.

Within a month after the test, though, Russell's embarrassment turns to humiliation when he is one of two managers stripped of their VP title and demoted to senior director. He's allowed to keep the same salary, but he's no longer part of the weekly direct reports meeting and he starts to feel as though he's being "put out to pasture." More than anything, he feels lost in the new world that Justin is leading.

Rather than stewing in his humiliation, Russell decides to create an Emotional Equation that will help him understand what's at play in order to develop a response to the hole he's fallen into. As he takes an inventory of his bodily feelings and emotions, he notices that he feels less manly. He's been stripped of his pride and, on a deeper level, feels anger in his belly because he feels mistreated and powerless at the same time. Still, the word that keeps resonating for him is humiliation.

Russell's wife suggests that he go online and check www .visualthesaurus.com for the word "humiliation" to see what comes up. He sees the words "shame," "disgrace," and "chagrin." The latter two words don't resonate for him, but the first one—the hollow stab of shame—is almost painful to read. On some core level, he feels ashamed to be in this situation and to have his coworkers see him demoted and his family see him so weak. His Internet-savvy wife then suggests they do a Wikipedia review on shame, and he sees that the emotion is beyond guilt (what you feel when you think you've done something wrong). Given that he feels like an old-timer in what's become a young person's industry, he feels that his problem is more intrinsic to who he is (shame being what you feel when you're sure there is something wrong with you). But he also realizes that he feels a lot of anger about it, and the feelings resonate in his gut.

As he tries to piece together an Emotional Equation that will be helpful, Russell realizes that the two most powerful emotions he's feeling are shame and anger, so they must be two ingredients in the humiliation stew. But that doesn't feel like the whole recipe. Based upon reading chapter 7 on anxiety, he knows that powerlessness is also in the mix. So, a bit like a jigsaw puzzle, Russell puts together the following equation, understanding that shame and anger combined are combustible. The irony is that this powerful multiplication is completely diluted by a lack of power:

$$Humiliation = (Shame \times Anger) - Power$$

As he surveys this equation and breathes deeply, he feels a sense of power that comes from seeing the truth in black and white. But it's one thing to know and quite another to shift the self-abasing emotion of humiliation. First, Russell spends some time reading about how to tame shame. He reviews his relatively successful twenty-year run with the bank and makes a list of all his accomplishments. In fact, doing this, knowing that he may need to put together a résumé, helps him feel a little more power and understand where he has historically added the most value to the organization.

As he starts making his case for why he deserves some pride and power in the workplace, he realizes that he's very angry with Justin for publicly sharing the technology test results and dismissing him to a lower position in a disrespectful manner. But rather than just staying angry, he decides that he'd like to meet with Justin to clear the air and outline what his greatest strengths in the organization have been. The goal would be to determine whether there's a future with Justin as his boss and, if not, to find out if there's an alternative place in the bank that can use his skill set more effectively. Taking this proactive step gives Russell a real sense of power. By turning humiliation into an equation, he was able to understand its components and start developing a game plan that could shift this disabling emotion into something he could work with in reshaping his life.

## CASE STUDY 3: EMPATHY

Thirty-year-old Alexis has mostly been running away from her feelings. She grew up in a textbook setting of the dysfunctional family—alcoholic father and victimized mother—and was thrown into the role of caretaker for herself and her younger brother. As a result of the chaos and violence she experienced, she was an adept survivor, learning how to bob and weave trouble by overcompensating in most situations and relationships. One of the ways this manifested in her life was hypersensitivity to everyone around her and what they were feeling and/or needing. Her acute sense of assessing what others needed, coupled with her refined caretaking skills, molded her into an extremely empathetic person.

In a healthy environment, a highly empathetic person is able to adapt profound feelings and manage them appropriately. But Alexis, having left home at age sixteen, learned most of life's lessons while in survival mode. Like many in her family, she turned to alcohol for comfort, and the numbing of her feelings served a purpose throughout her twenties—in the sense that she didn't have to look at who she was or how she really felt. Alexis was truly empathetic, but half the time she went overboard to help others, being so doggedly loyal and determined to rescue those she cared about that her intentions got lost and were often perceived as controlling and self-serving. She had the habit of giving advice with good intentions, but she'd also take up the lion's share of any conversation, which often left people not feeling cared for at all, as they couldn't get in a word edgewise. The other half of the time, she would find herself judging others—their actions, opinions, and weaknesses. At the end of the day, she judged herself the most, feeling unworthy and unlovable.

At twenty-six, Alexis found herself hitting bottom both emotionally and physically from the drinking, the running, and where it had all gotten her. She was finally able to admit the truth of her situation, facing her emotions for the first time without the elixir that kept her "safe" from feeling—including two of the emotions explored by Russell and Joan in our previous case studies: shame and surrender. When Alexis sat with our two sets of questions, she learned how important it was to breathe and to get in touch with what she was feeling in her body, which helped her identify shame and judgment.

Alexis had a therapist friend who had a lot of experience with how empathy and compassion can work in her clients' lives. One day she confronted Alexis when she was once again dominating their conversation and told her that although she knew her intentions were good, she felt that their relationship was out of balance and needed to change. This level of honesty (and love) brought up fearful feelings in Alexis and an impulse to feel shame. But her friend helped her see that her natural ability to empathize could be fine-tuned and save her from the self-serving motivations she'd relied on for protection all her life. Her friend was showing Alexis great compassion, which is often mistaken for empathy. But compassion is a more passionate emotion, as it usually manifests in action when we feel something *for* someone else—often taking action to help them—versus feeling *with* someone else—being fully present where no action is required.

In order for Alexis to harness her empathy, she had to feel her friend's compassion and then develop compassion for herself. This allowed her to become more attuned to her own feelings and those of others, without being judgmental. Putting herself into others' shoes, which is the common definition of empathy, allowed her to just listen and be present to the feelings of others and those that came up inside herself, waiting to see if a compassionate act was required or merely an empathetic posture, which is deep and meaningful all on its own.

So Alexis had experienced both resistance and humiliation, as Joan and Russell had. But her equation,

$$Empathy = Compassion\ (for\ self) + Presence\ (for\ others)$$

gave her a mantra to help tap into her predisposition to care for others—without the need to control, judge, or fix anything. That opened up an entirely new way to approach all of her relationships and relieved her of the responsibility to take on all the world's problems, keeping the core part of who she was—the most lovable part—intact.

## TURNING PRECARIOUS INTO PRECIOUS

It's been said that adversity reveals greatness, while prosperity masks it. That's easy to say when you're standing on a mountaintop, harder to feel when you're in the depths of the valley. But living through a difficult period in your life isn't a prison sentence. The author Gabrielle Roth says, "There is no true joy and compassion except through the difficult emotions—all we get without the experience of fear, anger, and sadness are cheap imitations of joy and compassion—pleasantness and sentimentality."

Our emotions let us know that we are alive and that we care about something. But modern life can be a form of "tri-zophrenia" when we think one thing, feel another, and act out a third. The more conscious we become about the ingredients of our emotions, the easier it is to transmute the more complicated, high-volume emotions into something more manageable. Anxiety and regret don't arise out of nowhere like a freak thunderstorm. There are component parts, or building blocks, that you can analyze to help you understand why the emotion is blocking you from the sun. Most important, a friend reminds me, emotions always win, especially when one works to avoid them. Our emotional body sends us a bill that accrues interest when we don't pay attention to it in the present. So know that creating your own Emotional Equations may even be fiscally responsible on your part.

I hope this book has helped you become more of an emotional alchemist as you transform precarious feelings and reactions into equations that will serve you well. There's no clear-cut numerical equation that's going to solve all of life's most challenging questions. And my "Jealous" or "Joy" equation may be different from yours (that's why you might want to go to www.emotionalequations.com to share your own equations). The variables in life are complex, subtle, and intangible, difficult to distill perfectly into a mathematical equation. But just as we learned in chapter 2, math is all about relationships, and that's true of our emotions as well. Some relationships zap our energy; others make us more powerful and resilient. You are being asked to step up and take command of your emotions. This new tool in your arsenal can help you stretch to meet the challenge.

Parasto Niakian, one of the senior learning and development managers in my company, emailed me an image from Prague while I was working on this book. It was a photo of some graffiti near the John Lennon Memorial Wall that simply stated, "Perfect Happiness = Enthusiasm − Expectations." Emotional Equations aren't just a way to make sense of our lives; they are part of a bigger movement toward creating insight as we take off our psychological blindfolds. I wish you all the best as you begin to see yourself and the world with a new clarity—assisted by the logic and lyricism that can be found in Emotional Equations.

# Acknowledgments

This is the story of two Jewish shrinks and two guys named Chip. When I most needed guidance during the capitalistic chaos of the past decade, I turned my attention to the wisdom of Abe Maslow and Viktor Frankl. I feel a bit cheated that I never got to spend any time in their presence. Fortunately, I was able to spend time with Chip Hankins—my mirror in life—but it was far too short. All I can say to him—wherever he is—is that his death helped me to appreciate life like never before. Thank you, Phillipa, for allowing me to tell Chip's story.

Whether thriving or just surviving, we all have emotions and I appreciate all of the following people who gave me such insightful and emotional feedback along the way: Zain Elmarouk, Denise Corcoran, Brian Johnson, Jim Canfield, Scott Annan, MeiMei Fox, Drew Banks, Avery Jessup, Matthew Fox, Srikumar Rao, Lindsay Kenny, Bryan Neuberg, Chip Heath, Peter Winick, Bill Wiles, Laura Galloway, Jeff Malone, Alan Lurie, Jean Knowles, Jim Sellner, Tom Blake, Nadia Allaudin, Edward Quinn, Edwin Jansen, Anne Kreamer, SARK, Mario Garces, Tommy Thomas, Kim Ann Curtin, Amy Pressman, Sue Funkhouser, Athena Katsaros, Kate Roeske, Rochelle Edwards, Eugene Dilan, Brother David, Anthony Chavez, Chade-Meng Tan,

Andrew Greenberg, Steve Levin, Sean Stephenson, Cathy Conley, Mike LaHorgue and my YPO forum, and Jon Staub (who reminded me on our juice fasts that how I handled the darkest period of my life proved I was a combination of Tenacity + Grace). And to Salliji and my Spiritual Salon group, I can't tell you how much your support has meant to me during this time of metamorphosis.

Thanks to Courtney Caccavo, a unique soul with graduate degrees in both psychology and business, who did quite a bit of research for me early in the project. Dr. Dan Russell, with his PhD in artificial intelligence and a life experience lived from the soul, kept me honest with my equations. Sandeep Sood taught me about wisdom and helped me break through to figure out the final equation in this book. My muse, Vanda Marlow, helped provide balance so that the seesaw didn't tilt too far toward equations and to the detriment of emotions. And Ben Davis gave me a creative spark by coming up with humorous new equations (Wisdom = Experience × Ear Hair) or imagining how to visualize *Emotional Equations,* while lifting my spirits when I was too deep in the trenches (and thanks to his WPI guys as well). A huge thank-you as well to Ian and Jeremi Karnell and their talented team at One to One Interactive, evangelists who are creating more evangelists.

The academic community has been very generous. I feel fortunate to have received great counsel along the way from Mike Csikszentmihalyi, Sonya Lyubomirsky, Barry Schwartz, Barbara Fredrickson, Jean Twenge, Jennifer Aaker (who helped me see that Coke and Pepsi are at emotional war with each other: happiness versus joy), Nicholas Christakis, Dan Goleman, and Phil Zimbardo (my college professor who introduced me to psychology and also created the "Humiliation" equation in the last chapter). Thanks to Mark Schulman and his colleagues at the Saybrook University who gave me an honorary doctorate in psychology while helping me hone this message. And to the author Raphael Cushnir for reminding me to feel first, think next, and act last.

I'm forever indebted to the senior leadership team at Joie de Vivre, many of whom have now gone through two "once-in-a-lifetime" downturns in the past decade: Ingrid Summerfield, Christian Strobel, Mike Wisner, Jane Howard, Karlene Holloman, Linda Palermo, Lori Lincoln, Morgan Plant, Michael Stano, and the Rock of Gibraltar, Anne Conley. Thanks to Gary Beasley for making the introduction to Geolo Capital and for filling my shoes as CEO less than three months after we'd become partners, which gave me the time and space to write this book. And, of course, thanks to my Joie de Vivre co-chairman and friend, John Pritzker, for being a role model in the business of being human. Rachel Carlton, Sara Pedersen, Valisa Dougherty, and Karen Klose—you've supported me through thick and thin (and forgiven my sometimes thick brain and thin skin).

Then there's the phenomenal team that helped birth this book: my literary agent Richard Pine, who believed in me even before I'd properly explained how I was going to find the time as a full-time CEO to write *Emotional Equations*. My champions at Free Press—Dominick Anfuso, Donna Loffredo, Suzanne Donohue, Laura Cooke, Carisa Hays, Claire Kelley, Meghan Cassidy—who without hesitation put the full weight of their organization behind the book. A special thanks to my editor, Leslie Meredith, who helped me over and over again to take off my blinders and see a better way to express myself. And to Kevin Small, Matt Miller, Ashley Davis, Peter Jacobs, and Olivia Metzger, thanks for helping to turn *Emotional Equations* into a movement.

Debra Amador, you bridge the waters between colleague and family because you are like blood to me at this point, having been my personal editor of four of my books and the center of my "Chip Inc." solar system. Thank you for being available to me twenty-four hours a day, whenever the genie is moving through me and I need counsel or some quick editing. Mom and Dad, what can I say other than the fact that I'm the luckiest son on Earth to have such support from you, especially in the past few years, when you've known that it was time for my transition in life. Damien Hall, my son and occasional external conscience, you and I have suffered through a few very painful years together in our emotional prisons. I hope you will continue to look within and focus on the meaning in life.

Finally, a profound thank-you to the premier people watcher of all time, Allen Funt. Long before Malcolm Gladwell was writing bestselling books about human behavior, Allen Funt was exposing the basic truths about human nature on television (in fact, *Candid Camera* premiered on CBS the year I was born, 1960). He was truly the first "street shrink" who made both psychology and our emotions accessible in a way that was far less threatening than lying down on an analyst's couch. Allen Funt's work taught me that Humanity + Humor = Great Entertainment.

# Notes

My purpose in sharing these notes is to illuminate the resources that were rattling around my heart and head when I was researching and writing *Emotional Equations*. This is neither bibliography nor endnotes. But these are an absolute necessity if you're a CEO writing a book on a subject—emotions—that isn't in your historical domain (in fact, I had to become an expert on each of the varied emotions—not an easy task). So I guess part of this exercise is to earn a little street cred. But the lion's share of why I've written this is to give you some clues for how you can explore a particular emotion or subject in more depth. A good book shouldn't be an end point in your search for wisdom. It should be just the beginning.

## CHAPTER 1: EMOTIONS = LIFE

This book might not have happened without Viktor Frankl's *Man's Search for Meaning*. Some readers struggle with the first half of his book because the story of life inside a concentration camp is painful and at times dauntingly depressing. But don't give up on it, as there's redemption in the first half and the second half gives some psychological underpinning to his logotherapy theory. I also like Frankl's *The Unheard Cry for Meaning*.

When it dawned on me that the whole range of human emotions resides inside us, I looked for a variety of books that could give me a metaphorical taste of emotions. I really enjoyed J. Ruth Gendler's *The Book of Qualities* for its poetic style and Michael Jawer and Marc Micozzi's *The Spiritual Anatomy of Emotion: How Feelings Link the Brain, the Body, and the Sixth Sense*.

The connection between emotional depression and economic depression was important for me in creating a context for why the times we live in are having such a psychological impact on us. A variety of research papers helped me understand this link, including Allan V. Horwitz's "The Economy and Social Pathology"; "Job Insecurity, Socio-Economic Circumstances, and Depression" by H. Meltzer, P. Bebbington, T. Brugha, R. Jenkins, S. McManus, and S. Stansfeld; and a *New York Times* article (November 21, 2009) by Robert J. Shiller called "What If a Recovery Is All in Your Head?" But the most encouraging source material was Glenn H. Elder, Jr., and Jeffrey K. Liker's study "Hard Times in Women's Lives: Historical Influences Across Forty Years," which demonstrates that the Great Depression was a healthy, yet difficult, warm-up for women's self-reliance and resilience, which they would need again when they began to typically outlive their husbands.

The company that analyzes hotel industry customer satisfaction is Market Metrix and they gave us the 2010 award cited at the end of the chapter.


## CHAPTER 2: EMOTIONS: *YOUR OWNER'S MANUAL*

How can I summarize all of the great books on emotions that helped make up my thinking for this chapter? At the top of the list is a book that was published just as I was finishing my manuscript, Anne

Kreamer's *It's Always Personal: Emotion in the New Workplace.* It was such a validation to read this well-researched book just as I was crawling across the finish line. Other books that were most important to me: *Buddha's Brain: The Practical Neuroscience of Happiness, Love and Wisdom* by Rick Hanson with Richard Mendius; *Descartes' Error: Emotion, Reason, and the Human Brain* by Antonio Damasio; *The Emotional Brain: The Mysterious Underpinnings of Emotional Life* by Joseph LeDoux; *What Is Emotion?* by Jerome Kagan; *Expression of Emotion in Man and Animals* by Charles Darwin; and *Molecules of Emotion: The Science Behind Mind-Body Medicine* by Candace Pert. Valuable research studies on emotions included "Can Mixed Emotions Peacefully Coexist?" by Patti Williams and Jennifer L. Aaker; "What Is an Emotion?" by William James; and "How Many Emotions Are There? Wedding the Social and the Autonomic Components" by Theodore D. Kemper.

My biggest satisfaction during the research process came when I discovered Robert Plutchik's work on the Multidimensional Model of Emotion that he evolved into the Wheel of Emotions, much as Newton did with his color wheel. I read many of Plutchik's books and spent some time talking with his widow, Anita, but found the most on-point material to be his book *Emotions and Life: Perspectives from Psychology, Biology, and Evolution* and his research paper in *American Scientist* called "The Nature of Emotions." It was at that time in my research that I realized that combining emotions wasn't just some parlor game and that, in fact, there was considerable research that showed how the spectrum of somewhat familiar emotions were building blocks for other, more complex, emotions.

To give some context to how emotions impact business decision making, leadership, and culture, I dove deep into Daniel Goleman's prolific work on Emotional Intelligence. I was pleased to find Dr. Matthew Lieberman's more recent studies on how our brain plays tricks on us when we make decisions in an emotionally reactive state, as this is particularly relevant to business leaders. And I've had the good fortune of getting to know Nicholas Christakis since we were fellow TED speakers in 2010. His book *Connected: The Surprising Power of Our Social Networks and How They Shape Our Lives* articulately outlines why organizations are like ponds and describes the caustic effect of bad psycho-hygiene on our emotions. One last piece of reference material on this subject is Jeremy Rifkin's RSA Animate video on empathy, belonging, and the power of mirror neurons entitled "The Empathic Civilization," which can be viewed online at www.youtube.com/watch?v=l7AWnfFRc7g.

## CHAPTER 3: DESPAIR

Of course, the source material for this chapter is virtually anything Viktor Frankl ever wrote. Anna S. Redsand's concise and visual *Viktor Frankl: A Life Worth Living* is a poignant portrait of this man's life. Some of my other favorites related to personal meaning include Alex Pattakos's *Prisoners of Our Thoughts* (a real deep dive into Frankl-ian thinking), Dan Millman's *The Way of the Peaceful Warrior,* Jonathan Haidt's *The Happiness Hypothesis,* and Bill Harris's *Thresholds of the Mind.* I learned a lot from a research paper by Ed Tronick called "Meaning Making, Open Systems and Pleasure."

In the organizational context, my favorite books regarding workplace meaning include *Meaning Inc.* by Gurnek Bains et al.; *Resonant Leadership* by Richard Boyatzis and Annie McKee; *The Hungry Spirit* by Charles Handy; *The Reinvention of Work* by Matthew Fox; and *The Workplace Revolution* by Matthew Gilbert.

## CHAPTER 4: DISAPPOINTMENT

Abraham Lincoln's life is a fascinating study in disappointment and redemption, and hundreds of authors have tried to plumb the depths of the man's psyche. Some of the best books include Michael Burlingame's *Abraham Lincoln's Emotional Life,* Joshua Shenk's *Lincoln's Melancholy,* and Doris Kearns Goodwin's *A Team of Rivals.*

Given how prevalent disappointment is in modern psychology, it's not surprising that there's a truckload of research you can review. I found the following to be most illuminating (all of these are research papers): "Affect Intensity: Separating Intensity and Frequency in Repeated Measured Affect" by Ulrich Schimmack and Ed Diener; "Blessed Are Those Who Expect Nothing: Lowering Expectation as a Way of Avoiding Disappointment" by Wilco W. van Dijk, Marcel Zeelenberg, and Joop van der Pligt; "I Never Had a Chance: Using Hindsight Tactics to Mitigate Disappointments" by Orit E. Tykocinski; "The Impact of Probability and Magnitude of Outcome on Disappointment and Elation" by Wilco W. van Dijk and Joop van der Pligt; and "To Warn or Not to Warn: Management Disclosures in the Face of an Earnings Surprise" by Ron Kasznik and Baruch Lev. You might also want to review the psychologist Suzanne Segerstrom's work on the effect of optimism on disappointment as well as Alex Michalos's work on people's perceived quality of experience.

Two books worth recommending in this area are Ian Craib's *The Importance of Disappointment* and Barry Schwartz's *The Paradox of Choice: When Winning at Work Means Losing at Life.* Barry's book is also amazing source material for the next chapter, on regret.

## CHAPTER 5: REGRET

If I had to limit myself to reading source material from only three different thought leaders on the subject of regret, it would be Barry Schwartz (mentioned above, but you might also check out the paper "Maximizing Versus Satisficing: Happiness Is a Matter of Choice," which he wrote with several others), Sheila Iyengar's *The Art of Choosing,* and anything written by the Dutch masters Wilco W. van Dijk,

Marcel Zeelenberg, and Joop van der Pligt (their research studies on this subject include "Reconsidering the Relation Between Regret and Responsibility" and "On Bad Decisions and Disconfirmed Expectancies: The Psychology of Regret and Disappointment"). I also like anything written by Dan Ariely.

Speaking of masters, you can't go wrong reading Daniel Kahneman and Amos Tversky's landmark research ("The Psychology of Preferences" is my favorite) or Thomas Gilovich and Victoria Husted Medvec's work in "The Experience of Regret: What, When, and Why," which is outlined in the chapter with respect to failures to act versus regrettable actions. I didn't have space to talk about Walter Mischel's famous marshmallow test with respect to kids and how we learn to delay gratification, but that's definitely a relevant subject in the literature on regret (check out Lauren M. Caldwell and Robert R. Mowrer's "The Link Between Procrastination, Delay of Gratification, and Life Satisfaction: A Preliminary Analysis"). Similarly, Charles Carver and Michael Scheier's work on self-regulation is worth exploring ("Origins and Functions of Positive and Negative Affect: A Control-Process View"). And then there's a fascinating study on entrepreneurs' predilection to regret: "Are Perseverance and Self-Efficacy Costless? Assessing Entrepreneurs' Regretful Thinking" by Gideon D. Markman, Robert A. Baron, and David D. Balkin.

If you're worn out with all these choices on what to read about regret, the best simple article I've found on the subject is called "You Choose" and was three succinctly written pages in *The Economist* (December 18, 2010).

## CHAPTER 6: JEALOUSY AND ENVY

The Israeli philosopher Aaron Ben-Ze'ev is one of the most provocative thought leaders in this area. He even created a conference called "Pleasure in Others' Misfortune," a perfect welcome mat for all the envious folks in the world (read his paper "Envy and Jealousy"). I mention Social Comparison Theory in the chapter, but I should give some attribution to Leon Festinger, who created the theory.

When it comes to jealousy, I'm a big fan of David Buss's writing, which includes *The Dangerous Passion: Why Jealousy Is as Necessary as Love and Sex* (a good portion of his work relates to how men and women process jealousy differently). The French psychiatrist Marcianne Blevis has an interesting perspective in *Jealousy: True Stories of Love's Favorite Decoy*. Lastly, I mention a *Psychology Today* article in the chapter, which is "The Heart of Jealousy" by Peter Salovey and Judith Rodin. Their research paper "The Differentiation of Social-Comparison Jealousy and Romantic Jealousy" is also worth reading.

## CHAPTER 7: ANXIETY

Most of the really thoughtful research on anxiety is focused on the neuroscience of what happens to our reptilian brain in a state of "fight, flight, or freeze." Many of the books I mention in my notes on chapter 2 will be valuable in understanding how our brain processes the emotions of fear and anxiety and how moving from the ancient part of our brain to the more newly formed prefrontal cortex makes all the difference. Check out Matthew Lieberman's studies from UCLA on this subject as well. And the Canadian neuroscientist William Colmers has published some interesting thoughts on pinpointing the anxiety trigger in the brain.

Any of the books written by Søren Kierkegaard (*The Concept of Anxiety*) or the theologian Paul Tillich will give a philosophical perspective on how to process anxiety in a transformative manner. The Buddhist nun Pema Chodron is the author who holds my hand through the hard times with her books that include *The Places That Scare You: A Guide to Fearlessness in Difficult Times*. Check out David

Barlow's article "Unraveling the Mysteries of Anxiety and Its Disorders from the Perspective of Emotion Theory" as well.

# CHAPTER 8: CALLING

For in-depth, thought-provoking reading on the various forms of pleasure in our lives, I can't recommend Aristotle's *Nicomachean Ethics* enough. Though written long ago, the message is still resonant in modern society with respect to whether pleasure is something we seek or avoid, especially in the context of our work. There was a fascinating cover story in *The New York Times*' Sunday business section (September 19, 2010) called "Just Manic Enough: Seeking the Perfect Entrepreneur" that outlines the fine line between a healthy calling and unhealthy workaholism. I also really like Douglas T. Hall and Dawn E. Chandler's research paper "Psychological Success: When the Career Is a Calling."

You can read more about Tal Ben-Shahar's "want-to" versus "have-to" equation in his book *Happier: Learn the Secrets to Daily Joy and Lasting Fulfillment.* A book that gives the sense of calling in work more of a religious perspective is Michael Novak's *Business as a Calling.*

# CHAPTER 9: WORKAHOLISM

It's good news that both the psychology and the organizational development fields have ramped up their study of workaholism in the past two decades. Some of the best source material includes "Workaholism: Definition, Measurement, and Preliminary Results" by Janet T. Spence and Ann S. Robbins; "Workaholism: Its Definition and Nature" by Itzhak Harper and Raphael Snir; "Workaholism: The 'Respectable' Addiction," www.medicinenet.com/script/main/art.asp?articlekey=51425; "On Being a Workaholic" by the guy who coined the word, Wayne E. Oates; "The Hidden Costs of Worka-holism" by Ray Williams, July 9, 2009, www.fastcompany.com/blog/ray-williams/leadership-edge/hidden-costs-workaholism; "Workahol-ism and Relationship Quality: A Spillover-Crossover Perspective" by Arnold B. Bakker, Evangelia Demerouti, and Ronald Burke; "The Relationship of Workaholism with Work-Life Conflict, Life Satisfac-tion, and Purpose in Life" by Cynthia A. Bonebright, Daniel L. Clay, and Robert D. Ankenmann; "The Work Alibi: When It's Harder to Go Home" by Fernando Bartolomé; "An Exploration of the Meaning and Consequences of Workaholism" by Kimberly S. Scott, Keirsten S. Moore, and Marcia P. Miceli; and "Workaholism Components, Job Satisfaction, and Career Progress" by Ronald J. Burke.

Some of the best books include *Chained to the Desk: A Guide-book for Workaholics, Their Partners and Children, and the Clinicians Who Treat Them* by Bryan E. Robinson; *The Workaholics Anonymous Book of Recovery* by Workaholics Work Service Organization; *Work-ing Ourselves to Death* and *The Rewards of Recovery* by Diane Fassel; and the seminal *The Overworked American: The Unexpected Decline of Leisure* by Juliet B. Schor. That's enough reading to keep a worka-holic busy for quite some time!

## CHAPTER 10: FLOW

This is the only chapter (and equation) in the book named after a psychological theory (other than possibly the "Thriving" chapter), so Mihaly "Mike" Csikszentmihalyi's theories and work would be your best starting point, especially his landmark book of the same name as the chapter. Some of Mike's other books that are worth check-ing out are *Beyond Boredom and Anxiety: Experiencing Flow in Work and Play; Finding Flow; The Evolving Self: A Psychology for the Third Millennium;* and *Good Business: Leadership, Flow, and the Making of Meaning.*

Of course, being a Maslovian, I find Abe Maslow's theories on self-actualization and peak experiences are relevant here, including the following books: *Toward a Psychology of Being; Maslow on Management; Religion, Values and Peak Experiences;* and *The Farther Reaches of Human Nature.* For an interesting comparison of Csikszentmihalyi's and Maslow's theories, check out Gayle Privette's paper "Peak Experience, Peak Performance and Flow: A Comparative Analysis of Positive Human Experiences."

Last, George Leonard's book *Mastery: The Keys to Success and Long-Term Fulfillment* is an insightful basic text on the idea that mastery requires a lifelong journey. More recently, Geoff Colvin's book *Talent Is Overrated: What Really Separates World-Class Performers from Everybody Else* amplifies the point that practice makes perfect—well, not exactly, but at least it has more of an impact on mastery and getting into the flow than does innate talent.

## CHAPTER 11: CURIOSITY

One of my heroes, Peter Drucker, has written about the importance of curiosity and constant learning in a number of articles and books (most specifically, *The Need for Continuous Learning*), but the best overview of his thinking comes from Bruce Rosenstein's book *Living in More Than One World: How Peter Drucker's Wisdom Can Inspire and Transform Your Life.* If Drucker wasn't one of your role models before reading this book, he will be after you've finished.

I highly recommend Todd Kashdan's book *Curious? Discover the Missing Ingredient to a Fulfilling Life* as it speaks to much more than the value of curiosity. He also wrote a paper, "Curiosity and Exploration: Facilitating Positive Subjective Experiences and Personal Growth Opportunities" with Paul Rose and Frank D. Fincham that explores this same subject. Carol Dweck's book *Mindset: The New Psychology of Success* will help you understand how you can train your mind to be more curious and open to growth. I stumbled upon a couple of intriguing papers on the subject as well: "Human Curiosity: How It Became the Primal Force to Create and Drive the Modern World" by Daniel Greenberg and "A New Look at Curiosity and Creativity" by Clarence Leuba.

Finally, for the more poetic side of wonder and awe, I really enjoyed both *Wonder, the Rainbow, and the Aesthetics of Rare Experiences* by Philip Fisher and *Born to Be Good* by Dacher Keltner, which is a fascinating read that suggests it's not just the fittest who survive but the kindest and the most curious. Speaking of curious, Sir Ken Robinson is an inquisitive educator on a mission, and his first TED talk—in which he argues that traditional schools are killing creativity—is hilarious and one of the best TED talks of all time; the video can be viewed at www.ted.com/talks/ken_robinson_says_schools_kill_creativity.html. Steve Jobs told the Smithsonian Institute that the eduational system "came close to really beating any curiosity out of me."

## CHAPTER 12: AUTHENTICITY

Virtually every self-help book ever written relates in some way to the subject of authenticity, so I dug into source material that's a little more foundational. The psychologist Carl Rogers's work on what it means to be "real"—a precursor of the positive psychology movement—ranks up there with the best of Abraham Maslow's work on humanistic psychology theory. Most of Rogers's books are more oriented toward therapists, but you might check out his last two: *On Personal Power: Inner Strength and Its Revolutionary Impact* and *A Way of Being*. A more recent book that covers the subject—and has received rave reviews from my friends—is Brené Brown's *The Gifts of Imperfection: Let Go of Who You Think You're Supposed to Be and Embrace Who You Are*.

Some other books that are worth seeking out are *Sincerity and Authenticity* by Lionel Trilling; *The Ethics of Authenticity* by Charles Taylor; and, for something a little controversial, *The Authenticity Hoax* by Andrew Potter. In the context of business, I love Bill George's *Authentic Leadership,* where he shares what it's like to be a public market CEO while staying true to oneself at the same time. And Jim Gilmore and Joe Pine's *Authenticity: What Consumers Really Want* speaks to authenticity in the marketplace.

Let me finish with a couple of scholarly journals on the subject: "The Role of Authenticity in Healthy Psychological Functioning and Subjective Well-being" by Brian Middleton Goldman and Michael H. Kernis and "Authentic Personality: a Theoretical and Empirical Conceptualization and the Development of the Authenticity Scale" by Alex M. Wood, P. Alex Linley, John Maltby, Michael Baliousis, and Stephen Joseph.

## CHAPTER 13: NARCISSISM

Space didn't allow me to tell the full mythological story of Narcissus in the chapter, but it's worth reading, as the supporting character of Echo (the perfect complement to a narcissist) may be familiar to some of you in your own relationship. As the myth goes, one day, Narcissus rejected the fawning Echo in the forest, so she retreated to a cave, which is where an echo would live ever after. While you can dust off the Roman poet Ovid's original telling of this story in Book III of *Metamorphoses,* I'd recommend Louise Vinge's *The Narcissus Theme in Western Literature Up to the Nineteenth Century.*

The best abbreviated deep dive into this subject is a *Psychology Today* cover story (July 5, 2011) by Scott Barry Kaufman, "How to Spot a Narcissist." I mention both Michael Maccoby's book *The Productive Narcissist: The Promise and Peril of Visionary Leadership* and Jean Twenge and W. Keith Campbell's book *The Narcissism Epidemic:*

*Living in the Age of Entitlement.* If you're looking for a more comprehensive read on the state of this condition in modern society, I'd definitely recommend the latter, even though it might occasionally infuriate you if you disagree with some of the overly broad assertions. I still really enjoyed the basic premise. I also mention Peggy Orenstein's column in *The New York Times Magazine* entitled "I Tweet, Therefore I Am" (June 30, 2010), which is an easy-to-read indictment of how high tech has helped us lose our sense of authenticity. Additionally, Sherry Turkle's recent *Alone Together: Why We Expect More from Technology and Less from Each Other* gives a sense of how lonely it can be between the parentheses—interesting to juxtapose with Christopher Lasch's landmark *The Culture of Narcissism* from the "Me Decade" thirty years ago.

Finally, consider doing a Narcissism movie night with *All About Eve, We Live in Public, American Psycho,* and *The Picture of Dorian Gray.* I'd recommend you invite some friends over, though.

## CHAPTER 14: INTEGRITY

One of my favorite books of the past couple of years was by the English poet David Whyte called *The Three Marriages: Reimagining Work, Self, and Relationship.* What I thought was going to be a lyrical operating manual for finding balance in my life became a deep, soulful lesson in how to integrate your passions and personalities in the three primary roles in your life: at work, in your romantic relationship, and with yourself. I can't say enough good things about this book as a primer for identity integration and lighting your heart on fire.

I mention a study in the chapter about the actual-versus-ideal-versus-ought self that comes from E. Tory Higgins's study "Self-Discrepancy: A Theory Relating Self and Affect." It's an academic read but worthy of a perusal. Additionally, I enjoyed Hazel Markus and Elissa Wurf's study "The Dynamic Self-Concept: A Social Psychological Perspective." Last, if you watch the MTV series *If You Really Knew Me* and enjoy it, go to the website of Challenge Day (the organization behind the series: www.challengeday.org) to learn more. The founders, Yvonne and Rich Dutra-St. John, have written a book called *Be the Hero You've Been Waiting For*.

## CHAPTER 15: HAPPINESS

We're experiencing a happiness epidemic, at least when it comes to publishing. There are a few dozen books I could recommend to you, but I'll limit them to a diverse collection of my favorites starting with the best "how-to" in the bunch, Sonja Lyubomirsky's *The How of Happiness: A New Approach to Getting the Life You Want*. Dan Gilbert's *Stumbling on Happiness* will teach you a few things about yourself you didn't know; check out his TED video as well, at www.ted.com/talks/dan_gilbert_asks_why_are_we_happy.html. Ed Diener and Robert Biswas-Diener wrote an encyclopedia on the subject, *Happiness: Unlocking the Mysteries of Psychological Wealth*. Can't forget the touchstone on the subject, Martin Seligman's *Authentic Happiness: Using the New Positive Psychology to Realize Your Potential for Lasting Fulfillment*. Note: Seligman and Sonja Lyubomirsky collaborated on a happiness equation based upon sizable evidence showing that 50 percent of our well-being is considered an innate, biological set point—much like your family tendencies toward height or weight. Ten percent is related to your circumstances and 40 percent is a function of the intentional activities you pursue. So, this equation (which is more complicated than most of those in this book) is Happiness = 50% (Innate Characteristics) + 10% (Circumstances) + 40% (Actions or Intentional Activities).

For a lighter, fun read, try Marci Shimoff's *Happy for No Reason: 7 Steps to Being Happy from the Inside Out*. Or Timothy Miller's *How to Want What You Have: Discovering the Magic and Grandeur of Ordinary Existence.* And then there's my separated-at-birth twin author Tony Hsieh with his great tale of Zappos' success, *Delivering Happiness: A Path to Profit, Passion, and Purpose.*

Though there are all kinds of happiness thought leaders, my preferred one is Jennifer Aaker at Stanford Business School. She's been the co-author of two great research studies that illuminate the subject: "The Shifting Meaning of Happiness" (with Cassie Mogilner and Sepandar D. Kamvar), which outlines how the nature of happiness changes as we age, and "If Money Doesn't Make You Happy, Consider Time" (with Melanie Rudd and Cassie Mogilner). "To Do or to Have? That Is the Question" by Leaf Van Boven and Thomas Gilovich is an interesting study on whether material possessions or experiences drive happiness. There's a *New York Times* Sunday business section cover story (August 8, 2010) entitled "But Will It Make You Happy?" that covers the same ground in a more mainstream, accessible fashion. And Jeff T. Larsen and Amie R. McKibban put the "Happiness" equation to the test with their research article "Is Happiness Having What You Want, Wanting What You Have, or Both?"

The Princeton study I mentioned about $75,000 per year being all it takes to be happy in the United States comes from the psychologist Daniel Kahneman and the economist Angus Deaton. This study got lots of ink in the mass media, but my two favorite magazine articles on the subject of happiness are *The Economist*'s cover story (December 16, 2010) on "The U-Bend of Life: Why, Beyond Middle Age, People Get Happier as They Get Older" and *Scientific American Mind*'s story on how happiness shows up in different parts of the world, "The Many Faces of Happiness" (September/October 2011). Part of the reason we become happier with time is that we stop resorting to what Srikumar Rao calls "if-then" thinking (check out his book *Are You Ready to Succeed?*). One of my favorite books of all time is Gregg Easterbrook's *How Life Gets Better While People Feel Worse,* a wake-up call for realizing that most of us have mixed up the difference between a hierarchy of needs and a hierarchy of wants, much to our detriment.

## CHAPTER 16: JOY

Happiness is overrated. Joy is underappreciated. And it's been much less written about, although I think Sri Nisargadatta Maharaj got it right in *I Am That* when he wrote, "You are love itself—when you are not afraid." That sums up this equation. Gregg Braden's powerful quote about love and fear in the chapter comes from his powerful book *The Spontaneous Healing of Belief: Shattering the Paradigm of False Limits.* And the biologist Bruce Lipton's research showing that cells can't both grow and protect themselves at the same time comes from *The Biology of Belief: Unleashing the Power of Consciousness, Matter and Miracles.*

I also mention the "Love on a Suspension Bridge" study, which comes from Donald Dutton and Arthur Aron. Jerry Jampolsky's pioneering book *Love Is Letting Go of Fear* supposedly helped Carlos Santana write the lyrics "Love. And fear. Love. And fear. That's all it is. That's all it is." Jampolsky's book and *A Course in Miracles* were early teachers for me that spirituality can be practical, not just ethereal, hocus pocus kind of stuff. A more recent book, *The Joy of Living* (which caught my eye based upon the name of my company) by the Buddhist teacher Yongey Mingyur Rinpoche, once again reinforces the fact that joy isn't just an emotion, it's an action. For a practical read on joy with a Buddhist perspective, look for James Baraz's *Awakening Joy: 10 Steps That Will Put You on the Road to Real Happiness* with Shoshana Alexander.

Finally, for those of you who truly want to understand some of the academic background for what separates happiness from joy, look up the Hungarian professor Zoltán Kövecses's paper from two decades ago, "Happiness: A Definitional Effort."

# CHAPTER 17: THRIVING

Nelson Mandela's *Conversations with Myself* is a compilation of letters, diary entries, and musings from this great man's life and gives a sense of how someone can create a thriving spirit based upon molding his emotions (although David James Smith's *Young Mandela* is a more literate and fresher overview of this modern-day saint). Similarly, spend a day with Maya Angelou's *I Know Why the Caged Bird Sings,* which has some uncanny similarities to Mandela's prison story.

At the heart of this equation is Barbara Fredrickson's phenomenal book *Positivity: Groundbreaking Research Reveals How to Embrace the Hidden Strength of Positive Emotions, Overcome Negativity, and Thrive.* The notes at the end of the book are a checklist of insightful reading on this subject. You also might read a study by her collaborator, Marcial Losada, about positivity ratios applied to business: "The Role of Positivity and Connectivity in the Performance of Business Teams." To understand the value of positivity during the most traumatic times, review Fredrickson's research paper "What Good Are Positive Emotions in Crises? A Prospective Study of Resilience and Emotions Following the Terrorist Attacks on the United States on September 11th, 2001" with Michele Tugade, Christian E. Waugh, and Gregory R. Larkin.

If you want to read a book that is truly one, big emotional equation over and over again, crack open *The Mathematics of Marriage* by John M. Gottman, James D. Murray, Catherine C. Swanson, Rebecca Tyson, and Kristin R. Swanson. It's a tough read but fascinating collaborative research between psychologists and mathematicians on the algebra of marriage.

I also mention the Nobel Prize–winning academics Daniel Kahneman and Amos Tversky in the chapter. To learn more about their theory that losses affect us more emotionally than gains, read their paper "Prospect Theory: An Analysis of Decision Under Risk." If you want to take a really deep dive into this subject, it's worth perusing Barbara Ehrenreich's *Bright-Sided: How the Relentless Promotion of Positive Thinking Has Undermined America*—although it kept reminding me of an equation for cynicism that somehow matches fear with intellectualism.

Finally, if you're having trouble coming up with things or ideas to stoke your positivity, check out www.1000awesomethings.com. It was started by a guy in Canada who went through a similar set of challenges as mine—his best friend took his life and his wife suddenly left him, etc. He sat down at his computer and started making a list of everything he could think of that was awesome. It's an inspired site.

## CHAPTER 18: FAITH

No chapter in this book strained my eyes more. I read a lot of books to get my mind and heart firmly connected to the slippery subject of faith. I'll out myself in telling you that I'm aligned with the former nun Karen Armstrong in a lot of my beliefs, so I found her *The Case for God* to be particularly compelling. The Dalai Lama's personal story in *My Spiritual Journey* with Sofia Stril-Rever is also worth reading.

For those of you who are more philosophical, try either of the following: Walter Kaufmann's *The Faith of a Heretic* or Pierre Teilhard de Chardin's *The Phenomenon of Man*. Some of the more skeptical books on faith that I read included Sam Harris's *The Moral Landscape: How Science Can Determine Human Values*, Bertrand Russell's *Why I Am Not a Christian*, Michael Krasny's *Spiritual Envy: An Agnostic's Quest*, and Thomas Henry Huxley's *Agnosticism and Christianity and Other Essays*. Three intellectually inclined books that helped me make the case for faith were George Vaillant's *Spiritual Evolution: A Scientific Defense of Faith*, Philip Yancey's *What Good Is God? In Search of a Faith That Matters*, and C. S. Lewis's epic *Mere Christian-*

*ity.* To get a sense of how the Dalai Lama and scientists are merging their efforts, check out Richard J. Davidson and Anne Herrington's book *Visions of Compassion: Western Scientists and Tibetan Buddhists Examine Human Nature.*

After all that serious reading, for a little humor about the insanity of literalism, seek out A. J. Jacobs's *The Year of Living Biblically: One Man's Humble Quest to Follow the Bible as Literally as Possible.* And for a little visual and heartfelt lyricism, rent Bill Moyers's documentary on the song "Amazing Grace" and marvel at Jessye Norman's ability to capture a drunken audience with this transcendent tune.

## CHAPTER 19: WISDOM

Socrates stated, "Wisdom begins with wonder," so this was the chapter that got my curiosity flowing like a raging river (and I was able to truly drop into that combination of wonder and awe in marveling at the nature of wisdom over the ages). I started with a reading of the Book of Wisdom by King Solomon. Then I moved on to Aristotle's *Metaphysics,* which defines wisdom as the knowledge of causes or why things exist in a particular fashion. Barry Schwartz and Kenneth Sharpe's book *Practical Wisdom: The Right Way to Do the Right Thing* helped give a modern spin to Aristotle's thinking.

I say the Serenity Prayer first thing every morning when I get up, so I'm deeply indebted to the theologian Reinhold Niebuhr, who crafted this mantra for his flock during a time when the economy was playing tricks similar to those it is playing right now. His daughter, Elisabeth Sifton, wrote an interesting biography on her father and his wisdom, *The Serenity Prayer: Faith and Politics in Times of Peace and War.*

As for other resources (beyond Dan Russell and Sandeep Sood, who really guided me through this equation), I'd recommend the following books: Tony Schwartz's *What Really Matters: Searching for*

*Wisdom in America; The Power of Collective Wisdom and the Trap of Collective Folly* by Alan Briskin, Sheryl Erickson, John Ott, and Tom Callanan; and Robert Sternberg's *Wisdom: Its Nature, Origins, and Development.* With respect to insight and how it comes upon us, you might review Jonah Lehrer's article "The Eureka Hunt: Why Do Good Ideas Come to Us When They Do?" To remind myself that age doesn't always mean sage, I take the poet David Whyte's advice: "Experience is not gained by erasing our sense of innocence."

## CHAPTER 20: CREATING YOUR OWN EMOTIONAL EQUATIONS

The parable of the coach is told in Eastern traditions with Gurdjieff recounting it in Ouspensky's *In Search of the Miraculous.* But it also appears in a slightly different form in the *Katha Upanishad* from nearly 3,500 years ago with the following advice:

> *Know the Self as lord of the chariot,*
> *The body as the chariot itself,*
> *The discriminating intellect as charioteer,*
> *And the mind as reins.*
> *The senses, say the wise, are the horses;*
> *Selfish desires are the roads they travel.*
> *When the Self is confused with the body,*
> *Mind, and senses, they point out, he seems*
> *To enjoy pleasure and suffer sorrow.*

There are all kinds of great books that can help you get in touch with healing yourself. From an emotional perspective, I love *The Emotional Hostage: Rescuing Your Emotional Life* by Leslie Cameron-Bandler and Michael Lebeau. I've also had the chance to speak with Raphael Cushnir and appreciate his approach to getting in touch with our emotions through sensing the body in *The One Thing Holding You Back: Unleashing the Power of Emotional Connection*. There are three great body-mind-focused self-help books you could review as well: *You Can Heal Your Life* by Louise Hay; *Anatomy of the Spirit: The 7 Stages of Power and Healing* by Carolyn Myss; and *Maps to Ecstasy: Teachings of an Urban Shaman* by Gabrielle Roth with John Loudon. And the Center for Nonviolent Communication has a wonderful website (www.cnvc.org) dedicated to enhancing compassion for self and our ability to communicate from that place with others.

The crowning validation for writing this book about the power of emotions came when the conservative mainstream author and columnist David Brooks unveiled his book *The Social Animal: The Hidden Sources of Love, Character, and Achievement* at the TED Conference in February 2011, just as I was finishing the first draft of my manuscript. This story of two characters—Erica and Harold—weaves in all kinds of modern psychological and sociological research that helps them understand the emotional building blocks that dominate their life. It is a seminal book that shines an intellectual light on our emotions, not to the detriment of reason but serving as a better means of creating character and great decision making as we saunter, skip, or stumble along our path in life. Brooks coined the phrase "emotional GPS," which I've been using liberally in talks about Emotional Equations.

# Index

actual self, 164, 165, 169–70
Adams, Abigail, 106
*Adventures of a Bystander* (Drucker), 125
Agassi, Andre, 147–48
Alcoholics Anonymous, 101
*All Things Shining* (Dreyfus and Kelly), 219
"Amazing Grace," 219–20
Angelou, Maya, 197
anger, 17, 18, 39, 62, 205, 244–45, 247
anticipation equation, 22
anxiety, 39, 73–83, 113, 124, 133, 154, 176, 200, 202, 238, 240, 244, 248
    equation for, 23, 73, 75–76, 80–83
Aristotle, 18, 89–90, 222–23, 224
Armstrong, Karen, 211, 218
Armstrong, Lance, 90
*Art of Choosing, The* (Iyengar), 51–52
atheism, 209, 210, 213, 214
Aurelius, Marcus, 238
Austen, Jane, 68–69
*Authentic Happiness* (Seligman), 181

authenticity, 137–46, 168
    as component of integrity, 160, 161, 162–63, 168
    equation for, 7, 137, 140, 145
    self-awareness and courage as tools of, 140–43, 145, 163
awe, 123, 127–32, 198, 205, 219

Beethoven, Ludwig van, 121–22
belief, 210–13, 214, 215, 217
Ben-Shahar, Tal, 96
*Bird by Bird* (Lamott), 111
Boehner, John, 166
*Born to Be Good* (Keltner), 128
Botton, Alain de, 27
Braden, Gregg, 187, 210
*Bright-Sided* (Ehrenreich), 201
Brooks, David, 148
Buber, Martin, 158–59
Buddha, Buddhism, 31, 32, 37, 72, 176, 208, 209
Burning Man festival, 129–30, 164

callings, 87–97, 121, 173, 190, 229
    workaholism vs., 97, 100, 102, 105

Campbell, Joseph, 97
Campbell, W. Keith, 151
*Case for God, The* (Armstrong), 211
Cashman, Kevin, 83
*Character Strengths and Virtues*
    (Peterson and Seligman),
    142–43
Child, Julia, 88
*Choosing the Right Pond* (Frank),
    182–83
Christakis, Nicholas, 182
Christianity, 160–61, 217, 219
Churchill, Winston, 7, 160
Clinton, Bill, 138, 185
Colette, 184
compassion, 157, 158, 218, 220,
    246–47
concentration camps, 6, 29–30, 32,
    36
Confucius, Confucianism, 200, 218
Conley, Stephen, Sr., 144–45, 230
contentment, 171, 175, 176, 178
Costanoa, 44–46, 166, 167
courage, 137, 140, 142–43, 145,
    146, 163
creativity, 124, 188, 189, 198
curiosity as fuel for, 125–26, 128,
    133
Csikszentmihalyi, Mihaly, 9, 90–91,
    111, 112, 114, 119, 128
Cunningham, Michael, 50
curiosity, 123–33, 198, 206, 217,
    219

Dalai Lama, 37, 208–9
Darwin, Charles, 16, 73–74
Dawkins, Richard, 210
*Death of Ivan Ilyich, The* (Tolstoy),
    36–37
*Delivering Happiness* (Hsieh), 16, 174
depression, 10, 17, 39, 76, 124, 133
Descartes, René, 127

despair, 9, 33
    equation for, 6, 23, 29, 33, 34,
        35–37, 207
disappointment, 38–48, 152, 176
    as component of regret, 49, 51
    equation for, 7, 23, 38, 41,
        46–48
    expectations in relation to,
        40–42, 44, 47–48, 58, 152,
        201
    regret vs., 40, 57
    sense of reality in relation to, 41,
        42–44, 46, 58
Disney, Walt, 123–24, 127
Disneyland, 123, 127, 128, 130
Dogen (Zen master), 121
Donahue, Phil, 138
Dreyfus, Hubert, 219
Drucker, Peter, 125–26, 132
Dutra-St. John, Yvonne and Rich,
    169
Dweck, Carol, 126

Eckhart, Meister, 90
Ehrenreich, Barbara, 201
Einstein, Albert, 124, 127, 212–13
Ekman, Paul, 16, 224
Eliot, George, 170
Eliot, T. S., 223
Ellis, Havelock, 62
Emerson, Ralph Waldo, 218–19
Emotional Equations, 6–7, 11–12,
    15, 238
    creating your own, 239–48
    math functions used in, 22–24,
        242
    and parallels between math and
        life, 8–10
    understanding and controlling
        emotions with, 9–10, 11, 16,
        20, 21–22, 247–48
    *see also specific emotions*

# Index

emotional intelligence (EQ), 14–15, 85

emotions, 14–25
  as contagious, 15, 182, 194
  distinguishing between, 19–20
  habitual responses of, 20–21
  Plutchik's wheel of, 18–19, 21, 22
  roots of, 16, 17
  *see also* Emotional Equations; *specific emotions*

empathy, 20, 72, 223, 245–47
  narcissist's lack of, 151, 154, 158

entitlement, 43, 177
  as component of narcissism, 147, 150, 151, 152–53
  humility and compassion in place of, 157, 158

envy, 66–72, 150, 205, 206
  equation for, 60, 68–69, 70, 71–72
  jealousy vs., 61–62, 66–67

Ericsson, K. Anders, 116

expectations, 38, 39, 40–42, 43, 152, 248
  disappointment and, 7, 40–42, 44, 47–48, 58, 152, 201
  managing of, 40, 41, 44, 47–48

Facebook, 153–54, 159, 161, 164, 175

failure to thrive (FTT), 198, 203

faith, 88, 208–20, 238
  belief vs., 210–13
  as cure for obsession, 215–17
  doubts and, 209, 218
  equation for, 208, 209, 212, 213, 217–20
  intellect and, 212, 214, 217

fear, 7, 18, 19, 20, 21, 23, 81, 128, 143, 194, 200, 205, 238, 246, 247

attachment as root of all, 191, 192
  author's experience with overcoming of, 190–92
  as barrier to joy, 185–86, 188, 192, 195
  evolutionary perspective on, 187–88
  masquerading as love, 188–90
  tips for overcoming of, 192–94

"flow," 9, 80, 90–91, 110–22, 174, 226

*Flow* (Csikszentmihalyi), 111, 128

Frank, Richard, 183

Frankl, Viktor, 5–6, 7, 20, 29–31, 36, 82, 168, 231

Franklin, Benjamin, 59, 171

Fredrickson, Barbara, 198, 199, 201, 205

Freud, Sigmund, 29, 150

Frost, Robert, 50

frustration, 40, 46–47, 200

Gandhi, Mahatma, 163

Geolo Capital, 230, 231

Gibran, Kahlil, 8, 88, 91

Gibson, Mel, 148

Gide, André, 62

Gilbert, Elizabeth, 92

Glide Memorial Church, 216

Goleman, Daniel, 14, 85

Gottman, John, 200, 206–7, 224

Graham, Katharine, 74, 221–22

gratification treadmill, 24–25, 177–80, 183

gratitude, 180, 198, 202, 205, 206
  as key to happiness, 24–25, 177, 183

Greenfield, Meg, 221

gross national happiness (GNH) indexes, 174–75

growth equation, 242

guilt, 39, 156, 165, 205
    shame vs., 155, 244

Haidt, Jonathan, 33
Hamilton, Bethany, 35
Hankins, Chip, 4–5
Hanson, Rick, 207
happiness, 173–84, 193
    equations for, 24–25, 173, 175,
        176, 177, 180, 181–84, 248
*Happiness Hypothesis, The* (Haidt), 33
Harris, Sam, 213
Hastings, Reed, 227–28
Hawking, Stephen, 43, 48
Hay, Louise, 240
*Heal Your Body* (Hay), 240
Hicks, Esther and Jerry, 194
Hill, Napoleon, 10–11
Hock, Dee, 169
Hoffer, Eric, 182
*Hours, The* (Cunningham), 50
Hsieh, Tony, 16, 174
humiliation, 62, 242–45, 247
humility, 128, 157, 163, 218

*I and Thou* (Buber), 158–59
ideal self, 164, 165, 169–70
*If You Really Knew Me* (TV show),
    169
Ignatow, David, 149
innovation equation, 188
insight, 226–28, 230, 231, 232–33
Insight Prison Project (IPP), 167–68
integrity, 143, 160–70
    AIR components of, 160, 161,
        162–63, 168
    equation for, 160, 168–70
    integration of identities and,
        161–62, 164–65, 167,
        168–70
intellect, 215, 223
    faith and, 212, 214, 217

intellectual capacity (IQ), 15, 85
Internet, 161, 164
    narcissism and, 153–54, 159
intimacy, fear of, 101, 103, 104
invisibility, 160, 161, 162, 163,
    168
Iyengar, Sheena, 51–52

James, William, 16–17, 151
Jampolsky, Gerald, 195
Japan, 98–99, 105
jealousy, 60–66, 248
    equation for, 60, 63, 65, 70
Jen Ratio, 200
Jobs, Steve, 130,
John Paul II, Pope, 88
Joie de Vivre (JdV), 4, 6–7, 11, 12,
    56, 70, 118, 186, 192, 228,
    229–31, 232
Jordan, Michael, 110, 111–12, 115
joy, 18, 19, 20, 22, 128, 185–95,
    198, 205, 247, 248
    equation for, 7, 185, 192–95
Jung, Carl, 141

Kahneman, Daniel, 52, 200
Kashdan, Todd, 124
Kelleher, Herb, 146
Keller, Helen, 173–74, 179
Kelly, Sean Dorrance, 219
Keltner, Dacher, 128, 129, 200
Kimpton, 70
Kniss, Mindie, 186
Kübler-Ross, Elisabeth, 215

Lamott, Anne, 111
Law of Attraction, 194, 195
*Law of Attraction, The* (Hicks and
    Hicks), 194
L'Engle, Madeleine, 218
Lennon, John, 177, 248
Leonard, George, 120

Lewis, C. S., 160–61, 163
Lincoln, Abraham, 38–40, 48
Lipton, Bruce, 187
*logos,* 211–12, 213, 215
Long, Tony, 153
Losada, Marcial, 199
love, 18, 187, 192, 193, 198, 202,
    205, 213, 246
    as component of joy, 185–86,
        194, 195
    fear masquerading as, 188–90
    jealousy masquerading as, 62
*Love Is Letting Go of Fear*
    (Jampolsky), 195
Lubbock, John, 180
Lurie, Alan, 158
Luther, Martin, 213
Lyubomirsky, Sonja, 183

McClure, Vimala, 171
Maccoby, Michael, 150
Mandela, Nelson, 196–97, 201
*Man's Search for Meaning* (Frankl),
    5–6, 29, 30
Maslow, Abraham, 4, 9, 89, 95, 179,
    187, 203
mastery, 115–17, 120–21, 226
*Mastery* (Leonard), 120
*Mathematics of Marriage, The*
    (Gottman), 200
meaning, 29–37, 39
    despair as suffering without, 6,
        7, 8, 9–10, 11, 23, 29, 34,
        35–37, 207
Mencken, H. L., 42
"metacognition," 114–15
Michalos, Alex, 42
Michelangelo, 137
Millman, Dan, 31
Morita, Akio, 125
Mother Teresa, 87–88
Moyers, Bill, 219

*Mrs. Dalloway* (Woolf), 49–50
*mythos,* 211–12, 213, 215

narcissism, 68, 140, 146, 147–59,
    163, 177, 238
    equation for, 147, 151, 152,
        156–59
*Narcissism Epidemic, The* (Twenge
    and Campbell), 151
negativity, 198, 199, 204, 205
    combating of, 202, 206
    positivity ratios and, 198,
        199–201, 205–6
    shifting focus from, 203–4
    strong impact of, 200, 207
Netflix, 228
Newton, Isaac, 8, 74
Niakian, Parasto, 248
Nicene Creed, 217
Niebuhr, Reinhold, 11, 231
Nietzsche, Friedrich, 29
Noble Truths, 32
Norkus, Art, 191–92
Norman, Jessye, 219–20
Nowak, Lisa Marie, 60–61, 62

O'Neil, John R., 132
*Open* (Agassi), 148
optimism, 22, 33, 44, 148, 180, 196,
    198
Orenstein, Peggy, 154
ought self, 164–65, 169–70

Paige, Satchel, 124
pain, 31, 32, 37
    of a calling, 90–91, 93, 94, 96
"paradoxical intention," 82–83
*Paradox of Choice, The* (Schwartz),
    41, 53, 58
*Paradox of Success, The* (O'Neil),
    132
Peale, Norman Vincent, 201

# Index

*Personal History* (Graham), 221
Peterson, Christopher, 142–43
Plato, 222
Plutchik, Robert, 18–19, 22
Pope, Alexander, 40
positional consumption, 178
positivity, 196–201, 204, 207
    forming habits of, 203–4
    positive thinking vs. true
      emotions of, 201–2
    ratios of, 198, 199–201, 205–7
    taking inventory of, 205–6
*Positivity* (Fredrickson), 198
powerlessness, anxiety and, 23,
    75–76, 77, 81, 83, 244
*Practical Wisdom* (Schwartz and
    Sharpe), 222–23
pride, 58–59, 71, 198, 205, 243
primary emotions, 11, 19, 22
Pritzker, John, 230
*Productive Narcissist, The* (Maccoby),
    150

*Real Enjoyment of Living, The*
    (Schachtel), 175
reality, sense of, 7, 38, 41–44, 46, 48,
    58, 71
regret, 20, 49–59, 97, 196, 213,
    248
    disappointment vs., 40, 57
    equation for, 23, 49, 57–59
reliability, integrity and, 160, 161,
    162, 163, 168
remorse equation, 51
resistance, 240–42, 247
    suffering influenced by, 31–32
responsibility, 139
    as factor in regret, 50, 52, 57
    narcissism and, 151
Rilke, Rainer Maria, 237
"Road Not Taken, The" (Frost), 50
Robinson, Ken, 128

romantic relationships, 199
    fear masquerading as love in,
      188–90
    jealousy in, 61, 62–63, 64–66,
      71
    narcissism and, 158
    positivity ratios in, 200, 206–7
    workaholism and, 106
Roosevelt, Franklin D., 193
Roth, Gabrielle, 247
Russell, Bertrand, 68
Russell, Dan, 223, 228

Salinger, J. D., 186
San Quentin State Prison, 3, 32,
    167–68
Sartre, Jean-Paul, 209
Schachtel, Hyman, 175
schadenfreude, 67–68, 72
Schwartz, Barry, 41, 53, 222–23
Schweitzer, Albert, 161
secondary emotions, 11, 18, 22
self-absorption, 151, 153–54,
    156–57, 158
    *see also* narcissism
self-awareness, 139, 144, 151, 168
    authenticity and, 137, 140–42,
      145, 163
    tips for developing of, 140–42,
      145–46
self-esteem, 17, 68, 102, 158
    diluting of, 156–57
    jealousy and, 63–64, 66, 71
    narcissism and, 147, 148, 149,
      151–52, 155
Seligman, Martin, 142–43, 181–82
Serenity Prayer, 9, 11, 231–32
Seuss, Dr., 135
Shakespeare, William, 66, 170
shame, 156, 165, 205, 243–44, 246
    guilt vs., 155, 244
    narcissism and, 151, 155

# Index

Sharpe, Kenneth, 222–23
Shimoff, Marci, 82
Shipman, Colleen, 61
social media, 153–54, 159, 161
Socrates, 171, 175
Solzhenitsyn, Alexander, 51
Sood, Sandeep, 223, 226
Stephenson, Sean, 185–86
suffering, 9, 32, 101, 216
    equation for, 31–32
    without meaning equals despair,
        6, 23, 29, 33, 34, 207
    pain vs., 31
    transforming of and finding
        meaning in, 35, 36, 37
suicide, 3, 4–5, 39, 104, 165–66,
    222
Sullivan, Anne, 173

TED Conference, 24, 78–80, 82,
    129
tertiary emotions, 11
*Think and Grow Rich* (Hill), 10–11
Thomas Aquinas, Saint, 105
thriving, 196–207
    equation for, 196, 198, 204
    positivity ratios as key to, 198,
        199–201, 205–7
*Time,* 153
*Titanic* (ship), 202
Tolle, Eckhart, 216
Tolstoy, Leo, 36–37
Toyota, 98, 99
Transcendentalists, 128, 218
Trump, Donald, 101
Truth and Reconciliation
    Commission (TRC), 197
Tutu, Desmond, 197
Tversky, Amos, 200
Twain, Mark, 54, 58, 75
Twenge, Jean, 151, 158
Twitter, 153, 154, 159, 161

Uchino, Kenichi, 98, 99, 108
uncertainty, anxiety and, 23, 75–76,
    77, 80–81, 83
"unemployment neurosis," 30–31

Vaillant, George, 210
vanity, 68–69, 148

*Washington Post,* 221, 222
Webber, Alan, 118
Wikipedia, 237, 244
Wilde, Oscar, 59, 139
Will, George, 179
Williams, Cecil and Jan, 216
Winfrey, Oprah, 92, 137–38
wisdom, 221–33
    equation for, 221, 224–27, 231
wonder, 123, 126–28, 131
    in group setting, 129–30
Woolf, Virginia, 49–50
Workaholics Anonymous, 108
workaholism, 97, 98–109, 148

Yancey, Philip, 238

# About the Author

**Chip Conley** founded Joie de Vivre Hospitality (JdV), what was to become America's second largest boutique hotelier, at the age of twenty-six. As CEO for nearly two dozen years, Conley guided the creation of more than fifty unique boutique hotels and built a company with close to a quarter billion dollars in annual sales. The *San Francisco Business Times* honored him as the Most Innovative CEO in the Bay Area and awarded JdV as a Best Place to Work (#2) in the Bay Area. An accomplished author and international speaker, Conley's book *Peak: How Great Companies Get Their Mojo from Maslow* forged new ground at the crossroads of psychology and business. He is also the author of *The Rebel Rules: Daring to Be Yourself in Business* and *Marketing That Matters: 10 Practices to Profit Your Business and Change the World.* He holds an honorary doctorate in psychology from Saybrook University and is the school's 2012 Scholar-Practitioner in Residence. Conley received his BA and MBA from Stanford University. He lives in San Francisco, California. Visit him at www.chipconley.com or www.emotionalequations.com.